Palgrave Studies in Maritime Politics and Security

Series Editor
Geoffrey F. Gresh, Springfield, USA

The world's oceans cover over 70% of the planet's surface area. Global shipping carries at least 80% of the world's traded goods. Offshore oil and gas account for more than one-third of world energy production. With the maritime domain so important and influential to the world's history, politics, security, and the global political economy, this series endeavors to examine this essential and distinct saltwater perspective through an interdisciplinary lens, with a focus on understanding the ocean historically, politically, and from a security lens. Through a spectrum of engaging and unique topics, it will contribute to our understanding of the ocean, both historically and in a contemporary light, as source, avenue, and arena: a source of food and energy; an avenue for the flow of goods, people, and ideas; and an arena for struggle and warfare. The series will use an interdisciplinary approach—integrating diplomatic, environmental, geographic, and strategic perspectives—to explore the challenges presented by history and the contemporary maritime issues around the world.

All manuscripts in the series undergo single blind peer review both at proposal and final manuscript stage, and have to abide by the Springer Nature ethical policy statement: https://www.springer.com/gp/editorial-policies/ethical-responsibilities-of-authors.

Paul Midford

The Senkaku Islands Confrontation and the Transformation of Japan's Defense

palgrave
macmillan

Paul Midford
Meiji Gakuin University
Yokohama, Japan

ISSN 2730-7972 ISSN 2730-7980 (electronic)
Palgrave Studies in Maritime Politics and Security
ISBN 978-3-031-77726-4 ISBN 978-3-031-77727-1 (eBook)
https://doi.org/10.1007/978-3-031-77727-1

© The Editor(s) (if applicable) and The Author(s), under exclusive license to Springer
Nature Switzerland AG 2025

This work is subject to copyright. All rights are solely and exclusively licensed by the
Publisher, whether the whole or part of the material is concerned, specifically the rights
of translation, reprinting, reuse of illustrations, recitation, broadcasting, reproduction on
microfilms or in any other physical way, and transmission or information storage and
retrieval, electronic adaptation, computer software, or by similar or dissimilar methodology
now known or hereafter developed.
The use of general descriptive names, registered names, trademarks, service marks, etc.
in this publication does not imply, even in the absence of a specific statement, that such
names are exempt from the relevant protective laws and regulations and therefore free for
general use.
The publisher, the authors and the editors are safe to assume that the advice and information in this book are believed to be true and accurate at the date of publication. Neither
the publisher nor the authors or the editors give a warranty, expressed or implied, with
respect to the material contained herein or for any errors or omissions that may have been
made. The publisher remains neutral with regard to jurisdictional claims in published maps
and institutional affiliations.

This Palgrave Macmillan imprint is published by the registered company Springer Nature
Switzerland AG
The registered company address is: Gewerbestrasse 11, 6330 Cham, Switzerland

If disposing of this product, please recycle the paper.

This Book is Dedicated to the Memory of Akitoshi Miyashita
A Great Scholar of Japanese Foreign Policy and International Politics,
Friend, and
Columbia University Graduate School Classmate

Preface

This book grew out of a project on Asian security funded by the Norwegian Defense Ministry, and I gratefully acknowledge the generous funding this book project received from the Ministry and through the Norwegian Institute for Defence Studies (IFS). I am indebted to Øystein Tunsjø of IFS for inviting me to join the Security in Asia Project. I also want to thank Rasmus Gjedssø Bertelsen and Steven F. Jackson for very useful comments on early drafts of portions of this book. Earlier versions of parts of this book were presented as papers at the International Studies Association's annual meeting in Montreal in March 2023, and at IFS's conference on Asian Security in May 2022. I thank other panelists and members of the audience at those two meetings for valuable comments and suggestions.

In Japan I would also like to thank the RIPS Fellows of the Research Institute of Peace and Security, and especially the convenors, Jitsuo Tsuchiyama and Matake Kamiya, where I was able to present an early version of this book in June 2023. In Oslo, I want to thank Henrik Hiim of IFS and Wrenn Yennie Lindgren of the Norwegian Institute of International Affairs (NUPI) for organizing a seminar at IFS where I presented an overview of my book in September 2023, and for the valuable comments they and other participants offered. In Stockholm I wish to thank Christopher Weidacher Hsiung and Oscar Almén, for organizing a seminar at the Swedish Defense Research Agency where I also presented an overview of this book in September 2023, and for the valuable comments I received. I want to thank Andrew Oros for valuable comments, and especially Tom Phuong Le and Garren Mulloy for exceptionally detailed and valuable comments on every chapter of this book.

I am indebted to four people for helping me prepare this book for publication. First, I would like to thank Imamura Maki of Meiji Gakuin University's Institute of International Affairs for truly incisive and expert editing of an early version of the manuscript that became this book. Second, I am indebted to Anca Pusca at Palgrave for her patience and help shepherding this book through the publication process. Finally, I would like to thank Preetha K Kuttiappan and Aishwarya Balachandar for their efficient and expert editing and other preproduction work. Nonetheless, the contents of this book, especially any errors, are the sole responsibility of the author.

Finally, I dedicate this book to the memory of Dr. Akitoshi Miyashita, a professor at Tokyo International University, who suddenly and unexpectedly passed away in January 2024. Aki was a great scholar of Japanese foreign policy and international politics, a kind but incisive critic, a friend, and a Columbia University graduate school classmate in the doctoral program of Political Science.

Yokohama, Japan   Paul Midford

Contents

1	**Introduction**	1
	Analytical Framework	8
	Competing Arguments	14
	Plan of the Book	17
2	**From Dispute to Tacit Cooperation to Confrontation Over the Senkakus**	19
	Introduction	20
	The 1978 Tacit Management Regime	26
	From Tacit Cooperation to Open Confrontation	31
	Final Collapse of the 1978 Tacit Regime	38
3	**The Impact of the New Confrontational Senkaku Status Quo on Japanese Politics and Policy**	45
	Introduction	46
	Changing Perceptions of China	46
	Influence on Japan's Overall Defense	51
	Senkaku Driven Strategy	57
	Challenges	65

X CONTENTS

4 Japan's Emerging A2/AD Strategy in the East China Sea — 73
Introduction — 74
What Is an Anti-Access/Area Denial (A2/AD) Strategy? — 74
Emergence of Japan's A2/AD Strategy — 76
   Building Out Japan's AD/A2 Strategy — 84
   Challenges to Japan's Emerging A2/AD Umbrella — 87

5 Japan's Emerging A2/AD Strategy and Its Offensive Missile Debate — 99
Introduction — 100
Counterstrike Debate Emerges — 100
Stand-off Capabilities — 102
Long-Range Missiles Surface in Domestic Politics — 103
Conclusions — 105

6 The Culmination: Japan's New Security and Defense Strategies of 2022 — 107
Introduction — 108
Counterstrike Capability — 108
Explicit Prohibition on Preemptive Strikes — 111
Senkaku Islands — 112
No Commitment to Defend Taiwan — 113
Increased Defense Spending and Autonomous Defense — 117
Public Reaction to the New Security Documents — 122
Counterstrike Missiles and Ryukyuan Public Opinion — 128

7 Conclusions: The Senkaku Islands, Japan's Defense Transformation and Regional Security — 131
Japan's East China Sea Strategy and a Taiwan Scenario — 134
Declining Confidence in the US Defense Commitment — 148
Summary — 149

Index — 153

ABOUT THE AUTHOR

Paul Midford is Professor of Political Science at Meiji Gakuin University in Yokohama Japan. He specializes in Japanese foreign and security policies, renewable energy politics and policy, and East Asian regional politics and security. Midford has published in *International Organization*, *International Studies Quarterly*, *Security Studies*, *The Pacific Review*, *Asian Survey*, and *Japan Forum*. He is co-editor of nine edited volumes, and author of *Rethinking Japanese Public Opinion and Security: From Pacifism to Realism?* (2011); and *Overcoming Isolationism: Japan's Leadership in East Asian Security Multilateralism* (2020).

LIST OF FIGURES

Fig. 2.1 Location of the Senkaku Islands (*Source* Akiyama Masahiro, "Geopolitical Considerations of the Senkaku Islands," OPRI Center of Island Studies, August 7, 2013, as accessed August 20, 2024 at https://www.spf.org/islandstudies/research/a00007.html) 25

Fig. 2.2 What Measures should the Kan Cabinet implement to respond to the situation around the Senkaku Islands? (*Source* Figure is author's creation. Data from NTV [Nippon Television], "2010 nen 10 gatsu teirei yoron chōsa" [October 2010], as accessed November 24, 2010, at http://www.ntv.co.jp/yoron/201010/question.html) 39

Fig. 2.3 Incursions into Senkaku Territorial Waters and Contiguous waters by Chinese Guard (CCG) vessels as of July 2023 (*Source* Japanese Ministry of Foreign Affairs, as accessed August 20, 2023, at https://www.mofa.go.jp/files/100537084.pdf) 42

Fig. 3.1 Japanese Threat Perceptions of China Overtake Those of North Korea (*Source Yomiuri Shimbun*, Nichibei kyōdō yoron chōsa, normally conducted in early December. Author created figure) 47

xiv   LIST OF FIGURES

Fig. 4.1   Map of Japan's Nascent A2/AD Umbrella As of April
2023 (*Source* Asia Maritime Transparency Initiative
(AMTI), "Remote Control: Japan's Evolving Senkaku
Strategy," July 29, 2020, as accessed February 29, 2024,
at https://amti.csis.org/remote-control-japans-evolving-
senkakus-strategy/)   80
Fig. 4.2   The Japanese Ground Self-Defense Forces Base on Ishigaki
Island (*Source* Author's photograph)   95

CHAPTER 1

Introduction

Abstract This chapter introduces the book and provides an overview of the pivotal decade of 2012 to 2022. This decade witnessed the final breakdown of the previous Sino-Japanese conflict management regime for the Senkaku (Diaoyu) islands that dated from the late 1970s, the emergence of a new status quo of continual confrontation between these two countries over these islands, and the transformation of Japan's defense in response. It argues that these two developments are linked, with the new status quo of China continually challenging Japan's control over the Senkaku islands prompting Japan to reassess China's intentions as hostile and causing Tokyo to begin a large-scale military buildup in order to defend its control of the Senkaku islands and the nearby Sakishima islands. It introduces defensive realism and balance of threat theory as explanatory frameworks for understanding Japan's response to this new status quo.

Keywords Senkaku islands · Defensive Realism · Balance of Threat Theory · Self-Defense Forces (SDF) · Anti-Access/Area Denial (A2/AD) · Sakishima islands

© The Author(s), under exclusive license to Springer Nature Switzerland AG 2025
P. Midford, *The Senkaku Islands Confrontation and the Transformation of Japan's Defense*, Palgrave Studies in Maritime Politics and Security, https://doi.org/10.1007/978-3-031-77727-1_1

The decade of 2012–2022 witnessed two major developments in Japan's security. The first has been the emergence of a new status quo of continuous confrontation between China and Japan over the Senkaku (known in China as the Diaoyu) islands. This started in September 2012 when China began continuously challenging Japan's control of these islands by regularly sending coast guard and other state vessels into the territorial waters around these islands, something it had almost never done before. China has continued to do so almost every month since that time, sometimes more than once a month. This is significant as the first physical challenge to Japan's territorial integrity (e.g., land that Tokyo controls) since the end of World War II.

The second major development since 2012 has been the transformation of Japan's defense policy overall. The main milestones in this transformation include Japan establishing a National Security Council and secretariat (2013), reinterpreting the constitution to allow for the right to Collective Self-Defense (2014–2015),[1] the withdrawal from unit-level participation in international peacekeeping (2017), and by the end of this period, in December 2022, committing to acquire offensive counterstrike missiles and increase its defense budget by over 60%.

This book argues that this ongoing challenge to Japan's territorial integrity and its defense transformation are very much related. Specifically, the new status quo of continuous threat to Japan's control of the Senkakus has had a transformative impact on Japanese defense politics and strategy, triggering the major changes in Japan's defense seen during the decade of 2012–2022. The post-2012 status quo of continuous confrontation in the East China Sea, especially around the Senkaku islands, between Japan and China, and its long-term impact, have received little systematic attention.

This book argues that this first direct and ongoing challenge to Japan's territorial integrity since 1945 has become a catalyst for the transformation of Japan's overall defense posture, and has produced significant change in its domestic politics. It focuses on Japan's emerging Anti-access/Area Denial (A2/AD) umbrella, modeled after China's A2/AD strategy, over the Senkaku and Sakishima islands, one designed to hold at risk any Chinese military and coast guard units operating in the vicinity of either. This study shows how this strategy and the threat

---

[1] In Japanese, 集団的自衛権.

to Japan's control of the Senkakus and growing concern about the Sakishima islands in case of a military conflict over Taiwan eroded the policy of not obtaining long-range missiles capable of striking enemy bases in neighboring countries. Moreover, it argues that the new National Security Strategy (NSS) and National Defense Strategy (NDS) adopted in December 2022 that mandate a 60% increase in Japanese defense spending up to 2% of GDP represent the culmination of the transformation of Japan's defense strategy set in motion by the Senkaku islands confrontation.

At the same time this strategy faces real challenges, including the limited geographical space of the Sakishima islands, and relations with a local population not used to, and often suspicious of, SDF bases and their implications. Finally, this study considers the implications of this strategy for Japan's involvement in a potential military conflict over Taiwan between China and the US. This book argues that the attitudinal defensive realism of the Japanese public and many elites explains why the confrontation over the small and remote Senkaku islands led to a transformation of Japanese defense, and why this transformation has been limited to territorial defense and is not leading Japan to play an active military role beyond its borders.

Obsession and Confrontation over "small stakes." The past quarter of a century has witnessed growing obsession over the Senkaku/Diaoyu (hereafter referred to as Senkaku islands as Japan currently controls them) islands in both China and Japan. This trend has been especially pronounced in Japan since 2010. To outsiders this dispute is especially striking given that these islands appear to be essentially barren rocks. What Thomas Schelling, the deterrence theorist, once said about Quemoy, an island held by the Republic of China (Taiwan) near to the coast of the People's Republic of China, could arguably apply equally well to the contemporary attitudes of US policymakers, if not those of Chinese and Japanese policymakers, regarding the Senkaku islands: "Almost everyone in America, surely including the President and the Secretary of State, would have been relieved in the late 1950s if an earthquake or volcanic action had caused Quemoy to sink slowly beneath the surface of the sea."[2] Likewise, Michael O'Hanlon has coined the term "Senkaku Paradox" to

---

[2] Thomas C. Schelling, *Arms and Influence* (New Haven: Yale University Press, 1966), p. 83, note 24.

describe the generic case of risking great power war over "small stakes," or "a few barren pieces of land with little if any inherent importance."[3]

This post-2010 obsession is a significant change, given that from the normalization of Sino-Japanese relations in 1972 both sides had cooperated to avoid having this territorial conflict harm the larger bilateral relationship. The recent and novel obsession regarding these islands appears to be fueled by growing nationalism on both sides that powers a spiral of growing tension and in turn further fuels this nationalism. This trend is especially pronounced in Japan, where, in contrast to China, the Senkaku islands had relatively low salience among the general public and elites before 2010. Although Japanese public opinion remains very opposed to using military force overseas, there is a broad consensus that military power has utility for defending national territory,[4] and Japanese overwhelmingly see the Senkakus as Japanese territory.[5] A second underlying factor driving this action-reaction spiral and nationalist fervor on both sides has been a legal dynamic internal to the dispute itself, where both sides have seen the actions of the other as undermining their own claim to the islands under western international law. Paul O'Shea has labeled this type of political dynamic as the "sovereignty game."[6] This has led both sides to compete in demonstrating effective control over the islands (mostly Japan) or to disrupt the other's exercise of effective control (mostly China).

A third variable that has been exacerbating the confrontation over the Senkakus since 2010 is that it has been occurring during a period of geopolitical power transition, as China rises, and Japan and the US have experienced relative decline. This creates growing uncertainty regarding the balance of military capabilities between China on the one hand, and Japan and the US, on the other hand. Moreover, US interest in this territorial dispute itself is low, and Washington has manifested concerns about

---

[3] Michael E. O'Hanlon, *The Senkaku Paradox: Risking Great Power War Over Small Stakes* (Washington, DC: Brookings Institution Press, 2019), p. 95 and back cover.

[4] Paul Midford, *Rethinking Japanese Public Opinion and Security: From Pacifism to Realism?* (Stanford, California: Stanford University Press, 2011).

[5] NTV (Nippon Television), "2010 nen 10 gatsu teirei yoron chōsa" (October 2010), http://www.ntv.co.jp/yoron/201010/question.html.

[6] Paul O'Shea, "Sovereignty and the Senkaku/Diaoyu Territorial Dispute," *EIJS, Stockholm School of Economics Working Paper 240* (September 2012), pp. 8–12.

1 INTRODUCTION 5

becoming entrapped in a military conflict there. The Trump administration's erratic foreign policy during its first term (and now during its second) has created further uncertainty about the balance of interest, and specifically the US commitment to deterring threats to Japanese control over the Senkaku islands. On the one hand, President Donald Trump issued the strongest US promise to defend Japan's control early in his first term. On the other hand, Trump's public questioning of the US-Japan alliance and pressure for a dramatic increase in host nation support from Japan has raised questions about US commitment to the alliance during his two administrations and more generally.[7]

Power transition also creates incentives for the parties to this dispute to act more aggressively in staking their sovereignty claims, thereby destabilizing and exacerbating the conflict. China, as a rising power, might perceive that a shift in the balance of power in its favor allows it to become more territorially assertive in exercising effective control.[8] On the other

---

[7] Sheila Smith, *Japan Rearmed: The Politics of Military Power* (Cambridge, MA: Harvard University Press, 2019), pp. 232–233; "Trump Rips U.S. Defense of Japan as One-Sided, Too Expensive," *Japan Times*, August 6, 2016.

[8] Power transition theory argues that a transition in the relative capabilities of major powers can increase the risk of war and encourage aggressive behavior by both the rising power and the status quo power. Some of the leading works in this literature include A.F.K. Organski and Jacek Kugler, *The War Ledger* (Chicago: University of Chicago Press, 1980); Jacek Kugler and Douglas Lemke, "The Power Transition Research Program: Assessing Theoretical and Empirical Advances," in Manus I. Midlarsky, ed., *Handbook of War Studies II* (Ann Arbor: University of Michigan Press, 2000), pp. 129–179; and Jack Kugler and Douglas Lemke, eds. *Parity and War: Evaluations and Extensions of the War Ledger* (Ann Arbor: University of Michigan Press, 1996). Regarding Sino-US power transition and the possibilities for conflict versus peaceful transition see Ronald Tammen and Jacek Kugler, "Power Transition and China–US Conflicts," *The Chinese Journal of International Politics* 1, no. 1 (Summer 2006), pp. 35–55; Graham Allison, *Destined for War: Can America and China Escape Thucydides Trap?* (Boston: Mariner Books, 2018); Avery Goldstein, "Power Transitions, Institutions, and China's Rise in East Asia: Theoretical Expectations and Evidence," *Journal of Strategic Studies* 30, no. 4–5 (2007), pp. 639–82; and Steve Chan, *China, the US, and the Power-Transition Theory: A Critique* (New York: Routledge, 2008). Regarding the debate about whether China is becoming more assertive, see Alastair Iain Johnston, "Is China a Status Quo Power?" *International Security* 27, no. 4 (2003), pp. 5–56; Alastair Iain Johnston, "How New and Assertive Is China's New Assertiveness?" *International Security* 37, no. 4 (Spring 2013), pp. 7–48; and Björn Jerden, "The Assertive China Narrative: Why It Is Wrong and How So Many Still Bought into It," *The Chinese Journal of International Politics* 7, no. 1 (2014), pp. 47–88.

hand, a Japan in relative decline and pessimistic about the future direction of the balance of power vis-à-vis China would have an incentive to act more aggressively, at least tactically, in order to consolidate a relatively favorable territorial *status quo* before the distribution of capabilities shifts further against it. Recent research indicates that the period of Japan's relative decline beginning in the 1990s corresponds with a rising assertiveness in staking and consolidating its maritime territorial claims, and not just vis-à-vis China. For example, James Manicom observed already in September 2010 that "developments in Japan... point to a more activist, if not assertive, Japanese posture toward its maritime realm."[9]

The spiral of nationalist tensions and the action-reaction dynamic that emerged between the two countries since 2010, and especially since 2012, one that involves frequent, if by now somewhat ritualized, confrontations between the coast guards of China and Japan, has arguably become the most dangerous territorial dispute in East Asia and the most likely regional trigger of a great power military confrontation outside of the Korean peninsula, possibly eclipsing even the Taiwan issue.[10] Unlike the many other maritime territorial disputes in East Asia, the Senkaku islands are unique in the sense that they are the only one where the US is bound by treaty commitment to become involved in the case of military conflict. Article 5 of the Treaty of Mutual Cooperation and Security Between Japan and the US, signed in 1960 and still in force today, states that

[9] James Manicom, "Japan's Growing Assertiveness at Sea," *Wall Street Journal* (online), September 20, 2010, as accessed August 20, 2023 at https://www.wsj.com/articles/SB10001424052748703556604575502830616192158. Also see James Manicom, "Japan's Ocean Policy: Still the Reactive State?" *Pacific Affairs* 83, no. 2 (2010), pp. 307–326; James Manicom, *Bridging Troubled Waters: China, Japan and Maritime Order in the East China Sea* (Washington, DC: Georgetown University Press, 2014); Johnston, "How New and Assertive Is China's New Assertiveness?" p. 22; Jeffrey A. Bader, *Obama and China's Rise: An Insider's Account of America's Asia Strategy* (Washington, D.C.: Brookings Institution Press, 2012), p. 106 and Paul O'Shea, "Sovereignty and the Senkaku/Diaoyu Territorial Dispute."

[10] For a more optimistic view of the stability of the current confrontational status quo see Yun Yu and Ji Young Kim, "The Stability of Proximity: the resilience of Sino-Japanese relations over the Senkaku /Diaoyu Dispute," *International Relations of the Asia Pacific* 19, no. 2 (2018), pp. 327–355. Tensions over Taiwan may currently be as likely or perhaps more likely to spark a great power conflict between China and the US, but depending on the orientation of the administration in Taipei toward mainland China, cross-strait relations have experienced periods of détente (e.g., during the Ma Ying-jeou administration from 2008 to 2016) as well as confrontation, with the current period being one of heightened confrontation.

the two parties recognize that "an armed attack against either Party in the territories under the administration of Japan would be dangerous to its peace and safety and declares that it would act to meet the common danger." Although the US does not take a position regarding which claimant has sovereignty over the Senkaku islands, it does recognize Japan's administrative control there, which means a Chinese armed challenge to that control would be grounds for US military intervention. This makes this dispute uniquely dangerous, as it is perhaps the only territorial conflict at present that could directly trigger a Sino-US military conflict.[11]

Because this threat is a direct one to Japan, not an indirect one that largely flows through Japan's connection to the US, as is the case with the threat from North Korea, Japan has focused more on developing its own independent capabilities, and worries more about abandonment than entrapment, whereas the US for the first time in its alliance with Japan has had to focus seriously on the risk of entrapment. These risks are being exacerbated over time by gradual escalation by both China and Japan.

This book focuses on Japan's long-term response to the new status quo of continuous, if often ritualized confrontation around the Senkakus. It argues that this new status quo of confrontation has had a large impact on Japan's military strategy in the East China Sea, with broader implications for Japan's overall security policy, and even its domestic politics. The reason for this significant if not radical impact on Japan is that the ongoing regular Chinese incursions into the territorial waters of the Senkaku islands (essentially creating a gray zone conflict) is the first time that Japan has been confronted by a direct physical threat to its territorial integrity and territory under its control since the end of World War II.

Moreover, the Senkaku confrontation is essentially the only credible source of potential military conflict for Japan that does not flow through a bilateral conflict between the US and another state. Essentially all other scenarios, most notably those involving China, North Korea, or Russia, and which could conceivably lead to strikes on Japanese territory, including those aimed at Japanese as well as US military bases, and are predicated on the assumption that Japan will support US war efforts, are conflicts that do not directly involve Japan and at least begin as bilateral conflicts between the US and another state. For example, despite their

---

[11] Japan has made it a top priority to press successive US administrations for promises to defend its control over the Senkakus, and has realized significant success in doing so. See Smith, *Japan Rearmed*, pp. 209, 310.

very chilly and even hostile relationship, it is hard to see a plausible purely bilateral conflict between Japan and North Korea that could spiral into military conflict. At the same time, it is important to remember that unlike the South China Sea, where the US does not have a treaty commitment to defend Manila's control over Spratly islands (or geographic features) it controls, the US does have a treaty commitment to defend Japan's control over the Senkakus, despite being neutral about the sovereignty dispute between China and Japan.

This book identifies an emerging Japanese strategy to create an "Anti-Access/Area Denial" (henceforth A2/AD) umbrella[12] over the Ryukyu and Senkaku islands designed to hold at risk any Chinese military and coast guard assets operating in the vicinity of either. It also considers some of the challenges Japan faces in fully developing this A2/AD strategy. It also argues that this new strategy so far has only limited implications for possible Japanese involvement in a military conflict over Taiwan, which would necessitate the development of different capabilities.

ANALYTICAL FRAMEWORK

This book uses defensive realism to explain how and why China's continual challenge to what Japan defines as its territorial integrity in the Senkaku islands since 2012 has caused Japan to respond as it has, and why this has had a radicalizing impact on Japan's defense. It shows specifically why this has led Japan to double down on territorial defense and withdraw from direct military contributions to international security, and further reenforce its skepticism about the use of offensive military power overseas as a foreign policy tool, even to defend nearby states

---

[12] Anti-Access and Area Denial (A2/AD, in Japanese 接近阻止/領域拒否) capabilities refer to long-range kinetic capabilities, usually precision-guided missiles, to block adversaries from entering or maneuvering in a designated zone. See Chapter 4. One of the earliest arguments that Japan "should" develop its own A2/AD strategy and capabilities in the East China Sea is Grant Newsham, Ryo Hinata-Yamaguchi and Koh Swee Lean Collin, "Japan Should Steal a Strategy from China's Playbook: How Tokyo Can Build Its Own A2/AD Network in the East China Sea," *National Interest*, May 11, 2016 as accessed August 8, 2023 at https://nationalinterest.org/feature/japan-should-steal-strategy-chinas-playbook-16159. For a more recent and broader argument that places Japan's emerging A2/AD umbrella in the framework of a strategy of deterrence by active denial, see Eric Heginbotham and Richard J. Samuels, "Active Denial: Redesigning Japan's Response to China's Military Challenge," *International Security* 42, no. 4 (Spring 2018), pp. 128–169.

such as Taiwan.[13] Stephen Walt's balance of threat theory argues that states balance against military capabilities[14] and perceived aggressiveness. Although Walt's theory does not specify which matters more, military capabilities or perceived aggressiveness, this book uses a balance of malevolence corollary to balance of threat theory,[15] which hypothesizes that perceptions of perceived aggressiveness matter more than aggregate capabilities. When there is an imbalance in perceived aggressiveness the state will choose to align with another state perceived as having more benign intentions. As Walt himself notes, this is why the US and the UK do not feel threatened by each other's nuclear weapons, and why the states of Western Europe aligned with the US during the Cold War, despite a clear imbalance of power in favor of the US.[16]

In East Asia, where the US was more dominant than in Europe during the Cold War, Japan nonetheless aligned with the US rather than balancing against (US) power. The importance of imbalances of aggressiveness is even clearer in Japan's balancing against a modest North Korean nuclear arsenal versus its seeming lack of concern (at least before Moscow's all out invasion of Ukraine caused Japan to reassess the aggressiveness of Russia's intentions) about Russia's vastly larger nuclear arsenal and overall military power. As this book will show, Japan also looked upon China's economic and military rise with a significant degree of equanimity until the Senkaku crises of 2010–2012 caused Japan to reevaluate China's intentions toward its territorial integrity as aggressive.

[13] Thomas Berger, who rather describes Japan's defense strategy as defensive liberal, also notes that Japan remains reluctant to use force overseas. Thomas U. Berger, "The Pragmatic Liberalism of an Adaptive State," in Thomas U. Berger, Mike M. Mochizuki and Jitsuo Tsuchiyama, eds., *Japan in International Politics: The Foreign Policies of an Adaptive State* (Boulder, Colorado: Lynne Rienner, 2007), pp. 259–300, esp. 260.

[14] Walt's original formulation included aggregate material capabilities, geographic proximity and offensive military capabilities as independent variables along with perceived aggressiveness. Stephen Walt, *Origins of Alliance*, pp. 22–26. For the sake of simplicity these material variables are subsumed into military capabilities.

[15] For an earlier discussion of balance of malevolence theory see Paul Midford, "China Views the Revised US-Japan Defense Guidelines: Popping the Cork?" *International Relations of the Asia-Pacific* 4 (2004), pp. 118–120.

[16] Walt, *Origins of Alliances*, Chapter 1. US balancing against very weak powers such as Saddam Hussein's Iraq, Muammar Gaddafi's Libya, or North Korea are other examples suggesting that perceptions of malevolence matter far more than the balance of material capabilities.

Another tenet of defensive realism is that most states are socialized to the implications of anarchy, and therefore understand that attempts to achieve hegemony are futile and self-defeating. Moreover, the offense-defense balance normally favors the defense, meaning that the best defense is usually a good defense, not a good offense. Because the fine-grained structure of power is benign, security is plentiful, and consequently socialized states should pursue defensive strategies that focus on defending national territory.[17]

On the other hand, Stephen Van Evera finds that states, especially great powers, not infrequently misperceive the offense/defense balance as favoring the offense, and therefore believe offensive military action is easier and more advantageous than defensive military action. Recent wars illustrate both the frequency of this misperception and the failure of offensive wars. The Vietnam War, two invasions of Afghanistan, the invasion of Iraq, and most recently Russia's invasion of Ukraine are all cases of great powers underestimating the difficulty of offensive military action and conquest, and ultimately being defeated by far weaker opponents fighting wars of national defense backed by nationalist mobilization. However, below the level of polar powers this misperception appears to be less prevalent among lesser great powers and middle powers, in part because they are less capable of mounting offensive military operations.

Security Isolationism. This book finds that Japan's grand strategy is firmly focused on territorial defense. In part this is because of Japan's inability to reemerge as a great power,[18] and in part this is because of the lessons Japan learned when it attempted to conquer East Asia by force in the 1930s and 1940s. Post-war security isolationism appears to be another factor: a sense that as an island nation Japan stands apart from other nations and can therefore have a degree of isolation from international politics and security. Of course, this did not prevent Japan from maintaining an alliance with the US during the Cold War, but the US was exceptional as Japan's sole security partner in what was otherwise a posture of security isolationism. Since the end of the Cold War Japan has greatly reduced its security isolationism and decentered to an extent from

[17] This argument is most clearly developed by Stephen Van Evera, *Causes of War* (Cornell University Press, 1999), pp. 7–11.

[18] For a comprehensive analysis on the constraints limiting Japan's reemergence as a major military power see Tom Phuong Le, *Japan's Aging Peace: Pacifism and Militarism in the Twenty-First Century* (New York: Columbia University Press, 2021).

the US as its sole security partner by building security partnerships of various kinds with a range of countries, and Japan started making unit-level contributions of SDF troops to UN peacekeeping.[19] During the past fifteen years military exercises with non-US partners in Japan have begun in earnest.[20]

At the same time, isolationism remains a potent, if generally unrecognized, force in Japan's defense politics, as illustrated by the Abe's administration decision to entirely withdraw Japan from unit-level military participation in international peacekeeping in 2017 after a quarter century of nearly continuous participation.[21] This book will argue that China's looming territorial threat to the Senkakus, if not the Sakishima islands, was also a crucial motivating factor behind the Abe's administration's decision to end unit-level participation in UN peacekeeping. Nonetheless, this return to the Cold War equilibrium focus on the defense of Japanese territory also reflects an isolationist strain in Japanese and Abe

---

[19] On Japan's isolationism during the Cold War see Paul Midford, *Overcoming Isolationism: Japan's Leadership in East Asian Security Multilateralism* (Stanford, California: Stanford University Press, 2020), pp. 28–46; and Paul Midford and Wilhelm Vosse, "Introduction," in Paul Midford and Wilhelm Vosse, eds., *New Directions in Japan's Security: Non-U.S. Centric Evolution* (London: Routledge, 2020), pp. 1–3. Regarding the origins of Japan's post-war security isolationism see Hideo Ōtake, "Defense Controversies and One-Party Dominance: The Opposition in Japan and West Germany," in T. J. Pempel, ed., *Uncommon Democracies: The One-Party Dominant Regimes* (Ithaca: Cornell University Press, 1990), p. 139, where he observes that "Yoshida never considered such politico-military integration with neighboring nations possible or desirable... Although he was eager for international economic integration, he wished to maintain a distinctive cultural identity for the Japanese people." Also see Kenneth B. Pyle, *The Japanese Question: Power and Purpose in A New Era* (Washington, DC: The American Enterprise Institute Press, 1992), pp. 24; and John Welfield, *An Empire in Eclipse: Japan in the Post-war American Alliance System* (London and Atlantic Highlands, NJ: The Athlone Press, 1988), p. 90.

[20] Ibid., Midford, "Introduction," and more generally Midford and Vosse, eds., *New Directions in Japan's Security.*

[21] Paul Midford, "Abe's Pro-Active Pacifism and Values Diplomacy: Implications for EU-Japan Political and Security Cooperation," in Axel Berkofsky, Christopher W. Hughes, Paul Midford and Marie Söderberg, eds., *The EU-Japan Partnership in the Shadow of China: The Crisis of Liberalism* (London: Routledge, 2018), pp. 40–58 esp. pp. 42–45; and Paul Midford, "The Abe administration's passive pacifism," *Japan Today*, March 4, 2020, at https://japantoday.com/category/features/opinions/the-abe-admini stration's-passive-pacifism.

12   P. MIDFORD

administration thinking that sees contributions to global security more as a luxury than a necessity for this island nation.[22]

Attitudinal Defensive Realism. Reenforcing the defensive and isolationist orientation of most of Japan's political elites is the attitudinal defensive realism of the Japanese public, attitudes that appear widely shared by elites as well. Attitudinal defensive realism is the belief that the utility of military power is limited to defense of national territory in the face of imminent threats.[23] By contrast, attitudinal offensive realism is the belief that strategically offensive military power has utility for pursuing a wide range of state interests beyond defense of national territory.[24] These can include traditional security objectives such as suppressing terrorist networks or weapons of mass destruction proliferation, defense of a neighbor, or so-called offensive liberal objectives such as promoting the

---

[22] As will be touched on in subsequent chapters, isolationism and the return to the Cold War equilibrium focus on territorial defense has coexisted with an expanding range of security partnerships. For Japan, these partnerships have value by expanding opportunities for joint training, weapons sales, weapons co-development, and attracting political support from security partners. Nonetheless, they do not involve any obligation or implication that Japan will use military force to defend its security partners, or that these security partners will defend Japan. In this book Japan's defense isolationism means an unwillingness to use military force beyond Japan's territory to defend partners or as a foreign policy tool. Regarding Japan's security partnerships, see Midford and Vosse, eds., *New Directions in Japan's Security*.

[23] Paul Midford, *Rethinking Japanese Public Opinion and Security*, pp. 16–20. Academic defensive and offensive realism have a more probabilistic and less absolutist view about the utility of offensive military force. Jack Snyder suggests the difference between academic defensive and offensive realism is that the former believes strategically offensive military action can advance the state's interests about 20% of the time while offensive realists believe it can advance state interests about 30% of the time. See Jack Snyder, "Defensive Realism and the 'New' History of World War I," *International Security* 33, no. 1 (Summer 2008), pp. 174–185, at 183. By contrast, the attitudinal defensive realism of the Japanese public views strategically offensive military power as always lacking in utility.

[24] I use the modifier "strategic" before "offensive military force" to distinguish this from "tactically" offensive military force within the context of homeland defense. The latter could include Japanese counterstrikes on North Korean missile bases, while the former would include a Japanese-initiated attack on North Korea with the aim of achieving regime change or a preventive war to suppress weapons of mass destruction (WMD) development from eventually threatening Japan.

spread of democracy.[25] The common denominator is that offensive military action is seen as having utility for advancing national interest,[26] however that might be justified.[27]

The implications of attitudinal defensive realism on the part of most of Japan's public and a significant portion of its governing elites is to reenforce the focus and priority on defending Japanese territory and to see Japanese military power as lacking utility for other objectives, including the defense of even a neighbor such as Taiwan. This focus on territorial defense has been institutionalized in Japan's military doctrine of "defensive defense," or *Senshu Bōei*, which mandates force shaping of the SDF to deprioritize offensive capabilities and tactics in favor of those most useful for territorial defense.[28]

At the same time, as discussed later, Japanese overwhelmingly see the Senkaku islands as Japanese territory, meaning that contrary to preexisting stereotypes about supposed Japanese "pacifism," the Japanese public strongly supports the use of force to defend Japan's control

[25] Berger, "The Pragmatic Liberalism of an Adaptive State," esp. pp. 261, 291–292, footnote 4.

[26] This definition of the differences between defensive and offensive realism reflects more the defensive realist definition of the differences between the two schools. See Jack Snyder, *Myths of Empire: Domestic Politics and International Ambition* (Ithaca, New York: Cornell University Press, 1991), pp. 10–11; and John Mearsheimer, *The Tragedy of Great Power Politics* (New York: W.W. Norton & Company, Updated edition, 2014), pp. 19–21.

[27] Although differing views of the utility of offensive military power largely capture the divide between defensive and offensive realists, this does not mean that academic offensive realists necessarily support all justifications for offensive military action, or that the motivations of Japan's offensive realists necessarily correspond to academic Offensive Realism's theory of state motivation. As discussed above, academic offensive realists are only marginally more optimistic about the utility of offensive military power than are academic defensive realists. John Mearsheimer, for example, has opposed the invasion of Iraq and the eastward expansion of NATO as being too provocative of Russia to serve the US national interest. See Snyder, "Defensive Realism and the 'New' History of World War I," pp. 175. Mearsheimer regards liberal rationales for offensive military action as a device by which US policymakers conceal their true offensive realist motivations and seek support from the American public. See John Mearsheimer, *The Tragedy of Great Power Politics*, pp. 25–27; and John Mearsheimer, *The Great Delusion: Liberal Dreams and International Realities* (New Haven, Connecticut: Yale University Press, 2018). When applied to public opinion, the key question is whether not public opinion believes that offensive military power has utility for national interests.

[28] For a description and critique of this doctrine, see Yumi Hiwatari, *Senshu Bōei kokufuku no senryaku: Nihon no anzenhoshō wo dō toraeru ka* (Kyōto: Mineruva Shobō, 2012).

14   P. MIDFORD

of the Senkakus, even while not supporting Japan's military intervention in conflicts beyond its borders, even regionally.[29] It is precisely because of the defensive realist focus on territorial defense that China's ongoing threat to Japan's territorial integrity has become the key driver in the transformation of Japan's defense since 2012. This transformation happened at two levels. First, China came to be seen as harboring aggressive intentions against Japanese territory. Second, a broad domestic consensus emerged over the importance of building up Japan's military capability to defend against China's perceived threat to Japanese control of the Senkakus and the nearby Sakishima islands.

Competing Arguments

The claims made in this book about Japan's focus on territorial defense stand in contrast to some scholars and many media pundits, who, adopting implicitly a more offensive realist approach, see Japan transforming into a "normal" military power capable and willing to use military force overseas to pursue its foreign policy aims and support its US ally in global armed conflicts. For these observers China's direct challenge to Japan's control of the Senkakus is not a central driver of change in Japan's defense. Many of their arguments focus on Taiwan as a driver instead.

For example, Christopher Hughes argues that Japan has emerged as a "global military power:" "Japan is demonstrating all the indicators of becoming a more capable military actor and of going not just regional but also global in its military profile," but in the process is also becoming more subordinated to the US: "Japan is willing to venture further outwards to the Indo-Pacific, other regions, and globally for international military cooperation but only so far as compatible with US-Japan alliance objectives," starting with helping the US defend Taiwan.[30] Similarly, Giulio Pugliese claims "the Japanese government has gone to great lengths to integrate its own security into deterring a kinetic attack

[29] Midford, *Rethinking Japanese Public Opinion and Security*. Also see chapter 2.

[30] Christopher W. Hughes, *Japan as a Global Military Power: New Capabilities, Alliance Integration, Bi-lateralism Plus* (Cambridge: Cambridge University Press, 2022), pp. 54, 74–75. Strikingly Hughes does not provide any details about where or under what conditions Japan would be willing to use force beyond Japanese territory with the partial exception of a Taiwan scenario.

across the Taiwan Strait."[31] Commentator Ryan Ashley claims "Tokyo is signaling that it is willing to support Taiwan's sovereignty, up to and including joining a military defense of the island against Chinese attack."[32] Likewise, Zack Cooper and Eric Sayers make an even more sweeping claim that Japan is in a "transition from pacifism to regional protector."[33] The boldest claim comes from Axel Berkofsky, who declares flat out: "The gloves are off. Japan would – in the case of an unprovoked Chinese attack against Taiwan – get involved defending Taiwan militarily."[34] Many of these claims appear to reflect the preferences of policy elites in Washington and other western capitals, rather than careful analysis of the drivers of Japanese defense policy or the current state of Japanese defense.

More common are claims not that Japan "*will*" defend Taiwan, but that it "*should.*" Responding to an article in *The Wall Street Journal* that Japan is not willing to commit to militarily defending Taiwan and that Japanese elites have refused to try building a consensus in favor of such a

---

[31] Giulio Pugliese, "In It Together: Taiwan's and Japan's Security Are Linked," in Bonnie S. Glaser, ed., *Next-Generation Perspectives on Taiwan: Insights from the 2023 Taiwan-US Policy Program* (August 2023), p. 41, as accessed August 26, 2023 at https://www.gmfus.org/news/next-generation-perspectives-taiwan-insights-2023-taiwan-us-policy-program. However, Pugliese does not provide any detail about this integration beyond suggesting that US Marines would have access to military and civilian facilities in the Sakishima islands (although as discussed in Chapter 4, access to such facilities south of Okinawa island might be difficult).

[32] Ryan Ashley, "Japan's Revolution on Taiwan Affairs," *War on the Rocks*, November 23, 2021, as accessed August 11, 2023, at https://warontherocks.com/2021/11/jap ans-revolution-on-taiwan-affairs/. Also see Richard Lloyd Parry and Didi Tang, "Japan Pledges to Defend Taiwan If China Attacks, Says Deputy Prime Minister Aso," *Times*, July 7, 2021, as accessed February 29, 2024, at https://www.thetimes.co.uk/article/ japan-would-defend-taiwan-if-china-invaded-says-deputy-pm-l7dnhdfn0.

[33] Zack Cooper and Eric Sayers, "Japan's Shift to a War Footing," *War on the Rocks*, January 12, 2023, as accessed July 7, 2023, at https://warontherocks.com/2023/01/jap ans-shift-to-war-footing/.

[34] Axel Berkofsky, "Japan: All Dressed Up and Ready to Go (to the Taiwan Strait)?" *ISPI*, September 23, 2022, as accessed August 17, 2023, at https://www.ispionline.it/ en/publication/japan-all-dressed-and-ready-go-taiwan-strait-36244. For claims that Japan will definitely not defend Taiwan militarily, see Zhuoran Li, "No, Japan Will Not Defend Taiwan," *Diplomat*, March 18, 2024 as accessed March 25, 2024 at https://thediplomat. com/2024/03/no-japan-will-not-defend-taiwan/; and Julian Ryall, "Japan Troops Won't Get Involved If China Invades Taiwan, PM Yoshihide Suga Says," *South China Morning Post*, April 21, 2021, as accessed March 11, 2024 at https://www.scmp.com/week-asia/ politics/article/3130423/japan-troops-wont-get-involved-if-china-invades-taiwan-pm.

16   P. MIDFORD

commitment,[35] pundit Alexander Hughes bluntly argued in the conservative *National Review* that Japan *should* directly defend Taiwan so that China does not attack Japan next: China "would be all too happy to rule the Land of the Rising Sun."[36] Writing in *The Washington Post*, Oriana Skylar Mastro, after observing a "mismatch in talk and walk" among Japanese political elites observed: "Japan seems to be prepared to push back against only Chinese assets that are clearly poised to attack its sovereign territory. Those heading toward Taiwan? Not so much." She went on to argue that Japan *should* abandon its focus on self-defense: "Japan must broaden its vision of self-defense to encompass priorities and declaratory policies that will avert calamity in the region... Tokyo must make clear at home and abroad that defending Taiwan is no longer off the table." Notably, she argued Japan should be ready to send submarines into the Taiwan Strait at the start of any conflict to interdict a Chinese invasion force.[37]

Another set of competing arguments downplays the impact of the new status quo of continual confrontation over the Senkakus on Japanese defense and the risk of conflict. This view sees China and Japan as having avoided obsessing over this territorial conflict and having adopted rational and pragmatic approaches to managing the conflict to prevent damage to the bilateral relationship and escalation to armed conflict. Notably, Yun Yu

[35] Alastair Gale, "Would Allies Fight With U.S. for Taiwan? Japan Is Wary," *The Wall Street Journal*, July 15, 2023, as accessed August 17, 2023 at https://www.wsj.com/articles/would-allies-fight-with-u-s-for-taiwan-japan-is-wary-d90dd924. For other analyses suggesting Japan will not intervene to defend Taiwan see "Will to Fight? America's Ally Nervous About Waging War to Defend Taiwan," *The Economist*, May 10, 2023, as accessed August 11, 2023 at https://www.economist.com/asia/2023/05/10/will-japan-fight; Francis Pike, "Would Japan Defend Taiwan from a Chinese attack?" *Spectator*, August 27, 2021, as accessed August 17, 2023 at https://www.spectator.co.uk/article/would-japan-defend-taiwan/; Erin Hale, "Despite Tough Words, Japan Might Not Enter a Taiwan War," *VOA*, October 16, 2022 as accessed August 17, 2023 at https://www.voanews.com/a/despite-tough-words-japan-might-not-enter-a-taiwan-war/6791868.html.

[36] Alexander Hughes, "Japan Should Prepare to Defend Taiwan," *National Review*, July 17, 2023, as accessed August 11, 2023 at https://www.nationalreview.com/corner/japan-should-prepare-to-defend-taiwan/.

[37] Oriana Skylar Mastro, "Opinion: Japan Must Do More, and Faster, to Avert War Over Taiwan," *The Washington Post*, February 2, 2023, as accessed August 17, 2023 at https://www.washingtonpost.com/opinions/2023/02/02/japan-join-us-defend-taiwan/. Mastro inaccurately claims that anti-ship and anti-aircraft missiles have been deployed to Yonaguni, and that the US Navy and the MSDF together outnumbers the Chinese navy in the number of naval vessels by three to one.

and Ji Young Kim argue that China and Japan "have successfully engaged in bilateral crisis management by operating political, diplomatic and military exchanges to prevent further escalation." Rejecting what they call the "ticking time bomb" view of the dispute, they argue that "the possibility of an armed conflict is extremely low"[38] It should be noted however that two of their three case studies are before the start of continuous confrontation from September 2012, when, as argued in the next chapter, the two sides were indeed more successful in managing flare-ups.

Similarly, Mike Mochizuki and Jiaxiu Han note that Japanese and Chinese coast guards have been acting to minimize incidents involving private actors from both China and Japan in the territorial waters of the Senkakus. Arguing that reports of Chinese escalation around 2020 appear to be unjustified, the two authors concluded that "Tokyo should avoid inflating the Chinese threat."[39] Similarly, "Asia's Future Research Group," in a report recommending that Japan adopt a strategy for promoting peace and regional stability, suggests that the ongoing status quo of confrontation surrounding the Senkakus has reached a level of stability that can be enhanced through bilateral diplomacy.[40]

PLAN OF THE BOOK

The rest of this book is divided into six chapters. Chapter 2 outlines the break down of the previous conflict management regime during 2010–2012 and the emergence of a new status quo of continual conflict.

---

[38] Yu and Kim, "The Stability of Proximity," pp. 327–328. For earlier optimistic analyses of the risk of conflict over the Senkaku Islands see Linus Hagström, "'Quiet Power:' Japan's China Policy in regard to the Pinnacle Islands," *The Pacific Review* 18, no. 2 (2005), pp. 159–188; M. Taylor Fravel, "Explaining Stability in the Senkaku (Diaoyu) Islands Dispute," in Gerald Curtis, Kokubun Ryosei, Wang Jisi, eds., *Getting the Triangle Straight: Managing China-Japan-US Relations* (Tokyo: Japan Centre for International Exchange, 2010) pp. 144–156; and Kentaro Sakuwa, "A Not So Dangerous Dyad: China's Rise and Sino-Japanese Rivalry," *International Relations of the Asia–Pacific* 9, no. 3 (2009), pp. 497–528.

[39] Mike Mochizuki, "Is China Escalating Tensions With Japan in the East China Sea?" *The Diplomat*, September 16, 2020, as accessed July 23, 2023, at https://thediplomat.com/2020/09/is-china-escalating-tensions-with-japan-in-the-east-china-sea/.

[40] Yoshihide Soeya and Mike Mochizuki, et al., *Asia's Future at a Crossroads: A Japanese Strategy for Peace and Sustainable Prosperity* ("Asia's Future" Research Group, 2023), accessed July 31, 2023, at https://bpb-us-e1.wpmucdn.com/blogs.gwu.edu/dist/d/3083/files/2023/07/Asias-Future-at-a-Crossroads-English.pdf.

Chapter 3 considers the broader impact of the new Senkaku status quo of continuous conflict on Japanese public and elite opinion, and the changes it has triggered in Japanese security policy, and even in overall politics. This chapter also analyzes Japan's military buildup (apart from its A2/AD strategy) to defend the Senkaku islands and the challenges this buildup faces. Chapter 4 examines Japan's emerging A2/AD strategy, and the challenges Japan faces fully developing this strategy. Chapter 5 considers the impact of this new strategy on Japan's traditional policy of not acquiring offensive missiles capable of hitting targets in other countries. Chapter 6 examines the three new fundamental defense documents issued in December 2022 as representing the culmination of a decade of transformation of Japan's defense for the purpose of achieving autonomous defense of the Senkaku islands, and increasingly of the Sakishima islands as well. Chapter 7, the concluding chapter, considers the relevance of Japan's defense transformation for US regional military strategy and for regional security, especially for a military conflict over Taiwan.

CHAPTER 2

From Dispute to Tacit Cooperation to Confrontation Over the Senkakus

Abstract This chapter traces the background of the bilateral territorial dispute between China, Japan, and Taiwan over the Senkaku (Diaoyu) islands. It focuses on the emergence of this dispute as a result of the US reversion of Okinawa, including these islands, to Japan in 1972, and the subsequent emergence of a tacit Sino-Japanese conflict management regime following the normalization of relations between the two countries, and the conclusion of a bilateral peace treaty in 1978. It also examines the gradual decline and breakdown of this bilateral tacit conflict management regime from the 1990s. Finally, this chapter analyzes how this regime broke down because of two bilateral confrontations over the islands in 2010 and 2012, after which China began sending coast guard vessels through the territorial waters of these islands at least once a month.

Keywords Japan Coast Guard (JCG) · Senkaku islands · Okinawa Reversion · Taiwan · Territorial waters · US

© The Author(s), under exclusive license to Springer Nature Switzerland AG 2025
P. Midford, *The Senkaku Islands Confrontation and the Transformation of Japan's Defense*, Palgrave Studies in Maritime Politics and Security, https://doi.org/10.1007/978-3-031-77727-1_2

19

Introduction

This chapter introduces the Senkaku/Diaoyu islands territorial dispute and then analyzes the rise and fall of the tactic bilateral conflict management regime that China and Japan established in the wake of their 1978 Peace and Friendship Treaty. It identifies two reasons for the decline and eventual breakdown of this conflict management regime between 1992 and 2012. First, this chapter argues that growing obsession in the domestic politics and national identity of both countries over these islands, beginning in China and then in Japan, contributed to the breakdown of this tacit regime. The second cause it identifies are power transition dynamics as Japan and its US ally have declined relative to China's rising national capabilities. Power transition, along with growing obsession over the islands caused both China and Japan to adopt increasingly hardline tactics that ultimately led to the conflict management regime's collapse in September 2012, and its replacement by a new status quo of continual confrontation in the territorial waters around the Senkaku islands. Since 2012 China has regularly (often several times a month) sailed Chinese Coast Guard (CCG) vessels of increasing armament as it attempts to disrupt Japan's assertion of control over these islands.

Overview of the Islands. The dispute is over the Pinnacle Islands, called the Senkaku islands (尖閣諸島) by Japan, the Diaoyutai/Tiaoyutai islands (釣魚臺列嶼) by Taiwan (the Republic of China, or ROC), and Diaoyu island and its affiliated islands (钓鱼岛及其附属岛屿) by the People's Republic of China (PRC). The largest Senkaku island, Uotsuri island (魚釣島 by Japan, 釣魚台 by Taiwan, 钓鱼岛 by China)[1] is 3.6 km^2 in area. The next largest island, called Kubashima (久場島) by Japan, Huangwei (黄尾嶼) by Taiwan and Huangwei Yu (黄尾屿/黄尾嶼) by China, is 0.87 km^2. The combined area of the next six islands (geographic features) that make up the Senkakus is less than 1 km^2.[2]

---

[1] The three claimants have essentially the same name in Chinese characters for Uotsuri Island, or fishing island. The Taiwanese and Chinese name for the whole group of islands is based on the name of this largest island, while Japan's name for the entire chain appears to be based on the British name for the islands, the Pinnacles. Unryu Suganuma, *Sovereign Rights and Territorial Space in Sino-Japanese Relations* (University of Hawaii Press, 2000), p. 89. The coordinates for these islands are 25°44′42″N 123°29′06″E.

[2] Ministry of Foreign Affairs, "Japan's Basic Position on the Senkaku Islands and Facts" (October 2012).

None of the islands, including Uotsuri, has a natural fresh (drinkable) water supply.[3] None of these islands are populated, although during the first decades of the twentieth century there was a small Japanese settlement on Uotsuri associated with a fish processing facility, and in the 1960s fishermen and salvage workers from Taiwan occasionally resided temporarily on the islands (see below). These islands' resources include guano and fishing. They are unsuited for agriculture.[4] As such, under the United Nations Convention of the Law of the Sea (UNCLOS), they do not qualify for their own EEZ because they cannot naturally support human habitation (Article 121).[5] Moreover, since these islands are already inside of the overlapping EEZ claims of both China and Japan, even a finding that they are entitled to an EEZ would likely have little practical impact. However, as the Senkakus are above high-tide geographic features, they therefore qualify for 12 nm of territorial waters. Although the Senkakus today have essentially nothing in terms of natural resources apart from fishing, in their pristine undeveloped state they do have ecological value. In particular the Senkakus have hosts a diverse range of birds, including the rare short-tailed albatross. BirdLife International recognizes the Senkakus as an Important Bird Area (IBA), implying that one solution to the dispute could be the creation of a binational nature preserve.[6]

History of the Dispute. The Senkakus are controlled by Japan. The dispute between China, Japan, and Taiwan regarding sovereignty over these islands is largely based on historical claims dating back to the

---

[3] OPRI Center of Island Studies, "Water Quality on the Senkaku Islands," February 17, 2015, as accessed February 25, 2022, at https://www.spf.org/islandstudies/info_library/senkaku-islands-06-env--06_env001.html.

[4] Constantinos Yiallourides, "Senkakus/Diaoyus: Are They Islands? Yes, No, Maybe," *Blog Post* (University of Aberdeen, School of Law), April 24, 2016, as accessed February 25, 2022 at https://www.abdn.ac.uk/law/blog/senkakusdiaoyus-are-they-islands-yes-no-maybe/.

[5] Under the 2016 Court of Arbitration's ruling on the South China Sea, none of the Spratly islands were judged to be capable of naturally supporting human habitation, including Taiping Island, an island controlled by Taiwan that includes a freshwater supply and agriculture. By that standard clearly the Senkakus do not qualify as able to naturally support human habitation, and hence, do not qualify for their own EEZ.

[6] Manicom, *Bridging Troubled Waters*, pp. 64–67; and BirdLife International, "Senkaku Islands," as accessed February 27, 2022, at http://datazone.birdlife.org/site/factsheet/senkaku-islands-iba-japan.

22   P. MIDFORD

Sino-Centric system of international relations that managed the international relations of East Asia for many centuries before the arrival in force of Western imperial powers in the mid-nineteenth century.[7] During this period these islands lay between Imperial China and the Kingdom of Ryukyu based on Okinawa. Chinese investiture envoys reportedly used these islands as a navigational aid when visiting Ryukyu to invest Ryukyuan kings as the legitimate rulers of their realm. Japanese pirates (called Wako, although frequently they were multi-ethnic and multi-national, including Chinese elements) used the remote and barren Senkaku islands as a base for launching pirate attacks on shipping. On at least one occasion Imperial Chinese forces attacked this pirate base.[8] Above all, under the Sino-Centric tributary system these islands were a remote and barren territory in the border zone between China and Ryukyu. Unlike the Westphalian international state system that is characterized by precise borders and division of all land territories among states, the Sino-Centric tributary system featured border and buffer zones rather than precise borders.[9]

Following the Meiji Restoration in 1868, Japan began to rapidly modernize and westernize. Meiji leaders embraced Western (European) international law not just as "barbarian ritual" and a one-way street, as China was still to a significant extent viewing it, but as potentially a basis for bargaining and even making gains. Japan used pirate attacks on the Ryukyuan kingdom in 1875 as a pretext to attack Taiwan, which was part of the Qing Chinese Empire, and then as a further pretext under international law to annex Ryukyu.[10] This annexation brought Imperial Japan into proximity to the unpopulated Senkaku islands.

Subsequently, there were several proposals during the 1880s and early 1890s in Japan for the country to annex the Senkaku islands, but no action was taken for fear that this would create a conflict with China.

---

[7] Regarding the history of this dispute, see Suganuma, *Sovereign Rights and Territorial Space in Sino-Japanese Relations*; Kimie Hara, *San furanshisuko heiwa jyōyaku no mōten-Ajia taiheiheyō chiiki no reisen to 'sengo mikaiketsu no shomondai'* (Keisuisha, 2005); and Yabuki and Selden, "The Origins of the Senkaku/Diaoyu Dispute between China, Taiwan, and Japan."

[8] Suganuma, *Sovereign Rights and Territorial Space in Sino-Japanese Relations*, p. 67.

[9] Ibid., 97.

[10] Ryukyu had been under the de facto control of the Satsuma feudal domain, based in Southern Kyushu in modern day Kagoshima, since 1610.

Nonetheless, during the Sino-Japanese War of 1894–1895, specifically on January 14, 1895, three months before this war ended, Japan annexed the Senkaku islands, claiming they were terra nullius. In the subsequent Treaty of Shimonoseki ending the war, China ceded to Japan "the island of Formosa, together with all islands appertaining or belonging to the said island of Formosa."[11]

These two facts are central to the sovereignty dispute to this day, as Article 2 of the 1952 San Francisco Peace Treaty required Japan to surrender all territories it had acquired through the Sino-Japanese War of 1894–1895, including Taiwan. For the ROC, and then for the PRC, this meant the Senkaku islands had to be returned to China as they were a part of Taiwan and had been taken as a result of Japan's aggression in the Sino-Japanese War, as per the Treaty of Shimonoseki. In Japan's view, on the other hand, these islands had been annexed because they were terra nullius and this act, although happening during the Sino-Japanese War, was unrelated to it.[12]

Japan maintained continuous control of the Senkaku islands for 50 years, from 1895 until 1945, a period that coincided with its colonization of Taiwan. At the end of World War II Japan surrendered control of Taiwan to the ROC, and the US took control of the Senkaku islands along with Okinawa and the Ryukyu islands. The Senkaku islands remained under US administration until the return of Okinawa in 1972. During that period the US used two of the smaller Senkaku islands as bombing ranges, but otherwise left the islands in an unpopulated and pristine state. Fishermen from Taiwan frequently, and occasionally government-affiliated ships from the ROC or mainland China (PRC), showed up in Senkaku waters, and ROC ship salvage workers on at least one occasion in the late 1960s resided for a few months in tents on the islands. Nonetheless, the US exercised administrative, if not always effective control, over these small and remote islands.[13]

---

[11] Suganuma, *Sovereign Rights and Territorial Space in Sino-Japanese Relations*, pp. 97–98, 106–107; Manicom, *Bridging Troubled Waters*, p. 44.

[12] Suganuma, *Sovereign Rights and Territorial Space in Sino-Japanese Relations*, p. 98.

[13] Eldridge, *The Origins of US Policy in the East China Sea Islands Dispute*, pp. 58–59, 72–73, 78. Eldridge recounts that 45–60 workers from Taiwan lived on the Senkakus for several months while they salvaged a wrecked Panamanian freighter. Albatross egg and herb gatherers and fishermen from Taiwan also occasionally resided on the islands.

In the late 1960s three events happened almost simultaneously. First, Japan and the US reached an agreement for the reversion of Okinawa to Japanese sovereignty. The US had continued to occupy Okinawa and the rest of the Ryukyus even after Japan regained its sovereignty in April 1952. The issue of Okinawa's return to Japanese sovereignty and administration became an increasingly contentious issue in Japan-US relations following Japan's recovery of sovereignty. The 1960 Japan-US Security Treaty, the treaty of alliance that remains in effect to this day, was affected by this tension. The US refused to concede Japanese sovereignty over Okinawa and the Ryukyus in this treaty, and Japan refused to agree to anything that would call Japan's sovereignty into question. Japan also refused to help defend US control of Okinawa, in part because US military bases there were very much involved in confrontations with China over the ROC-held islands of Quemoy and Matsu. The eventual compromise that was reached meant that in Article 5 of the Security Treaty the US committed to defend territories under "the administration of Japan" (i.e., Japan's four main islands and subsidiary islands under its control).[14] This language would have the unforeseen effect decades later of obligating the US to defend Japan's control of the Senkaku islands.

During the same period when it became clear that the US was going to return Okinawa and the Ryukyu islands to Japan the Emery survey of May 1969 covering the East China Sea sponsored by the UN-funded Economic Commission for Asia and the Far East found potentially rich deposits of oil and gas in the East China Sea, including near the Senkaku islands. In September 1970 the ROC on Taiwan claimed sovereignty over the Senkaku islands. Days later Japan issued its own formal claim of sovereignty over these islands. Shortly thereafter, and following the ROC's lead, the PRC claimed sovereignty over these islands.[15] The Emery survey has become an important talking point for Japan, as those supporting Japan's claim often argue that the ROC and PRC were motivated to claim sovereignty over the Senkaku island merely because of the discovery of potential oil and gas deposits nearby, in an act of economic opportunism (Fig. 2.1).

---

[14] Regarding these negotiations, see Tetsuya Kataoka, *The Price of a Constitution* (New York: Crane Russak, 1991), pp. 190–192, 194–195, 200–201.

[15] Manicom, *Bridging Troubled Waters*, pp. 43–44.

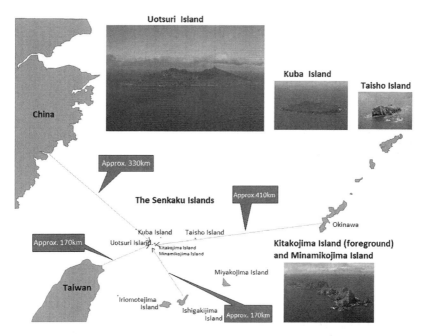

Fig. 2.1 Location of the Senkaku Islands (*Source* Akiyama Masahiro, "Geopolitical Considerations of the Senkaku Islands," OPRI Center of Island Studies, August 7, 2013, as accessed August 20, 2024 at https://www.spf.org/islandstudies/research/a00007.html)

However, another factor appears to be as much, if not more, important: the achievement of an agreement between Japan and the US in November 1969 regarding the return of Okinawa and the Ryukyus to Japanese sovereignty. The ROC, a US ally with US troops then stationed on its soil, had not pressed a sovereignty claim against US control of these islands, especially as two of them had been used as bombing ranges that presumably contributed to ROC's defense. Indeed, the ROC made clear that while it did not object to US administration of these islands or the Ryukyus, it did not view Japan as having any rights in these islands, and it questioned Japan's "residual sovereignty" over the Ryukyus as well.[16]

---

[16] Eldridge documents the ROC's position of accepting US administration over the Senkakus while opposing Japan's residual sovereignty there in August 1968, before the

In short, the timing of the ROC's claim to these islands can be linked to the envisaged return of Okinawa and the Ryukyus to Japan, which the ROC objected to, as much, or perhaps even more, than it can be linked to the discovery of oil and gas resources in the East China Sea. Moreover, it has never been clear, especially since UNCLOS was concluded in 1982 (as discussed above) and subsequently ratified by both China and Japan, that sovereignty over the Senkakus would confer any right to develop the hydrocarbon resources of the East China Sea beyond the 12 nm territorial waters that these islands have, an area probably too small to hold much in the way of significant hydrocarbon resources. It is even less clear that economic opportunism, instead of nationalism, has been a driving force behind the claims of China, Taiwan or Japan on the Senkakus over the decades since they laid claim to these islands.

In the end the US returned control of the Senkakus to Japan in 1972. At the same time the US adopted a position of neutrality regarding who possesses sovereignty over these islands. The US position was that it returned the islands in the same state that it took them, namely to Japanese control, arguing that the US could neither confer nor subtract from the validity of preexisting sovereignty claims over these islands. As a US State Department legal expert put it "The United States cannot add to the legal rights that Japan possessed before it transferred administration of the islands to us, nor can the United States, by giving back what it received, dimmish the rights of other claimants."[17]

The 1978 Tacit Management Regime

After the reversion of Okinawa and the Ryukyus from the US to Japan in 1972 the Senkakus emerged as an irritant in Japan's relations with Taiwan and especially with China. Sino-Japanese relations were normalized in 1972, and after that the two sides commenced negotiations on a peace and friendship treaty, during which the territorial dispute over these

---

Emery survey and Taiwan′s sovereignty declaration that came in the wake of that reversion agreement. Eldridge, *The Origins of US Policy in the East China Sea Islands Dispute*, p. 77.

[17] Letter by Robert I. Starr, Acting Assistant Legal Advisor for East Asian and Pacific Affairs of October 20, 1971, as reproduced in Yabuki and Selden, "The Origin of the Senkaku/Diaoyu Dispute between China, Taiwan and Japan." Eldridge documents various efforts by the US to avoid taking actions that favored or disfavored the sovereignty claims of Japan or any other claimants, especially the ROC. See Eldridge, *The Origins of US Policy in the East China Sea Islands Dispute*, pp. 83–95.

islands came up. In April 1978, during the final phases of negotiating the treaty China sent a large flotilla of 80 to 100 fishing boats to the Senkakus in a show of force. In the end the 1978 Treaty of Peace and Friendship did not settle the issue. Chinese leader Deng Xiaoping proposed that the territorial issue be "shelved."[18] Japan did not publicly endorse or refute this statement but appeared to tacitly accept it.[19] Some in Tokyo apparently misperceived Deng's statement as de facto Chinese recognition of Japanese sovereignty.[20]

In fact, after the conclusion of the Sino-Japanese Treaty of Peace and Friendship the two nations cooperated to keep bilateral tensions over the Diaoyu/Senkaku islands from damaging bilateral relations, especially economic relations. For example, bilateral fisheries cooperation was traditionally insulated from the territorial dispute; fishing around the islands (as per the 1975 and 1997 bilateral fisheries agreements) was defined as a fisheries issue, not a territorial one. This was one part of the tacit bilateral conflict management regime.

The basis of this conflict management regime was China's recognition of Japan's control of the islands, in exchange for a Japanese promise to leave these islands unoccupied and undeveloped. Japan tacitly agreed to China's "three no's:" no entry, no survey, and no use. The latter included no development. In exchange China tacitly agreed to Japan's "three no's:" no landing, no entry into islands' airspace, no entry into their waters.[21] Apart from the 1997 agreement on fisheries in surrounding waters, other resources were left undeveloped and largely unexplored, most notably hydrocarbon resources. When the issue flared up, both countries acted to quickly tamp down tensions and insulate the rest of the relationship.[22]

---

[18] This is known as "tana-age ron" (棚上げ論) or shelving theory in Japanese. Ukeru Magosaki, "Senkaku shotō, 'tana-age ron,' wa mada yūkō," *Nikkei Onrain*, November 28, 2012, as accessed May 7, 2019 at http://business.nikkeibp.co.jp/article/interview/20121121/239737/?rt=nocnt.

[19] The late senior LDP politician Nonaka Hiromu, who participated in normalization talks with China in 1972, confirmed the shelving agreement. See Niwa Uichiro, *Chugoku no daimondai* (Tokyo: PHP, 2014), p. 154.

[20] Manicom, *Bridging Troubled Waters*, pp. 45–46.

[21] Kazuhiko Togo, *Rekishi ninshiki wo toinasu: Yasukuni, ianfu, ryōdo mondai* (Tokyo: Kakugawa Shoten 2013), pp. 43–46.

[22] Michael J. Green, *Japan's Reluctant Realism: Foreign Policy Challenges in an Era of Uncertain Power* (Palgrave Macmillan, 2003), pp. 84–87.

Although both China and Japan used the tacit shelving and conflict management regime to prevent the Diaoyu/Senkaku dispute from dominating their important bilateral relationship, the dispute flared up several times between August 1978 and 2004. These flare-ups were driven by civil society groups from Japan, Hong Kong, Taiwan, and in later years increasingly from China.

The first challenge came in August 1978, before the two countries had even signed their newly completed Peace and Friendship Treaty, when *Nihon Seinensha* (Japanese Youth Federation), a right-wing Japanese group installed a small lighthouse on Uotsuri island. Japan responded by refusing to have the Japanese Coast Guard (JCG, then known as the Maritime Safety Agency, MSA) register this lighthouse as an official navigation marker. The conservative Liberal Democratic Party (LDP) government in Tokyo found it legally, but especially politically, difficult to act against this group, as its cause was popular among some party members and supporters.[23]

In 1988 the same group improved the lighthouse in order to gain approval from the JCG. In 1990 their application for recognition of this lighthouse generated great controversy, including a formal diplomatic protest from China. Approximately 10,000 Hong Kong residents held public demonstrations against Japanese control of the islands, and protesters from Taiwan visited the islands and planted the ROC flag. After the flag was removed by Japanese law enforcement, the demonstrators returned to the Senkakus but were blocked by JCG patrol ships from approaching the islands. Prime Minister Kaifu Toshiki defused the controversy by publicly stating that Japan would refuse to recognize the lighthouse. Kaifu's Chief Cabinet Secretary (the second highest-ranking official in the cabinet) publicly affirmed support for Deng's idea of shelving the dispute for posterity. Nonetheless, China was criticized by overseas Chinese activists for not being stronger in opposing Japan's position over the islands.[24]

The next flare-up was not caused by activists, but by China enacting a Law on the Territorial Sea and Contiguous Zone in February 1992.

---

[23] Suganuma, *Sovereign Rights and Territorial Space in Sino-Japanese Relations*, pp. 136, 139–140; Manicom, *Bridging Troubled Waters*, p. 47.

[24] Suganuma, *Sovereign Rights and Territorial Space in Sino-Japanese Relations*, pp. 136, 139–140; Manicom, *Bridging Troubled Waters*, p. 47; "Spokesman Favors Leaving Senkaku Islands Issue to Posterity," *Kyodo News International*, October 23, 1990;

Unlike a previous declaration from 1958, this law explicitly listed the islands as Chinese territory. While Chinese leader Jiang Zemin argued this law was consistent with "shelving" the dispute for future generations to solve, and while Japanese Prime Minister Miyazawa Kiichi also expressed support for this solution, Japan's Foreign Ministry responded to China's new law by starting to deny that there was any agreement about "shelving," and even going so far as to correct Miyazawa's statement.

The Japanese government also began leasing some of the land on the islands from their Japanese owners as a way of further strengthening its control over the islands, in part to make it more difficult for right-wing groups to continue landing on the islands.[25]

In 1996 the dispute flared up again as both China and Japan ratified UNCLOS and made their EEZ claims official in the East China Sea, reaffirming their claims over the Senkakus in the process. Nihon Seinensha built a lighthouse on Kita Kojima (which China calls Bei Xiaodao), one of the smaller islands, raised a Japanese flag over it, and applied to MSA for official recognition, recognition that was denied. A few months later this group returned to repair the lighthouse after a typhoon damaged it. This produced diplomatic protests from China and large public protests in Hong Kong. Meanwhile, protests on the mainland were suppressed, but websites dedicated to defending China's claims to the Diaoyu sprung up. Hong Kong protestors attempted to land on the islands, were blocked by the JCG, and one of four protestors who attempted to swim to the

and "10,000 Protest in Hong Kong over Japan's Islands Claim," *Kyodo News International*, October 28, 1990; "Chinese Press turns Critical Eye Toward Japan," *New York Times*, November 22, 1990, p. C-8.

[25] Manicom, *Bridging Troubled Waters*, pp. 48–49, 60, 65; Suganuma, *Sovereign Rights and Territorial Space in Sino-Japanese Relations*, pp. 142–143; Reinhard Drifte, "China Sea—Between Military Confrontation and Economic Cooperation," *LSE Asia Research Centre, Working Paper* no. 24 (2008), p. 7, as accessed March 16, 2014, at http://www.lse.ac.uk/collections/asiaResearchCentre/pdf/WorkingPaper/ARCWorkin gPaper24Drifte2008.pdf; Ukeru Magosaki, "Senkaku shotō, 'tana-age ron,' wa mada yūkō," *Nikkei Onrain*, November 28, 2012, as accessed May 7, 2019 at http://business. nikkeibp.co.jp/article/interview/20121121/239737/?rt=nocnt; Kazuhiko Togo, *Rekishi ninshiki wo toinasu: Yasukuni, ianfu, ryōdo mondai* (Tokyo: Kakugawa Shoten 2013), pp. 43–46. As Togo recounts the initial agreement in 1972, and again in 1978, to shelve the territorial dispute was a tacit, if not secret, agreement. So too was Japan's agreement to China's "three nos." Also see Niwa Uichiro, *Chugoku no daimondai* (Tokyo: PHP, 2014), p. 154.

30   P. MIDFORD

islands drowned. A week later Taiwanese activists successfully landed on the islands and hoisted both Taiwanese and mainland flags, apparently the JCG did not try to stop them.[26] Overall, Japan, China, and Taiwan tacitly cooperated to keep challenges from nationalists from upsetting the status quo or damaging relations.

In 2000 Nihon Seinensha again landed on Uotsuri and built a small Shinto Shrine, drawing condemnation but little escalation from China as the two sides again managed the crisis. However, on March 24, 2004, several activists from the mainland (as opposed to Taiwan and Hong Kong) landed on the Senkakus for the first time and burnt down the Shinto Shrine. They were arrested by the Japanese police on suspicion of damaging property. However, in the face of protests from China and to avoid escalation that could damage the larger bilateral relationship Japan refrained from applying domestic law to prosecute the Chinese activists, despite their destruction of the small Shinto shrine there. Instead, after Prime Minister Koizumi Junichiro publicly stated that he advised prosecutors in Okinawa to handle the issue so that it would not negatively impact Sino-Japanese relations, the activists were quickly deported to China. After the 2004 incident the Japanese government bought some of the privately held land on these islands from their Japanese owner to gain a stronger legal basis for blocking rightists from landing on the islands.[27] However, the Koizumi administration and China also acted to try shoring up the tacit bilateral conflict management regime by reaching a secret agreement under which Japan agreed not to prosecute Chinese activists

---

[26] Manicom, *Bridging Troubled Waters*, pp. 51–52, 78. A senior Japanese diplomat from the Asia bureau of the Foreign Ministry told the author that Japan allowed the demonstrators to land as a form of consolation for the drowned protestor.

[27] James Manicom, *Bridging Troubled Waters: China, Japan, and Maritime Order in the East China Sea* (Georgetown University Press, 2014), pp. 47–53; Björn Jerden, "The Assertive China Narrative: Why It Is Wrong and How So Many Still Bought into It," *The Chinese Journal of International Politics* 7, no. 1 (2014), pp. 58–59; "Nyukan ni watasazu danzoku sōsa, 7 nin sōken he: Chugoku wa shyakuhō yōkyū, Senkaku shotō jōriku," *Asahi Shimbun*, March 26, 2004 (chōkan), p. 1; "'Hō de handan,' seifu kyōchō: Senkaku jōriku no 7 nin sōken sezu," *Asahi Shimbun*, March 27, 2004 (chōkan), p. 2; "Hōshin kyūten, tomadō genba chūgokujin senkaku jōriku jiken de 7 nin kyōsei sōkan," *Asahi Shimbun* (chōkan) March 27, 2004, p. 4; O'Shea, "Sovereignty and the Senkaku/Diaoyu Territorial Dispute," p. 21; "Senkaku jyōriku/kyōsei sōkan: 'tokurei' tekiyō, kecchyaku isogu, 'kaimei sezu sōkan, futekisetsu' no koe mo," *Yomiuri Shimbun*, March 27, 2004 (chōkan), p. 3.

2 FROM DISPUTE TO TACIT COOPERATION ... 31

who land on the islands, and China undertook to prevent activists from landing on the islands in the first place.[28]

From Tacit Cooperation to Open Confrontation

Thus, since the conclusion of the 1978 Treaty of Peace and Friendship between China and Japan, the two nations worked to keep tensions over the Senkaku islands from damaging overall bilateral relations, especially economic relations.[29] This conflict management regime, which had already been weakening since 1992, broke down completely as a result of bilateral confrontations in 2010 and especially because of a subsequent confrontation in 2012 that destroyed the previous bilateral tacit conflict management regime and established the new status quo of continual confrontation over the islands. The first decisive blow against the 1978 management regime occurred in September 2010 due to an altercation between JCG patrol vessels and a Chinese fishing boat. This incident had profound implications for Japanese perceptions of China. This incident raised the Senkaku Island dispute to the top of the political agenda in Japan.

On the morning of September 7th this Chinese fishing boat, the Minjinyu 5179, collided with two JCG vessels (the Yonaguni and the Mizuki).[30] These two JCG vessels were attempting to make the boat leave

---

[28] "Nicchu 'Senkaku mitsuyaku' atta sukkupu, Seiji shudō no otoshi ana," *Aera*, October 25, 2010, p. 12. Strikingly, this produced a negative reaction from Taiwan which had not been included in this deal. See Chris Wang, "Taiwan Investigating Reported China-Japan Deal on Disputed Islands," *Focus Taiwan*, October 19, 2010, p. 1.

[29] Suganuma, *Sovereign Rights and Territorial Space in Sino-Japanese Relations*; Kimie Hara, *San furanshisuko heiwa jyōyaku no mōten*; and Susumu Yabuki and Mark Selden, "The Origins of the Senkaku/Diaoyu Dispute between China, Taiwan, and Japan," *The Asia-Pacific Journal*, 12, no. 2, 3 (January, 2014), http://japanfocus.org/-Mark-Selden/4061?rand=1392958972&type=print&print=1.

[30] Initially these two collisions were widely described in Japan and the Western media as the fishing boat deliberately ramming the two JCG vessels. Influencing this discourse might have been Transportation Minister, and subsequently Foreign Minister, Maehara Seiji, who, after seeing a video of the collisions soon after they happened described them as "clearly a ramming." For an argument in support of this interpretation see Satoshi Amako, "The Senkaku Islands Incident and Japan-China Relations," *East Asia Forum*, October 25, 2010, as accessed August 11, 2023 at http://www.eastasiaforum.org/2010/10/25/the-senkaku-islands-incident-and-japan-china-relations/. However, the video tape of this incident, which was subsequently leaked to the public, is inconclusive as it shows

32 P. MIDFORD

the territorial waters of the Senkaku islands that Japan claims and effectively controlled, resulting in minor damage to the JCG guard cutters. In response, the JCG vessels seized control of the Chinese boat and took it and all 14 crew members to Ishigaki Island, where the captain, Zhan Qixiong, was arrested on suspicion of obstructing the official duties of JCG personnel, a crime that carries a sentence of up to three years in jail. On September 10 an Okinawan court granted Ishigaki prosecutors' request to extend the captain's detention for ten days to prepare for possibly filing criminal charges. On September 19th, the captain's detention was extended for another ten days and it appeared that prosecutors were preparing to file charges.[31] Moreover, Foreign Minister Maehara Seiji stated not only that no territorial dispute existed, but stated for the first time that Japan had never agreed to "shelve" the dispute.[32]

At this point the issue of the captain's detention escalated into a bilateral confrontation, with China demanding that the ship's captain be released, as the crew and the boat had been. China rejected Japan's jurisdiction to indict the captain, citing their own territorial claims to the Senkaku islands, and started canceling bilateral meetings, and began deploying fisheries protection vessels in contiguous waters just outside the territorial waters of the islands. Beijing also suspended rare earth shipments to Japan, and four Japanese company employees were arrested in China for illegally videotaping in a restricted military zone. These developments were widely seen in Japan as an attempt to "intimidate" Tokyo into releasing the captain,[33] although whether either development was

---

the collision as filmed from one of the JCG vessels, and hence it does not show how that vessel was moving relative to the Chinese fishing boat. Subsequently, the Foreign Ministry in its annual diplomatic Bluebook and the Ministry of Defense in their Defense of Japan used the term "collision" (*shōtotsu jiken*) to describe what happened. See *Diplomatic Bluebook 2011* (Tokyo: Ministry of Foreign Affairs, 2011), p. 7; and *Defense of Japan 2011* (Tokyo: Ministry of Defense, 2011), pp. 7, 8, 106, 107; and Linus Hagström, "Power Shift in East Asia? A Critical Appraisal of Narratives on the Diaoyu/Senkaku Islands Incident in 2010," *Chinese Journal of International Politics* 5 (2012), p. 274.

[31] Masami Ito, "Trawler's Collisions, JCG Arrest of Skipper Near Senkakus Protested," *Japan Times*, September 9, 2010; "Editorial: King of the Islands Tiff," *Japan Times*, September 10, 2010; and Kyodo, "Chinese Vessel Asks Survey Ship to Stop," *Japan Times*, September 11, 2011; Hagström, "Power Shift in East Asia?" p. 272.

[32] Manicom, *Bridging Troubled Waters*, p. 59.

[33] See for example "Govt Leaders Flinch at China Intimidation," *Daily Yomiuri*, September 26, 2010, p. 3.

related to the bilateral dispute over captain's arrest (rather than being a coincidence) has been questioned.[34]

In late September the Ishigaki prosecutor's office, citing "the effects on the people of Japan and the future of Japan-China relations," announced the release of the ship's captain without filing charges.[35] The reaction from opposition parties was vociferous, with the Kan administration standing accused of pressuring prosecutors. In response to Kan's claim that "the decision was made by the prosecutor's office," the LDP's shadow defense minister, Onodera Itsunori claimed the captain's release was Japan's "biggest foreign policy blunder in the postwar era."[36] *Yomiuri Shimbun* cited a senior disgruntled DPJ member as claiming that neither Kan nor his ministers "knows anything about diplomacy. They just released the skipper in a flutter after being intimidated by China. China will probably continue to make unreasonable demands on Japan...

[34] Ibid., pp. 281–283. For a skeptical account about whether China actually imposed a rare-earths embargo in retaliation for the captain's arrest, see Alastair Iain Johnston, "How New and Assertive Is China's New Assertiveness?" *International Security* 37, no. 4 (Spring 2013), pp. 23–28. China announced restrictions on rare-earth exports to all countries a month earlier, apparently as part of a strategy to encourage high-tech industries that rely on rare earths to relocate production to China. See Tatsuo Kotoyori, Noriyoshi Ohtsuki and Takeshi Kamiya, "Japan Alarmed by China's Policy on Rare Metals," *Asahi Shimbun*, August 21, 2010, p. 2; Tatsuo Kotoyori, Koichi Furuya, and Takeshi Kamiya, "Chinese Adamant on Rare-Earth Metal Cuts," *Asahi Shimbun*, August 30, 2010, p. 3; "Rare-Earth Furor Overlooks China's 2006 Industrial Policy Signal," *Bloomberg*, October 21, 2010; and "Digging in China Restricts Exports of Some Obscure but Important Commodities," *Economist*, September 2, 2010, as accessed August 17, 2023 at https://www.economist.com/finance-and-economics/2010/09/02/digging-in.

[35] "Prosecutors to Release Trawler Captain," *Asahi.com*, September 25, 2010, http://www.asahi.com/english/"TKY201009240209.html; and "China Still Patrolling Senkaku Islands," *Asahi.com*, September 29, 2010, http://www.asahi.com/english/TKY201009 280282.html.

[36] "Senkaku shingi semerujimin 'sengo saigo no gaikōteki haiboku,' seifu wa kire waruku," *Yomiuri Shimbun*, October 1, 2010 (chōkan), p. 4; "Prosecutors to Release Trawler Captain," *Asahi.com*; "China Still Patrolling Senkaku Islands," *Asahi.com*. The LDP's sharp attack on the Kan administration for allegedly pressuring prosecutors to release the captain is ironic given that LDP Prime Minister Koizumi had openly done exactly that when Chinese activities were arrested on the Senkakus six years earlier (see the previous discussion of the 2004 incident). For more on LDP criticism of the Kan administration's response, see Hagström, "'Quiet Power:' Japan's China Policy in regard to the Pinnacle Islands," p. 278.

34   P. MIDFORD

[because] of this country's lack of mettle."[37] The perception that the Kan administration had given into Chinese intimidation created pressure to not compromise in future crises.[38]

The public was more convinced by the arguments of DPJ critics than Kan's counter-arguments. A *Yomiuri Shimbun* poll conducted shortly after the captain's release showed that 72% found the captain's release "inappropriate," versus only 19% who thought it "appropriate." In a follow-up question for those answering "inappropriate," 41% said the release created the image that Japan could be intimidated, while 30% cited the severity of the incident, and 14% expressed concern that the release would strengthen China's territorial claims. 83% of respondents were unconvinced by Kan's explanation that the decision to release the captain had been made by prosecutors, versus 11% who were convinced. Also, 71% answered that in order to respond to the Senkaku issue Japan needed to strengthen the alliance with the US, versus 19% who did not think so. Finally, in answer to a *Yomiuri* question about whether the "DPJ administration's security and foreign policies make you worried," 84% responded that they felt very (39%) or somewhat (45%) worried, versus only 14% who responded that they felt little (11%) or no (3%) worry. In the wake of the Kan administration's handling of this incident, its overall approval rating also fell significantly to (a still relatively high) 53% (versus 37% who disapproved).[39]

However, this fall in support for the Kan cabinet gathered momentum during the following month. A *Nihon Keizai Shimbun* poll found a drop in approval for Kan from 71% in mid-September to 40% by late October, with the disapproval rate hitting 48%, the first time it exceeded the disapproval rate during Kan's tenure as prime minister. Of respondents who disapproved of the Kan cabinet's performance, 28% cited poor handling of foreign and security policies, up from a mere 7% who gave this reason

---

[37] "Senkaku shingi semerujimin 'sengo saigo no gaikōteki haiboku,'" *Yomiuri Shimbun*. Hagström, "'Quiet Power:' Japan's China Policy in Regard to the Pinnacle Islands," p. 278.

[38] Arguably, China honored the spirit of the bilateral conflict management agreement after Japan released the fishing boat captain by revoking the captain's license, leaving him unemployed. "Senkaku gyosen shōtotsu, asu 1 nen: 'eiyū' senchō, ima wa kago no tori," *Mainichi Shimbun*, September 6, 2012 (yūkan), p. 1. Also see O'Shea, "Sovereignty and the Senkaku/Diaoyu Territorial Dispute," p. 14.

[39] "Naikaku shiji rakka 53%, Honsha zenkoku yoron chōsa kekka, shitsumon to kaitō," *Yomiuri*, October 4, 2010 (morning edition), p. 9.

in August, the number one reason given for disapproval (it is rare for disapproval of foreign and security policies to be the number one reason for disapproval).[40] A week later a Kyodo poll found Kan's support rate had dropped from 47.6% a month earlier to 32.7% (a drop of 14.9%), while his disapproval rate had reached 48.6%. The same poll found 74% disapproved of Kan's diplomacy, with disapproval of diplomacy toward China apparently playing a large role.[41] Similarly, an *Asahi Shimbun* poll conducted around the same time found that Kan's support rate had fallen from 45 to 27%, with 77% of respondents negatively evaluating Kan's foreign policy, versus a mere 11% who positively evaluated it.[42] The shock of the September 2010 confrontation surrounding the Senkaku islands, the widespread perception that the Kan administration had mishandled this crisis and retreated in the face of hardball tactics from the Chinese government, had large political reverberations, doing lasting damage to the foreign policy reputation of the Kan administration and more generally the DPJ. It also set in motion a long-term reevaluation of China's intentions toward Japan.

In fact, the Kan administration adopted a tougher approach to this incident than had previous LDP governments, especially the Koizumi administration in 2004, and may have even made some important gains, such as gaining a strong statement from US Secretary of State Hillary Clinton that the US would help Japan defend its control of the Senkakus.[43] The LDP's sharp attack on the Kan administration for allegedly pressuring prosecutors to release the captain is ironic given that LDP Prime Minister Koizumi had openly done exactly that when Chinese activists were arrested on the Senkakus six years earlier (see the previous discussion of the 2004 incident).

[40] "Gaikō he no fuman kyūkakudai: naikaku hyōka shinai riyū 1 ichi," *Nihon Keizai Shimbun*, November 1, 2010, (chōkan), p. 2. In English see "Boat sinks on Kan's approval rating," *Nikkei Weekly*, November 8, 2010, p. 2.

[41] "Naikaku shiji 32% ni kyūraku, Kyōdōtsūshin yoron chōsa," *Nihon Keizai Shimbun*, November 8, 2010 (chōkan), p. 2.

[42] "Asahi shimbunsha yoron chōsa shitsumon to kaitō," *Asahi Shimbun*, November 16, 2010 (chōkan), p. 4.

[43] Hagström, "Power Shift in East Asia?" pp. 283–290; Jeffrey A. Bader, *Obama and China's Rise: An Insider's Account of America's Asia Strategy* (Washington, D.C.: Brookings Institution Press, 2012), p. 106; Jerden, "The Assertive China Narrative," p. 58; Johnston, "How New and Assertive Is China's New Assertiveness?" p. 22.

This more hardline and assertive Japanese approach to territorial disputes had been building for years. In April 2007 the Diet passed the Basic Law on Oceans Policy (海洋基本法), which created a legal framework for deploying the JCG and even the MSDF to protect Japanese facilities harvesting resources in its claimed EEZ, although this law did not directly change the status quo for fishing around the Senkakus.[44] The DPJ's response appeared to depart from previous practice from the perspective of Chinese and some outside observers because the captain was not immediately released without charge, as had been the practice previously (specifically in 2004) and asserted jurisdiction to try the captain. That was notable because Sino-Japanese fisheries agreements from 1975 and 1997 explicitly, rather than implicitly, avoided the territorial issues in these waters by specifying flag-state jurisdiction (not coastal state jurisdiction) would apply in waters south of 27N (i.e., including waters around the Senkaku islands), meaning China was responsible for policing its own fishing boats. Consequently, the territorial waters around these islands were treated as high seas in the case of fishing vessels.[45]

Behind the difference between the DPJ's hardline versus the LDP's softer approach lay two very different party cultures, perhaps DPJ ignorance due to having never been in power before, and lacking good connections and working relations with career bureaucrats.[46] The DPJ

[44] James Manicom, "Japan's Growing Assertiveness at Sea," *Wall Street Journal* (online), September 20, 2010, as accessed August 20, 2023 at https://www.wsj.com/articles/SB10001424052748703556604575502830616192158.

[45] Sourabh Gupta, "China-Japan Trawler Incident: Japan's Unwise—And Borderline Illegal—Detention of the Chinese Skipper," *East Asia Forum*, 30 September 2010, as accessed 14 January 2014 at http://www.eastasiaforum.org/2010/09/30/china-japan-trawler-incident-japans-unwise-and-borderline-illegal-detention-of-the-chinese-skipper/; Manicom, *Bridging Troubled* Waters, pp. 71, 81; Reinhard Drifte, "The Japan-China Confrontation Over the Senkaku/Diaoyu Islands—Between 'Shelving' and 'Dispute Escalation,'" *Japan Focus* 12, no. 30 (July 27, 2014), p. 7, as accessed March 21, 2016 at http://apjjf.org/2014/12/30/Reinhard-Drifte/4154/article.html. It was common practice, however, for JCG ships to escort Chinese fishing vessels out of territorial waters (12 nm) around the Senkaku islands, and China did not object to this.

[46] Reflecting on the handicap of the lack of information on foreign policy that the DPJ had been privy to, and how this negatively affected foreign policy making under the DPJ is Kitazawa Toshimi, *Nihon ni jieitai ga hitsuyouna riyū* (Tokyo: Kakugawa, 2012), p. 126. Kitazawa served as Defense Minister in the Kan administration during this crisis. Regarding inadequate communication between DPJ administration officials and bureaucrats, and within the DPJ administration itself, see Niwa, *Chugoku no daimondai* (Tokyo: PHP, 2014), pp. 146–148, 151–152. Regarding the 2004 secret agreement see

during its long gestation period as an opposition party developed norms of transparency, openness, and even formality that contrasted with the LDP's long practice, both domestically and internationally, of relying on informal private negotiations to hammer out agreements.[47] In this sense, the LDP was perhaps more attuned to the informal back-door consultative networks among elites that have dominated conflict prevention and resolution mechanisms in East Asia.[48] The DPJ by contrast was almost legalistic in its approach. A related problem for the Kan administration is that it lacked good "pipes" to China, or DPJ members who could act as unofficial back channels of contact. The one DPJ politician well positioned to engage in informal diplomacy with China, Ozawa Ichirō, had become Kan's main rival (and also tainted by scandal) and hence estranged from the cabinet.

A final reason for the DPJ's harder line was the growing salience of the Senkaku and other maritime disputes for public opinion in Japan as well as China. Manicom argued "both states confront powerful disincentives for conciliation in light of the growing domestic salience of these issues."[49] Yves Tiberghien argues that this confrontation "was the result of a dynamic interaction between two highly charged domestic arenas...and actors who were mainly concerned with domestic issues caused the crisis."[50] On Japan's side Tiberghien blames the political

above. For an argument about how the DPJ's policies to reduce bureaucratic influence (such as by eliminating the bureaucratic vice ministers meeting, or *jimujikan kaigi*) ended up damaging the policy making process see Tomohito Shinoda, *Contemporary Japanese Politics: Institutional Changes and Power Shifts* (New York: Columbia University Press, 2013), chpts. 5–7. It is not clear whether in this case there was just poor communication between the DPJ and bureaucrats, as per Shinoda's argument, or whether bureaucrats tried to sabotage DPJ policy.

[47] The author's own experience meeting with LDP and DPJ party officials confirms this: DPJ officials were keen to take notes and ensure that nothing said during the meetings would be "secret."

[48] For a comprehensive description and analysis of these mechanisms and norms see Mikael Weissmann, *The East Asian Peace: Conflict Prevention and Informal Peacebuilding* (New York: Palgrave Macmillan, 2012).

[49] James Manicom, "Growing Nationalism and Maritime Jurisdiction in the East China Sea," *China Brief: A Journal of Analysis and Information* 10, no. 21 (2010), p. 7/8.

[50] Yves Tiberghien, "The Puzzling 2010 Diaoyu Crisis: Centrifugal Domestic Politics, Shifting Balance of Power, and Weak Regional Institutionalization," *Harvard Asia Quarterly*, December 24, 2010, http://asiaquarterly.com/2010/12/24/the-puzzling-2010-diaoyu-crisis-centrifugal-domestic-politics-shifting-balance-of-power-and-weak-regional-institutionalization/, pp. 77, 78.

38 P. MIDFORD

entrepreneurialism and ambition of Transportation Minister, and subsequently Foreign Minister, Maehara, for making the fateful decision to arrest the captain as a way to appeal to domestic nationalist sentiment.[51]

Regardless of whether a more assertive Japanese approach contributed to the exacerbation and extension of the September 2010 fishing boat confrontation over these very small islands, this confrontation had a big impact on Japanese perceptions of China. China's rising military as well as economic power had already been clearly perceived. Yet, China was not seen as harboring aggressive intentions toward Japan. What was seen in Japan as a bullying response during this crisis became an inflection point that started to change perceptions of China's intentions, which came to be seen as aggressive. This started to shift the balance in Japan's China policy away from reassurance and toward deterrence and an emphasis on being prepared to use coercive force to defend what Japan sees as its sovereign territory.[52]

This perception that deterrence if not physical force would be needed to maintain Japan's control over the Senkakus became visible not only among elites, but also among the public. When asked how the Kan cabinet should respond to the situation surrounding the Senkaku islands in a Nippon TV poll conducted a month after the confrontation, over 40% supported involving the SDF either through MSDF destroyer patrols (24.4%) or by stationing GSDF personnel on the islands (17.8%). 30.7% supported strengthened JCG patrols. In other words, over 70% of respondents favored strengthened coercive (military or police) measures. By contrast, only 1.2% supported talking with China about the Senkaku islands. In answer to another question in the same NTV poll, 61% of respondents stated that the fishing boat incident had caused their view of China to worsen somewhat or very much.[53] See Fig. 2.2.

Final Collapse of the 1978 Tacit Regime

Following the release of the fishing boat captain Sino-Japanese relations on the surface recovered and the situation around the Senkaku/

[51] Ibid., pp. 74, 77.

[52] This was in addition to the pre-September 2010 nationalist trend in Japan regarding the Senkakus identified in the previous paragraph. Also, see the analysis of the 2010 NDPG in Chapter 3.

[53] NTV (Nippon Television), "2010 nen 10 gatsu teirei yoron chōsa" (October 2010).

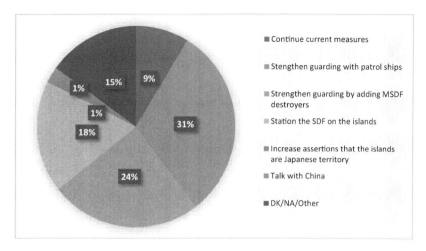

Fig. 2.2 What Measures should the Kan Cabinet implement to respond to the situation around the Senkaku Islands? (*Source* Figure is author's creation. Data from NTV [Nippon Television], "2010 nen 10 gatsu teirei yoron chōsa" [October 2010], as accessed November 24, 2010, at http://www.ntv.co.jp/yoron/201010/question.html)

Diaoyu islands returned essentially to the pre-crisis status quo. However, as indicated at the end of the last section, this tranquility masked deeper changes occurring, especially new perceptions of Chinese aggressiveness, perceptions that magnified all Chinese actions around the Senkakus and increased demands in Japan for stronger policies to secure Japanese control over the islands and ensure that Japan would "never again" give in to "intimidation."

This environment encouraged the then nationalist governor of Tokyo Ishihara Shintarō in April 2012 to provoke a new crisis over the Senkaku dispute, resulting in a new long-term status quo of continuous confrontation. Ishihara proposed buying the islands from their private Japanese owner and developing them. He justified this initiative by claiming that the DPJ was not doing enough to ensure effective Japanese control of the islands. Ishihara's proposal promised to fully destroy the already ailing 1978 conflict management regime, notably the status quo of Japanese control, but non-occupation, a development that would be exceptionally provocative for China.

40 P. MIDFORD

The Noda cabinet responded by announcing that it was considering purchasing the remaining private land on islands in order to preempt Ishihara. A May NTV poll found that 65% of respondents thought the central government should purchase the Senkakus, versus 17% who thought Tokyo or the city of Ishigaki (the islands are included within its city limits) should buy them, and 9% who wanted to maintain the status quo of the government renting the islands.[54] In July the Noda cabinet decided to buy the remaining private land on the Senkakus from their Japanese owner, effectively nationalizing them.[55]

Although the Noda cabinet's decision was intended to preserve the 1978 regime, instead it provoked China, which saw the purchase as another attempt by Japan to overturn the status quo by exercising effective control over the islands. In early September China took the nearly unprecedented step of sending six maritime patrol vessels beyond the contiguous waters near the islands and directly into the territorial waters of the Senkaku islands, a move Beijing justified as enforcing "China's jurisdiction over the Diaoyu Islands and its affiliated islets and ensure the country's maritime interests."[56] The next day the largest anti-Japanese protests since bilateral relations were normalized swept through 50 cities in China. For the first time Japanese-owned factories were attacked and damaged.[57] A mass boycott movement of Japanese goods was also organized in China, one that lasted for several months and was surprisingly effective; it reportedly lowered Japanese economic growth in fiscal year 2012 by up to 0.6%.[58]

The confrontation that began in September 2012 continued well past the end of the Noda administration and DPJ rule in late December

[54] NTV, "2012 nen 5 gatsu teirei yoron chōsa" (May 2012).

[55] Manicom, *Bridging Troubled Waters*, pp. 187–188; and Paul Midford, "Sino-Japanese Conflict and Reconciliation in the East China Sea," in Tim F. Liao, Kimie Hara and Krista Wiegand, eds., *The China-Japan Border Dispute: Islands of Contention in Multidisciplinary Perspective* (Surrey: Ashgate, 2015), pp. 183–184.

[56] Kyodo, "Six Chinese ships crowd Senkakus," *Japan Times*, September 14, 2012; Chico Harlan, "Six Chinese Ships Enter Japanese Waters Near Disputed Islands," *Washington Post*, September 14, 2012.

[57] Kyodo, "Anti-Japan Protests Spread Across China, Turn Violent," *Japan Times*, September 16, 2012; "Han nichi demo, chugoku 50 toshi ni kakudai, nikkei kōjyō yakiuchi," *Asahi.com*, September 16, 2012.

[58] Kyodo, "ADB lowers projection over China tensions," *Japan Times*, December 8, 2012, http://www.japantimes.co.jp/text/nb20121208a2.html. Ishihara was subsequently

2012, and throughout the subsequent Abe Shinzō administration and beyond. In other words, the regular cycle of confrontation between the coast guards of the two countries in the territorial waters of the Senkakus has become the new "normal." This permanent confrontation is what has replaced the collapsed 1978 conflict management regime. Long after the demonstrations and even the Chinese boycott of Japanese goods died down, the confrontation has continued in waters surrounding the Senkaku islands as China regularly sends CCG vessels into the territorial waters of these islands, thereby challenging Japan's effective control. Overtime the size and frequency of Chinese patrols through the Senkaku islands rose and fell, leading some observers to argue that China has been using the frequency of its patrols to signal escalation or deescalation in response to Japanese actions.[59]

Figure 2.3 captures the collapse of the Sino-Japanese tacit conflict management regime in September 2012 and its replacement with the new status quo of continual confrontation. Most significant are the red bars, which depict the number of times CCG (or similar Chinese state) vessels have entered the territorial waters around these islands. The blue line is less significant in that it merely shows Chinese state vessels' navigation through contiguous waters surrounding the territorial waters. Contiguous waters are considered high seas for the purpose of navigation (UNCLOS Article 33), so the navigation of CCG vessels there does not challenge Japan's sovereignty claim over the Senkakus. Nonetheless, the frequent presence of CCG vessels in contiguous waters, as depicted in this figure, although not illegal, probably exacerbates Japanese public and even elite perceptions of Chinese aggressiveness.

The red show that Chinese state vessels had very rarely entered Senkaku territorial waters before September 2012, but since that time multiple ships have entered these waters to challenge Japan's effective control over the islands nearly every month. This graph thus has become a salient and widely disseminated visualization of the new status quo of continual confrontation between Japan and China over exercising effective control and sovereignty over these islands.

---

criticized in the Japanese media for seriously damaging Japan's national interest. See "Sentaku Magazine: Island Issue Strands Ishihara," *Japan Times*, October 8, 2012, http://www.japantimes.co.jp/text/eo20121008a1.html.

[59] Taylor Fravel and Alastair Iain Johnston, "Chinese Signaling in the East China Sea?" *The Monkey Cage*, April 12, 2014.

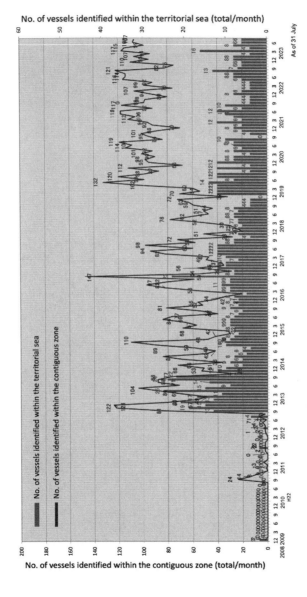

Fig. 2.3 Incursions into Senkaku Territorial Waters and Contiguous waters by Chinese Guard (CCG) vessels as of July 2023 (*Source* Japanese Ministry of Foreign Affairs, as accessed August 20, 2023, at https://www.mofa.go.jp/files/100 537084.pdf)

The result of the Chinese Coast Guard's (CCG) and other Chinese state vessels' monthly incursions into the territorial waters of the Senkaku islands has thus been to crystalize Japanese perceptions of Chinese aggressiveness. Their regular entry is a clear and direct physical challenge to Japan's control over the islands and its surrounding waters, control it had maintained since 1972 when the US returned control to Japan. From Japan's perspective this was the first time that its territorial integrity (i.e., territory it controls) had been directly threatened since it regained independence in 1952. Figure 2.3, which has been regularly updated and is widely distributed by the Japanese government and widely cited in both English and Japanese versions, visualizes the new status quo of confrontation, with a sharp break from the pre-September 2012 past of almost no CCG or other Chinese state maritime patrol vessels entering the territorial waters of the Senkaku islands, as denoted by the red bars.

Adding to the spike in Japanese perceptions of Chinese aggressiveness, and concern about Japan being unprepared to defend the Senkakus, was an incident in December 2012 when a Chinese State Oceanic Agency Y-12 patrol plane flew over the Senkakus. The JADGE air defense radar 200 km away at Miyako that had recently replaced the older BADGE radar failed to detect the Chinese aircraft until notified by the JCG. Eight ASDF fighters then scrambled from Naha 400 km away but arrived too late to intercept.[60]

In some cases, Japanese perceptions of Chinese aggressiveness have resulted from action-reaction dynamics between the two sides. For example, media reports in Japan in spring and summer 2020 suggested that after the outbreak of the COVID-19 pandemic China became more aggressive in challenging Japan's sovereignty by entering the territorial waters of the Senkakus for longer periods. However, this appears to have been a Chinese reaction to the right-wing Sakura TV channel sending a boat into Senkaku waters, and to more fishing in Senkaku waters from fishing boats from Ishigaki and Yonaguni, itself partially a result of reduced alternative tourist-related sources of income because of the COVID-19 pandemic. The greater CCG presence during this period thus appears to have been a reaction to more Japanese fishing and other

---

[60] Garren Mulloy, *Defenders of Japan: The Post-Imperial Armed Forces 1946–2016* (London: Hurst & Company, 2021), p. 257.

boats around the Senkakus, rather than a pre-planned unilateral escalation. Nonetheless, the latter perception was widely disseminated in the Japanese media.[61]

[61] Mike Mochizuki and Jiaxiu Han, "Is China Escalating Tensions with Japan in the East China Sea?" *The Diplomat*, September 16, 2020, as accessed July 23, 2023 at https://thediplomat.com/2020/09/is-china-escalating-tensions-with-japan-in-the-east-china-sea/. Ishigaki has been a center of dissatisfaction over PRC and ROC fishers' competition, and local fishers' threatened access to Senkaku waters, thereby merging nationalism and fishing interests. See Brad Williams, "Militarizing Japan's Southwest Islands: Subnational Involvement, and Insecurities in the Maritime Frontier Zone," *Asian Security* 11, no. 2 (2015), pp. 145–147 and "Senkaku kaiiki he 2-seki shutsugyo jimoto gyosen, junshi-sen ga keigo," *Yaeyama Nippo*, June 21, 2020, as accessed July 4, 2023 at https://yaeyama-nippo.co.jp/archives/12263. A year later CCG ships again chased a Japanese fishing boat in Senkaku waters. See "Chugokusen ga 2 nichi renzoku shinnyū Senkaku shūhen de Nihon gyosen wo," *Yaeyama Nippo*, June 22, 2021, as accessed July 4, 2023, at https://yaeyama-nippo.co.jp/archives/15905.

CHAPTER 3

The Impact of the New Confrontational Senkaku Status Quo on Japanese Politics and Policy

Abstract This chapter analyzes the initial impact of China's challenge to Japan's physical control over the Senkaku (Diaoyu) islands on Japanese perceptions of China, Japan's politics, and security policy. It argues that the emergence of physical confrontation around the Senkakus played a significant role in the collapse of DPJ rule and Abe Shinzō's return as prime minister. This chapter also demonstrates how this confrontation set in motion a longer-term transformation in Japan's defense policies, prompting a major buildup of the JCG and the SDF in the Ryukyu islands. Japan returned to a security-isolationist focus on territorial defense that had characterized the country's security strategy during the Cold War, albeit one that had room for more security partners than just the US.

Keywords Senkaku islands · Democratic Party of Japan · Liberal Democratic Party of Japan · Abe Shinzō · JCG · Public opinion · SDF · Ryukyu islands

© The Author(s), under exclusive license to Springer Nature
Switzerland AG 2025
P. Midford, *The Senkaku Islands Confrontation and the Transformation of Japan's Defense*, Palgrave Studies in Maritime Politics and Security, https://doi.org/10.1007/978-3-031-77727-1_3

Introduction

This chapter analyzes the initial impact of the challenge to Japanese physical control over the Senkaku islands on Japanese perceptions of China, domestic politics, and security policy. It argues that the emergence of physical confrontation in the Senkakus played a significant role in the collapse of DPJ rule and Abe Shinzō's return as head of the LDP and as prime minister. This chapter also demonstrates how this confrontation set in motion a longer-term transformation in Japan's defense policies, including a retreat from playing a direct role in global security through SDF unit-level participation in UN peacekeeping operations. Rather, Japan returned to a security-isolationist focus on territorial defense that had characterized Japan's security strategy during the Cold War, albeit one that now had room for more security partners than just the US.[1] More specific responses to the new status quo of ongoing confrontation in the Senkakus included a significant upgrade in Japan Coast Guard (JCG) capabilities, most notably a new JCG flotilla dedicated solely to the defense of the Senkakus was established, and the creation of an amphibious assault unit in the Ground Self-Defense Force (GSDF) modeled after the US Marine Corp. Japan's development of an A2/AD strategy in response to the Senkaku confrontation will be discussed in the next chapter.

Changing Perceptions of China

Changing Public Perception. The pre-2017 annual *Yomiuri Shimbun* poll on Japan's bilateral relations, which was usually conducted in December, showed a large increase in public threat perceptions of China following the September 2010 bilateral confrontation over the Chinese ship captain's detention. The results can be seen in Fig. 3.1. In short, this poll found that between 2010 and 2012, China overtook North Korea as the most cited potential military threat to Japan. Given that North Korea had long been considered the leading threat, this shift is significant.

---

[1] As touched on in the introduction chapter, security isolationism as used in this book refers to a policy of not deploying one's military overseas for operations that involve the use of force. Overseas military exercises, military diplomacy, and weapons sales, or the lack thereof, are not included in this definition. Regarding Japan's new security partnerships, Wilhelm Vosse and Paul Midford, eds., *Japan's New Security Partnerships: Beyond the Security Alliance* (Manchester: Manchester University Press, 2018).

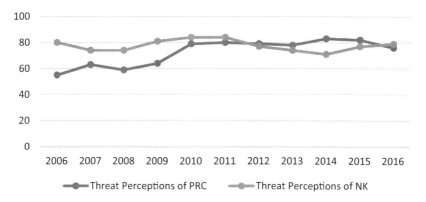

Fig. 3.1 Japanese Threat Perceptions of China Overtake Those of North Korea (*Source Yomiuri Shimbun*, Nichibei kyōdō yoron chōsa, normally conducted in early December. Author created figure)

More recent polling indicates that concern about China posing a military threat to Japan remains high among the Japanese public. An *Asahi Shimbun* poll conducted in spring 2022 found that 90% of respondents strongly (50%) or somewhat (40%) felt a military threat from China, versus 9% who somewhat (8%) or strongly (1%) did not feel a threat from China. By comparison 87% strongly (53%) or somewhat (34%) felt a threat from North Korea.[2]

Similarly, a poll conducted by Genron NPO during August–September 2022 found that Japanese threat perceptions toward China remain essentially tied with those toward North Korea. In 2022 72.1% of Japanese respondents identified China as posing a military threat, versus 72.8% who believed North Korea posed a military threat to Japan, a statistical tie. Moreover, when respondents were asked why they saw China as posing a military threat, the largest share, 64.7%, answered "intrusions into Japanese territorial waters," almost all of which happen in the territorial waters of the Senkakus. Another 50% cited "the existence of confrontation over the Senkaku islands and maritime resources" as the reason for seeing a military threat from China (multiple answers allowed). Clearly,

---

[2] "Fuanteina sekai, kenpō wa: Asahi shimbunsha chōsa," *Asahi Shimbun*, May 3, 2022 (chōkan), p. 6.

in 2022, ten years after the new status quo of continuous confrontation around the Senkakus had begun, most Japanese citizens still saw the regular intrusions of Chinese CG vessels into Senkaku territorial waters as reasons to see China as posing a military threat to Japan. By contrast, the possibility of China invading Taiwan was not a common answer given for seeing a Chinese military threat to Japan. Finally, a *Yomiuri Shimbun* poll conducted in spring 2024 found that 93% of respondents saw China's military buildup and intrusions into Japan's territorial waters greatly (59%) or somewhat (34%) threatened Japan's national security.[3]

Changing Elite Perceptions. There was a parallel shift in Japanese elite opinion as well. Before 2010, few Japanese elites had seen China as posing a direct military threat to Japan. Until September 2010 Japanese policymakers had growing concerns about China's military modernization, but did not have significant concerns about Chinese intentions or conduct.[4] This shift in public opinion and a shift in elite opinion resulting from the 2010 confrontation prompted the beginning of a major pivot in Japanese foreign and defense policies. Before then Japanese elites had watched China's military buildup with some concern but did not see China as having aggressive intentions toward Japan or its territory. As Bjørn Grønning argues, after the September 2010 confrontation Japan launched for the first time "counterbalancing" policies toward China, as concern over China's military build-up was mated with new "Japanese perceptions of aggressive Chinese behavior."[5] As Sheila Smith argues, "Tokyo saw Beijing's challenge to its administrative control over the Senkaku Islands as a grave risk to Japan's security…For the first time in the postwar era,

---

[3] The other common reasons given for seeing China as a threat include "Chinese military power is already becoming as strong as that of the US," and China is a "nuclear weapons state." See Genron NPO, *Dai 18-kai nitchū kyōdō yoronchōsa (2022-nen) kekka* (November 2022), pp. 20–21/57, as accessed August 3, 2023, at https://www.genron-npo.net/world/archives/13950-2.html; "Poll: 63% Support Constitutional Revision Amid Japan's Changing Security Environment; 93% Cite National Security Risk from China," *Japan News*, May 3, 2024, as accessed February 14, 2025 at https://japannews.yomiuri.co.jp/politics/politics-government/20240503-183778/.

[4] Based on the author's interviews of Japanese security elites in 2008 and 2013.

[5] Bjørn Elias Mikalsen Grønning, "Japan's Shifting Military Priorities: Counterbalancing China's Rise," *Asian Security* 10, no. 1 (2014), p. 15.

Japan could be the object of aggression...Defense of the Senkakus became equated with the defense of Japan."[6]

2010 NDPG. The first clear indication of Japan's new counterbalancing strategy came with the *2010 National Defense Program Guideline* (NDPG, or *Bōei Taiko*), which had been Japan's most basic defense policy document (until 2013). Up to 2010 Japan's post-Cold War *Bōei Taikos* (including the 1996 and 2004 NDPGs) were focused on responding to a perceived North Korean threat, or, in the case of the 2004 NDPG, nontraditional threats such as terrorism; none of them focused on a China threat. This NDPG, issued in December 2010, nearly 3 months after the September 2010 fishing boat confrontation, was the first to focus on China.[7] Notably, it called for strengthening the defense of the southern Ryukyu Islands (or Sakishima islands) near the Senkakus and Taiwan, a region that had no Japanese military bases, except for a radar and signals intelligence post established on Miyako Island in 2008. These islands had been called a "security vacuum" by Japanese defense officials. With the Democratic Party of Japan's (DPJ) 2010 *Bōei Taiko*, Japan decided to place a Ground Self-Defense Forces (GSDF) maritime radar unit on Yonaguni, the island closest to Taiwan and the Senkakus, to monitor a wide area including the Senkakus. This unit could theoretically act as a first responder to a crisis in the Senkaku islands. Discussions were also held about possibly deploying F-15s on nearby Ishigaki Island.[8]

At the same time the DPJ committed to Japan's development of its first amphibious assault unit in the GSDF, with help from the US Marine Corp, to enhance its ability to retake remote islands. Most significantly, the 2010 NDPG mandated an increase in Japan's submarine force by over

---

[6] Sheila Smith, *Japan Rearmed: The Politics of Military Power* (Cambridge: Harvard University Press, 2019), pp. 215–216.

[7] Cabinet of Kan Naoto, *National Defense Program Guidelines for FY 2011 and beyond*, approved December 17, 2010. Although this and all other NDPGs and the subsequent National Defense Strategy (NDS) from 2022 are all titled as applying from April in the following fiscal year, in this book I refer to these documents and other Japanese defense documents based on the year they were adopted, not the year they are supposed to take effect, as I believe that more accurately reflects their dating.

[8] Sado Akihiro, *The Self-Defense Forces and Postwar Politics in Japan* (JPIC: Tokyo, 2017), p. 215; and Paul Midford, "Japan's Defense Policy under the Democratic Party of Japan (DPJ)," *ISPI Analysis* (Istituto per gli Studi di Politica Internazionale) Vol. 81 (December 2011).

50   P. MIDFORD

a third, from 16 to 22, the largest submarine buildup in the Post-Cold-War era, and a buildup clearly aimed at China. This submarine buildup gives Japan greater capabilities to quietly monitor and control the seas around the Senkakus and Japan's other remote islands. It also allows the MSDF to exploit the Chinese navy's weakness in anti-submarine warfare (ASW) capabilities, while avoiding the threat posed by China's growing force of anti-ship ballistic missiles, which cannot target submarines.[9]

The scenario keeping Japanese defense planners and DPJ ministers awake at night was the nightmare of awaking the next morning to discover that Chinese troops or irregular forces had landed undetected on the Senkaku islands, thus presenting Japan with the unpalatable choice of accepting this *fait accompli* or undertaking major combat operations with the risk of escalation into war to retake the islands. They saw China use this strategy in 1995 when it seized Mischief Reef from the Philippines in the South China Sea when Manila's navy and coast guard were not watching. The focus of the 2010 *Bōei Taiko* on filling the "security vacuum" in the Sakishima Islands, and the new "Dynamic Defense" concept, which called for maintaining the SDF at a heightened state of readiness with enhanced mobility, information gathering capabilities, sustainability, and versatility for dealing with low-intensity conflicts short of war, were aimed at preventing a Mischief Reef type scenario on the Senkakus and other remote islands.[10]

The 2013 NSS. The focus on countering a Chinese threat to Japanese control of the Senkakus and defending the Sakishima islands that was evident in the 2010 NDPG was even clearer in the next NDPG approved by the LDP's Abe Cabinet in December 2013 along with a new higher level defense document that was issued at the same time, Japan's first ever National Security Strategy (NSS). Reacting to the new status quo of continual Chinese challenges to Japanese control of the Senkakus that had begun 15 months earlier, the NSS directly claimed: "China has taken actions that can be regarded as attempts to change the status quo by coercion based on their own assertions," and "has rapidly expanded and intensified its activities in the seas and airspace around Japan, including intrusion into Japan's territorial waters and airspace around

[9] *National Defense Program Guidelines for FY 2011 and beyond*, p. 20.

[10] Midford, "Japan's Defense Policy under the Democratic Party of Japan (DPJ)," p. 4; and *National Defense Program Guidelines for FY 2011 and beyond*, pp. 7, 11, 12.

the Senkaku Islands." The same document also complained that China's 2013-announced Air Defense Identification Zone (ADIZ) over the East China Sea "appears to unduly infringe the freedom of overflight above the high seas." China's new ADIZ covered the Senkakus.[11]

The 2013 NSS was thus clear in identifying aggressive Chinese behavior, if not Chinese aggressive intentions. Specifically, the 2013 *NSS* warned of "China's recent attempts change the status quo based on its unique assertion in its relations with neighboring countries, including Japan."[12] It singles out China's behavior around the Senkaku islands, specifically China's "intrusion into Japan's territorial waters and airspace around the Senkaku Islands."[13] In response, the *NSS* asserts that "Japan will proactively engage in the protection, management, and development of remote islands near national borders."[14]

Influence on Japan's Overall Defense

The long-term confrontation that emerged from September 2012 has come not only to dominate Japan's China policy, it also has come to dominate Japan's defense policy overall, and has even come to loom large in Japan's domestic politics. As the first direct kinetic threat to Japanese territory and its control thereof, the post-September 2012 Senkaku status quo of confrontation drove not only heightened threat perceptions of China, but also major changes in Japan's defense policy. According to Andrew Oros, "The most substantial and urgent threat perceived by Japan in connection with China's reemergence and military rise remains over China's claims to the uninhabited Senkaku islands. China's increasingly assertive claims to this territory and actions to challenge Japan's administrative control over them constitutes the principal driver of Japan's increased military capabilities and reform of long-standing practices and institutions that have limited Japan's effective use of its military power."[15]

[11] Cabinet Office, "National Security Strategy" (December 17, 2013, provisional translation), pp. 12–13.

[12] Ibid., p. 25.

[13] Ibid., p. 12.

[14] Ibid., p. 16.

[15] Andrew L. Oros, *Japan's Security Renaissance: New Policies and politics for the Twenty-First Century*, Columbia University Press, 2017, p. 83.

An example of the impact of the ongoing Senkaku confrontation on Japan's broader security policy was the Abe administration's reinterpretation of Japan's constitution to allow for the exercise of the right of collective self-defense, and the enactment of subsequent enabling legislation in 2014–2015. Although recognizing the right of collective self-defense allows Japan to defend other countries that come under attack, the restrictions enacted on this right are substantial. Ironically, possible military scenarios related to defense of the Senkaku islands and other Japanese remote islands featured prominently in the justifications the Abe administration made in trying to sell this change to the Japanese public.[16] As Smith argued in her book in 2019, "None of the legal changes made recently have fundamentally altered Japan's desire to limit the use of military force to tasks that enhance its own security."[17]

The birth of the hawkish Abe administration itself can be seen as another fruit of the 2010 and 2012 confrontations. These confrontations produced not only perceptions of Chinese aggressiveness but also perceptions that DPJ cabinets had been too weak in their response to this aggressiveness.[18]

Notably, the public negatively evaluated the DPJ Kan administration's decision to release a Chinese ship captain following an altercation with the JCG in September 2010 (see the previous chapter). A *Yomiuri* poll conducted shortly after the captain's release showed that 72% found the release "inappropriate," versus only 19% who thought it "appropriate." In a follow-up question for those answering "inappropriate," 41% said the release created the image that Japan could be intimidated, while 30% cited the severity of the incident, and 14% expressed concern that the release would strengthen China's territorial claims. 83% of respondents were unconvinced by Kan's explanation that the decision to release the captain had been made by prosecutors, versus 11% who were convinced. When asked if DPJ foreign and security policies made them feel uneasy (arguably a biased question), 84% answered that DPJ policies made them

[16] Paul Midford, "The Influence of Public Opinion on Foreign Policy in Asia: The Case of Japan," in Takashi Inoguchi, ed., *The SAGE Handbook of Asian Foreign Policy* (Thousand Oaks, California: Sage, 2019), pp. 381–404.

[17] Smith, *Japan Rearmed*, pp. 237–238.

[18] Paul Midford, "Foreign Policy as an Election Issue," in Robert Pekkanen, Steven Reed, and Ethan Scheiner, eds., *Japan Decides 2012*, New York: Palgrave, 2013, pp. 179–194.

feel very (39%) or somewhat (45%) uneasy, versus 14% who felt somewhat (11%) or not at all (3%) uneasy. Finally, 71% answered that in order to respond to the Senkaku issue Japan needed to strengthen the alliance with the US, versus 19% who did not think so.[19]

Similarly, a November 2010 NTV poll found that only 21% of respondents somewhat or strongly positively evaluated the foreign and security policies of the DPJ administration, versus nearly 75% who somewhat or very negatively evaluated these policies.[20] This confrontation clearly had a negative impact on the public's evaluation of the DPJ's foreign policy (also see Chapter 2 on this point). The DPJ's security policy brand was further damaged by the beginning of continual confrontation in Senkaku waters from September 2012. While Prime Minister Noda Yoshihiko's decision to effectively nationalize the Senkaku islands by buying all the remaining private property on the islands was strongly supported, this did nothing to reverse the image of DPJ weakness on foreign and security policies, and the resulting demand for tougher policies toward China.[21] The Senkaku confrontations of 2010 and 2012 thus helped create a public opinion environment that facilitated the return to power of the LDP and the hawkish Abe Shinzō.

The consistent annual increases in Japanese defense spending for eight years in a row during the Abe and Suga administrations after the confrontation began in 2012, following two decades of stagnation or decline in Japanese defense spending, is another fruit of this confrontation. Japan's defense spending had fallen for ten years in a row, from 2002 to 2012, a trend that was reversed the year after China's physical challenge to Japan's control of the Senkakus began. Japan's defense spending increased in real (if nonetheless relatively modest) terms every year during the Abe administration, beginning in 2013, although in some years higher economic growth meant that defense spending actually fell slightly as a percentage of GDP and stayed below the unofficial 1% limit on defense

[19] "Naikaku shijiritsu rakka 53%, honsha zenkoku yoron chōsa kekka, shitsumon to kotae," *Yomiuri Shimbun*, October 4, 2010, p. 9.

[20] NTV, November 2010: http://www.ntv.co.jp/yoron/201011/index.html.

[21] "Asahi Shimbunsha yoron chōsa, shitsumon to kotae," *Asahi Shimbun*, October 22, 2012 (morning edition), p. 3; "Honsha kinkyū zenkoku yoron chōsa kekka," *Yomiuri Shimbun*, October 3, 2012 (morning edition), p. 8; NTV, October 2012: http://www. ntv.co.jp/yoron/201207/index.html.

spending.[22] Nonetheless, in June 2017 an internal LDP policy report called for increasing defense spending to 2%, even while defense budgets continued to set nominal Yen-denominated spending records.[23]

The island dispute became a top, if not the dominant issue for Japan in its diplomacy toward China. Former Prime Minister Abe claimed that he used every meeting he had with President Xi Jinping to issue deterrent threats: "Whenever I met President Xi Jinping during my time as prime minister, I always made it a rule to convey clearly to him that he should not misjudge Japan's intention to defend the Senkaku islands and that Japan's intentions were unwavering."[24]

In addition to internal balancing in the form of this military buildup, Japan also turned to external balancing by strengthening its alliance with the US and building a series of new security partnerships with countries and actors as diverse as Australia, India, the UK, France, and the EU.[25] Japan succeeded in lobbying for ever stronger commitments from the Obama and Trump administrations to defend Japan's control of the Senkaku islands. The support that the US Marines have provided to the GSDF as Japan develops its first amphibious assault unit (see the subsequent discussion in this chapter) are a concrete manifestation of US assistance to Tokyo's efforts to ensure continued control of these islands even during a conflict. In November 2022 US Marines conducted joint remote island defense exercises with the GSDF, including its amphibious

---

[22] Edmund J. Burke, Timothy R. Heath, Jeffrey W. Hornung, Logan Ma, Lyle J. Morris, and Michael S. Chase, *China's Military Activities in the East China Sea: Implications for Japan's Air Self-Defense Force* (Santa Monica, CA: RAND Corporation, RR-2574-AF, 2018), pp. 14, 18; Tom Phuong Le, Japan's *Aging Peace: Pacifism and Militarism in the Twenty-First Century* (New York: Columbia University, 2021), pp. 207–215; and "EDITORIAL: Rapid growth in defense spending a hard sell to the public," *Asahi Shimbun*, January 4, 2022, as accessed April 11, 2022 at https://www.asahi.com/ajw/articles/14514817.

[23] Kyodo, "LDP Panel Calls for Boost in Defense Spending, Eying NATO's 2% GDP Target," *Japan Times*, June 20, 2017, as accessed February 2, 2024 at https://www.japantimes.co.jp/news/2017/06/20/national/politics-diplomacy/ldp-panel-calls-boost-defense-spending-eying-natos-2-gdp-target/; and Heginbotham and Samuels, "Active Deterrence," p. 159.

[24] Shinzo Abe, "U.S. 'Strategic Ambiguity' over Taiwan Must End," *Japan Times*, April 19, 2022, p. 6.

[25] Regarding these new partnerships, see Vosse and Midford, *Japan's New Security Partnerships*; and Paul Midford and Wilhelm Vosse, eds., *New Directions in Japan's Security: Non-US Centric Evolution* (Routledge, 2020).

assault detachment, on Yonaguni. In connection with this the US moved to reorganize a detachment of US Marines as a mobile unit that could be quickly deployed to the Sakishima Islands if not the Senkakus in order to help Japan defend its control over these islands. This new unit thus represents US reassurance to Japan in the form of a commitment to help Japan with remote island defense, especially to help Tokyo defend the Senkaku islands, and by extension the Sakishima islands,[26] rather than a Japan-US strategy for defending Taiwan as some analysts have suggested.[27]

Japan's new security partnerships linking up with the Japan-US alliance can be seen as an example of what could be called "federated defense," albeit just for training. For example, the French military together with the US military, held joint naval and amphibious exercises with Japan's SDF in May 2024. This exercise included simulated amphibious landings to practice defending and retaking remote and unpopulated islands, an exercise that explicitly had the Senkaku islands in mind.[28] Japan appears to think of its new non-American partnerships in terms of enhancing SDF training opportunities and encouraging its new security partners to

[26] Kyodo, "US Marines Set up Littoral Unit in Okinawa for Islands Defense," *Mainichi*, November 15, 2023 as accessed December 14, 2022 at https://mainichi.jp/english/articles/20231115/p2g/00m/0na/033000c; and Masayuki Shiraishi and Takeshi Takashima, "GSDF, Marines Retake Island in Joint 'Iron Fist' Drill in Oita," *Asahi Shimbun*, February 19, 2023, as accessed December 14, 2023 at https://www.asahi.com/ajw/articles/14843309.

[27] See Zack Cooper and Eric Sayers, "Japan's Shift to a War Footing," *War on the Rocks*, January 12, 2023, as accessed at July 7, 2023 at https://warontherocks.com/2023/01/japans-shift-to-war-footing/; and Giulio Pugliese, "In It Together: Taiwan's and Japan's Security Are Linked," in Bonnie S. Glaser, ed., *Next-Generation Perspectives on Taiwan: Insights from the 2023 Taiwan-US Policy Program* (August 2023), p. 41, as accessed August 26, 2023 at https://www.gmfus.org/news/next-generation-perspectives-taiwan-insights-2023-taiwan-us-policy-program.

[28] Xavier Vavasseur,"Japan, USA and France Set for Combined Amphibious Exercise," *Naval News*, December 7, 2020, https://www.navalnews.com/naval-news/2020/12/japan-usa-and-france-set-for-combined-amphibious-exercise/; "Nichibei futsu de hatsu no ritō jōriku kunren rainen 5gatsu, taichu hōimō wo kyōka, kakudai," *Sankei Shimbun*, December 5, 2020, as accessed February 14, 2024 at https://www.sankei.com/politics/news/201205/plt2012050016-n1.html; and "Nichibei Futsu ga kyōdō kunren, Chūgoku wo kensei Miyazaki Kagoshima, Kirishima enshū-ba," *Asahi Shimbun*, May 16, 2021 (chōkan), p. 2; and Mari Yamaguchi, "Japan, US, France, Hold First Joint Drills on Japanese Land," AP, May 11, 2021, as accessed August 11, 2024 at https://apnews.com/article/europe-france-japan-c2b9a90dcc8c5e681d4829075d7d1a97 Regarding the federated defense model, see Michael J. Green, and Zack Cooper, "Revitalizing the Rebalance: How to Keep U.S. Focus on Asia," *Washington Quarterly* 37, no. 3 (2014), pp. 25–46.

56   P. MIDFORD

engage in the defense of Japanese territory, politically if not militarily. Nonetheless, there are no indications that Japan intends to engage militarily in helping to defend its partners, and its new partners reciprocate this stance.

At the global level, the 2010 confrontation and especially the ongoing confrontation over the Senkaku islands since 2012 have shifted Japanese policy toward China and its overall defense policy fundamentally. One result, along with a public backlash in Japan against the SDF's deployment to Iraq, has been the deglobalization of the Japan-US alliance. Under the DPJ Japan withdrew from supporting US military operations outside of East Asia, a position that even Prime Minister Abe continued. Moreover, the Abe administration withdrew Japan from direct SDF unit-level participation in global security by withdrawing the SDF from all three UN peacekeeping missions Tokyo had been participating in when Abe returned to office in 2012. By May 2017 this returned Japan to zero participation in UN peacekeeping for almost the first time since 1992. Although Japan has continued to dispatch SDF several officers to the UN peacekeeping mission in South Sudan and to a non-UN-sponsored peacekeeping mission for the first time (in the Sinai Peninsula), these are not unit-level boots-on-the-ground deployments for peace-keeping.[29] Sending a few officers to the headquarters of peacekeeping missions involves little risk sharing and does not supply the boots on the ground that are in short supply for peacekeeping missions. To critics, these appear to be little more than token contributions. Prime Minister Abe's much promoted "proactive pacifism" in the context of global security ends up looking more like "passive pacifism."

Behind this change has been a return to the Cold War equilibrium in Japanese defense policy of focusing on territorial defense. Only the focal point of territorial defense has shifted, from defending Hokkaido from

---

[29] Garren Mulloy, *Defenders of Japan: The Post-Imperial Armed Forces 1946–2016* (London: Hurst & Company, 2021), pp. 226–227; Paul Midford, "The Abe Administration's Passive Pacifism," *Japan Today*, March 4, 2020, as accessed April 11, 2022 at https://japantoday.com/category/features/opinions/the-abe-administration-and-passive-pacifism; Paul Midford, "Abe Seiken no shōkyokuteki heiwashugi," *Kobe Joshi Tanki Daigaku Ronko* 67 (2022), pp. 53–65; and Midford, "Abe's Pro-Active Pacifism and Value Diplomacy: Implications for Eu-Japan Political and Security Cooperation," in Axel Berkofsky, Christopher W. Hughes, Paul Midford and Marie Söderberg, eds., *The EU-Japan Partnership in the Shadow of China: The Crisis of Liberalism* (Abingdon: Routledge, 2019), pp. 42–45.

the Soviet Union to a defense of the Senkaku and Sakishima islands from China.[30] Given the extraordinary impact that the ongoing confrontation over the Senkaku islands has had on not only Japan's policy toward China, but also its defense policy overall, and the large investments Japan has made in developing coast guard and A2/AD capabilities (see subsequent discussions) for defending these islands, policies that receive strong backing from the Japanese public, there is little reason to doubt that Japan, even on its own, but especially with backing from the US, would not hesitate to climb an escalation ladder to defend its control of these islands, not to mention the Sakishima islands.

Senkaku Driven Strategy

The 2013 *NDPG* focused on establishing air and naval "superiority" to prevent attacks on remote islands and developing the GSDF's amphibious assault capabilities in case it needed to retake remote islands, i.e., the Senkakus, that had been seized.[31] This emphasis reflects Japan's determination to defend the Senkakus and its position as the most likely trigger to a Sino-Japanese bilateral military conflict. As Eric Heginbotham and Richard J. Samuels observe: "The most likely flash point is the Senkaku Islands, but an expanded military campaign could see air, missile, and maritime activities play out over a much wider area—to include strikes against targets from areas just off Taiwan to Okinawa."[32]

In terms of the SDF and Japan's military strategy for defending the Senkakus and the Ryukyus, the large if gradual shift of GSDF and other SDF units from Hokkaido to the southwest of Japan, the promotion of "jointness" between the three SDF services (albeit with mixed results),[33] and the continued development of a GSDF amphibious assault unit, set

[30] Le, *Japan's Aging Peace*, pp. 111–112. However, as Le documents, this shift has been slowed by the difficulty of acquiring new bases in Japan's southwest.

[31] Cabinet of Japan, *National Defense Program Guidelines for FY 2014 and Beyond*, pp. 14, 19–20.

[32] Eric Heginbotham and Richard J. Samuels, "Active Denial: Redesigning Japan's Response to China's Military Challenge," *International Security* 42, no. 4 (Spring 2018), p. 148.

[33] Jeffrey W. Hornung, *Japan's Potential Contributions in an East China Sea Contingency* (Santa Monica, CA: Rand Corporation), pp. 80–83. On the problems caused for jointness by the lack of a joint command and GSDF dominance relative to the other services, see Heginbotham and Samuels, "Active Denial," pp. 163–164.

out originally in the *2010 NDPG* and enhanced in the *2013 NDPG*, "are all directly the result of the increased perception of threat from China."[34] Japan launched a large-scale military buildup in its southwest, in an area ranging from Kyushu to the Sakishima and Senkaku islands. In part, this resulted from doubts about the US commitment to helping Japan defend its control of the Senkakus (fear of abandonment), while US officials worried about entrapment in a potential conflict over tiny and barren islands of little material or military value. Higenbotham and Samuels argue that "some Japanese question the extent of the U.S. commitment to the defense of the Senkaku Islands...despite U.S. assurances, and U.S. officials ponder the risks of entanglement."[35] In Washington the term "Senkaku Paradox" was coined by Michael O'Hanlon as the archetype case of risking great power war over territory of inherently little value.[36]

JCG Senkaku Flotilla. The long-term Sino-Japanese confrontation over the Senkaku islands since 2012 has resulted in significant budget increases for the JCG for the sake of strengthening Japan's control over the Senkakus. The JCG assumes the first line of defense in maintaining Japan's control of the Senkakus and is more suitable than the MSDF for two reasons. First, the main threats to Japan's territorial control come from Chinese Coast Guard (CCG) vessels, reflecting China's gray-zone strategy of gradually asserting and expanding its control there without escalating to military force. Japan has been reciprocating this level of coercion to maintain control of the islands and territorial waters. Second, and as a complement to this strategy, non-state and quasi-non-state Chinese actors such as fishing boats also intrude into Senkaku territorial waters. The JCG is better equipped to deal with both types of low-intensity coercive challenges than is the MSDF, which remains in the background for backup in case armed conflict breaks out with the CCG or non-state actors and escalates.

[34] Oros, *Japan's Security Renaissance*, p. 84.

[35] Heginbotham and Samuels, "Active Denial," p. 136. For an argument that Japan's fear of abandonment by the US vis-à-vis China is one factor driving a more autonomous defense effort by Japan, see Lionel P. Fatton, "A New Spear in Asia: Why Is Japan Moving toward Autonomous Defense?" *International Relations of Asia Pacific* 19, no. 2 (2019), pp. 297–325.

[36] Michael E. O'Hanlon, *The Senkaku Paradox: Risking Great Power War Over Small Stakes* (Washington, DC: Brookings Institution Press, 2019), p. 95.

In April 2016, less than four years after the new status quo of continual confrontation had begun, the JCG launched a new flotilla exclusively dedicated to defending Japan's control of the Senkaku islands. The flotilla consists of 12 ships, 10 new 1500-ton fast patrol ships armed with 20 mm guns and water cannons, and two larger refurbished helicopter-carrying vessels that were transferred from other JCG regions. By comparison, the rest of the JCG's Okinawa Division consists of only six vessels larger than 1000 tons, and one helicopter-carrying patrol vessel for operations other than protecting Japanese control of the Senkaku islands. Of the 1722 JCG members assigned to the Okinawa Division, 606 are assigned exclusively to protecting the islands. A base consisting of piers, barracks, and other facilities was built for this flotilla on Ishigaki Island, making this the largest JCG base anywhere in Japan.[37]

Overtime the capabilities and size of the Senkaku Flotilla has increased. In FY 2017 the JCG's budget again increased, by 10 billion Yen to nearly 211 billion Yen to hire at least 200 new personnel and build five large patrol vessels and replace 13 old patrol and survey vessels. This was part of a plan to increase the number of JCG personnel to a record high of 13,744 in 2017, and to increase the JCG fleet of ships from 128 in 2015 to 142 by 2020. These increases were described as "measures to help deal with the continued incursions by Chinese vessels into the waters around the Senkaku Islands." Moreover the JCG dispatched personnel from other regions to reenforce Senkaku patrols.[38] The JCG also began acquiring maritime surveillance drones (UAVs) ahead of the MSDF.[39]

---

[37] Kyodo, "Japan Coast Guard Deploys 12 Ships to Patrol Senkakus," *Japan Times*, April 4, 2016, http://www.japantimes.co.jp/news/2016/04/04/national/japancoastgu arddeploys12shipstopatrolsenkakus/#VwMDxuKLTIU; Ben Dooley and Hisako Ueno, "The Island Paradise Near the Front Line of Tensions Over Taiwan," *New York Times*, December 16, 2021, as accessed December 17, 2021 at https://www.nytimes.com/2021/12/16/world/asia/ishigaki-japan-missile.

[38] "Japan Defense Spending to Hit Record High in Fiscal 2017," *Mainichi*, December 23, 2016, as accessed February 14, 2024, at https://mainichi.jp/english/articles/201 61223/p2a/00m/0na/005000c.

[39] Yoshihiro Inaba, "Japan Coast Guard and JMSDF Planning to Use UAVs for Ocean Surveillance," *Naval News*, November 18, 2020, https://www.navalnews.com/naval-news/2020/11/japan-coast-guard-and-jmsdf-planning-to-use-uavs-for-ocean-survei llance/. In late 2024 the JCG announced that it was increasing the number of large UAVs it used for patrol around the Senkakus from three to five. See Kathleen Benoza, "Chinese government vessels seen near Senkakus for record 353 days in 2024," Japan

In August 2021 Japan decided to deploy one of its largest JCG vessels to the Senkaku Flotilla, the 6500-ton Asazuki.[40] The size of the Senkaku Flotilla and its base indicates the very high priority Japan places on defending its control of these uninhabited islands. The JCG is now planning for a massively larger 30,000-ton vessel that is to be completed and deployed to the Senkaku flotilla by 2029.[41]

Japan has provided coast guard patrol vessels to the coast guards of Southeast Asian nations, especially to the Philippines and Vietnam since 2010, and has supplemented this with joint coast guard and naval exercises with both. Also, Japan transferred former SDF trainer aircraft to the Philippines that were repurposed for maritime surveillance. In December 2023 Japan provided the Philippines with a military quality radar to monitor airspace over the South China Sea. These policies are intended to put pressure on China's CG and indirectly counterbalance their deployments around the Senkaku islands. In this sense these policies are an extension of Japan's strategy for defending the Senkakus.[42]

Times, December 29, 2024, as accessed February 14, 2025 at https://www.japantimes.co.jp/news/2024/12/29/japan/japan-senkakus-china-record/.

[40] Dai 11-kanku kaijō hoanchō honbu "Junshisen 'asatsuki' no shūeki ni tsuite,"August 25, 2021, as accessed August 11, 2024 at https://www.kaiho.mlit.go.jp/11kanku/osirase/2021D/%E3%80%90%E6%B5%B7%E4%BF%9D%E5%BA%83%E5%A0%B1%E6%96%87%E3%80%91210825_%E5%B7%A1%E8%A6%96%E8%88%B9%E3%81%82%E3%81%95%E3%81%A5%E3%81%8D%E3%81%AE%E5%B0%B1%E5%BD%B9%E3%81%AB%E3%81%A4%E3%81%84%E3%81%A6.pdf; John Feng, "Japan to Deploy Largest Vessel to Guard Senkaku Islands From China Patrols," *Newsweek*, August 19, 2021, as accessed October 1, 2023, at https://www.newsweek.com/japan-deploy-largest-vessel-guard-senkaku-islands-china-patrols-1621024.

[41] Jun Tsuruta, "Japan to Build Major New Vessel for the Senkaku Islands," *The Diplomat*, July 27, 2024, as accessed August 11, 2024 at https://thediplomat.com/2024/07/japan-to-build-major-new-vessel-for-the-senkaku-islands/

[42] Xavier Vavasseur, "Japan to Build Six Patrol Vessels for Vietnam's Coast Guard," *Naval News*, August 8, 2020, https://www.navalnews.com/naval-news/2020/08/japan-to-build-six-patrol-ships-for-vietnams-coast-guard/; Reuters, "Abe, Aquino to Agree on Framework for Japanese Military Aid: Sources," *Japan Times*, November 16, 2015, as accessed December 26, 2015 at http://www.japantimes.co.jp/news/2015/11/16/national/politics-diplo...agree-on-framework-for-japanese-military-aid-sources/#.Vn7XZRYczeE; Prashanth Parameswaran, "Philippines to Receive First 2 Aircraft From Japan: The First Two of Five TC-90s Are Expected to Arrive Next Week," *The Diplomat*, March 23, 2017, as accessed June 25, 2017 at https://thediplomat.com/2017/03/philippines-to-receive-first-2-aircraft-from-japan/; Ramon Royandoyan, "Philippines Installs Japan-made

SDF Buildup.[43] In response to the new confrontational status quo, already before the end of 2012 Japan began an SDF buildup in the Southwest islands to protect the Senkaku islands and the Sakishima islands more generally. This is what retired GSDF Lieutenant General and former Commander of the Western Army, Banshō Kōichirō, has called the "Southwestern Wall Strategy."[44] Other Japanese defense officials referred to closing what they identified as a "security vacuum" in the Southwestern Ryukyus.[45]

Previously "China in the south had not been a top priority."[46] Already by November 2012, a mere two months after the new status quo of continual confrontation had begun, the DPJ Noda administration launched a large-scale (and unusually, closed to the media) exercise for defending remote islands, with the Senkakus the unstated objective in these exercises.[47] Over the following four years the GSDF engaged in intensive planning for remote island defense, planning both tactics and required equipment, and force shaping.[48] A year after the 2012 remote island exercise, the SDF held another large-scale exercise involving 34,000 SDF members, SAM and SSM missile units, 380 planes, and six naval

Radar to Track China's Moves," *Nikkei Asia*, December 20, 2023, as accessed February 29, 2024 at https://asia.nikkei.com/Politics/Defense/Philippines-installs-Japan-made-radar-to-track-China-s-moves More generally see Paul Midford, "Japan's Approach to Maritime Security in the South China Sea," *Asian Survey* 55, no. 3 (May/June 2015), pp. 525–547.

[43] This section analyzes the SDF buildup except for its A2/AD related buildup, which is the subject of the next chapter.

[44] Mulloy, *Defenders of Japan*, p. 249; and Robert D. Eldridge, "Organization and Structure of the Contemporary Ground Self-Defense Force," in Robert D. Eldridge and Paul Midford, eds., *The Japanese Ground Self-Defense Force*, p. 29; Smith, *Japan Rearmed*, p. 119.

[45] Xavier Vavasseur, "Japan's Type 12 SSM Deployed to Keep Watch On Miyako Strait," *Naval News*, April 3, 2020, https://www.navalnews.com/naval-news/2020/04/japans-type-12-ssm-deployed-to-keep-watch-on-miyako-strait/

[46] Zack Cooper and Eric Sayers, "Japan's Shift to a War Footing," War on the Rocks, January 12, 2023, as accessed July 7, 2023, at https://warontherocks.com/2023/01/jap ans-shift-to-war-footing/.

[47] "Nichibei kyōdō enshu, hikōkai de kaishi 16 nichi made," *Asahi Shimbun*, November 6, 2012 (chōkan). 4; and "Irei no Zenmen Hikokai Kunren," *Jiji*, November 5, 2012, as cited by Heginbotham and Samuels, "Active Denial," p. 157.

[48] Makoto Konishi, *Jieitai no tōsho senso: Shiryoshu, rikuji "kyou han" deyomu sono sakusen* (Tokyo: Shakai Hihyosha, 2017), pp. 37–149.

vessels. This SDF exercise was notable for being the first one that involved retaking a remote island that had already been captured by an unspecified enemy. This exercise set in motion a further series of exercises designed to defend remote islands, and exercises to retake those islands.[49]

These exercises came to feature the GSDF's new Amphibious Rapid Deployment Brigade (ARDB, *Suiriku kidō dan* 水陸機動小川). Established in March 2018, the ARDB has its home base in Sasebo, and an envisaged strength of 2400 troops. This amphibious brigade was itself in many ways a product of the new status quo of continual confrontation over the Senkakus. An infantry regiment of 650 members established by the Western Army (that covers Kyushu and Okinawa) in 2002 and based near Nagasaki developed some amphibious capabilities and received training from the US Marine Corp.[50]

The expansion of this regiment into a dedicated brigade of over 2000 troops faced political obstacles, as amphibious assault recalled memories from World War II and concerns that this was an offensive capability that could be used to attack other countries, and hence would be unconstitutional. However, the materialization of a constant physical threat to Japan's control of the Senkakus from China overcame this opposition as the Senkakus provided a concrete case of territorial defense where amphibious assault capabilities would be needed, a pattern that would be repeated with the acquisition of stand-off missiles a few years later (see the next two chapters). According to Grant Newsham, a US Marine Corp officer who helped the GSDF establish the ARDB, even Japan's left-of-center press was convinced by the defensive rationale of protecting Japan's control of the Senkakus.[51] The announcement of the ARDB's formation

---

[49] "Ritō bōei o sōtei, Okinawa de tōgō enshū chitaikan misairu tenkai," *Asahi Shimbun*, November 12, 2013 (chōkan, seibu), p. 38; and Heginbotham and Samuels, "Active Denial," p. 145.

[50] Bōeisho, "Riku jieitai suiriku kidō dantai," as accessed February 14, 2024 at https://www.mod.go.jp/gsdf/gcc/ardb/sp/; and Grant Newsham, "How Japan Got an Amphibious Rapid Deployment Brigade," *Asia Times*, March 27, 2018 as accessed October 1, 2023 at https://asiatimes.com/2018/03/japan-got-amphibious-rapid-deployment-brigade/; Robert D. Eldridge, "Organization and Structure of the Contemporary Ground Self-Defense Force," in Robert D. Eldridge and Paul Midford, eds., *The Japanese Ground Self-Defense Force*, p. 29; and Giuseppe A. Stavale, "The GSDF During the post-Cold War Years, 1989–2015," in Eldridge and Midford, eds., *The Japanese Ground Self-Defense Force*, pp. 220–222.

[51] According to Newsham, who played an advisory role in the creation of the ARDB, the leftist press accepted the Senkaku defense rationale of the ARDB: "Oddly, the reporters

came in the NDPG of December 2013, a little over a year after the new status quo of constant confrontation had started. The Medium Defense Program announced at the same time also called for Japan to acquire amphibious assault vehicles and seventeen tilt-rotor aircraft to enhance the ARDB's mobility.[52]

The development of the ARDB took place in the context of SDF planning for a conflict over the Senkakus expanding into armed combat engulfing the Sakishima islands, with specific planning for retaking Ishigaki island from a more numerous invasion force from China.[53] In 2019 a GSDF guard unit deployed to Miyako to defend the Sakishima and

---

who got it best were from one of Japan's leading leftist papers. And I knew we were on track when Japan Newsweek ran a cover story, 'Can Japan defend the Senkakus?'" Newsham "How Japan got an Amphibious Rapid Deployment Brigade," *Asia Times*, March 27, 2018 as accessed October 1, 2023 at https://asiatimes.com/2018/03/japan-got-amphibious-rapid-deployment-brigade/

[52] Cabinet of the Government of Japan, *National Defense Program Guidelines for FY 2014 and Beyond (2013 NDPG)*, p. 31; Cabinet of the Government of Japan, *Medium Term Defense Program: FY2014-2018*, December 17, 2013, p. 5; Stavale, "The GSDF During the post-Cold War Years, pp. 220–222; Eldridge, Organization and Structure of the Contemporary Ground Self-Defense Force," p. 29; "Senkaku yūji e sonae suiriku kidōdan, 2 sen-3 zen kibo de Sasebo ni shireibu," *Sankei Shimbun*, February 3, 2014, p. 1; Mulloy, Defenders of Japan, p. 250; and Newsham, "How Japan got an Amphibious Rapid Deployment Brigade." However, Heginbotham and Samuels, describing "the GSDF's tastes" as "particularly expensive," note that at $175 million per aircraft, the decision to acquire costly Ospreys came at the cost of other capabilities that were crowded out of the budget. "Active Deterrence," pp. 159, 165. The grounding of the Japanese and US fleets of Ospreys following a deadly accident in late 2023 revived questions about the reliability of this aircraft, especially during a military conflict, and questions about the alliance, especially in Okinawa. See Tara Copp, "US Military Grounds Entire Fleet of Osprey Aircraft Following a Deadly Crash Off the Coast of Japan, *AP*, December 7, 2023, as accessed February 14, 2024 at https://apnews.com/article/osprey-crash-grounded-japan-air-force-920c0ad16e005adbb0ff22548d7b11c4; and "VOX POPULI: Osprey Crash Shows Japan's Subservient Status to the U.S.," *Asahi Shimbun*, December 13, 2023 as accessed February 14, 2024 at https://apnews.com/article/osprey-crash-grounded-japan-air-force-920c0ad16e005adbb0ff22548d7b11c4

[53] Mulloy, *Defenders of Japan*, pp. 249; "Ishigakijima no shinkō sōtei bōei shōga sakusen bunseki," *Okinawa Times*, November 30, 2018, p. 2; "Nansei chiiki no jieitai kyōka: Jyūmin hogo ni no ni ji," *Ryukyu Shimpo*, June 23, 2019, p. 21; "Jūmin no inochi wa mushi ka'/Jieitai tenkai-an ishigaki shimin-ra ikidōri," *Okinawa Times*, November 30, 2018 (chōkan), p. 28; and "SDF Strengthening in Southwest Japan Includes Plan for Military Clash, Not Residents' Evacuation," *Ryukyu Shimpo*, June 23, 2019, as accessed October 1, 2023 at http://english.ryukyushimpo.jp/2019/06/28/30673/

Senkaku islands.[54] To further GSDF defense of the Senkakus and the Sakishima islands this service decided in 2021 to acquire for the first time its own transport ships by 2024, one medium-sized 2000-ton ship and two small-sized transports of 400 tons each for the transport of troops and supplies to the southwestern islands.[55]

Japan has been backing up the GSDF and its new ARDB by pushing for greater support from the US. As mentioned previously, the US Marine Corp has played a significant in training the ARDB and its predecessor regiment.[56] The US took a further step in late 2022 by agreeing to create a US Marine Littoral Regiment in Okinawa that will be operation from 2025. The formation of this unit is intended to reenforce Japan's defense of its Southwestern islands, including the Senkakus, and reassure Japan of the US commitment to defending those islands.[57]

Complementing the GSDF buildup in the Ryukyus, Japan also moved to reenforce the ASDF there. Four years after the breakdown of the tacit conflict management regime into continual confrontation around the Senkakus, Japan greatly increased the number of air superiority fighter jets in January 2016 when a second squadron of F-15s was deployed to the ASDF base at Naha on the main island of Okinawa. This was then designated as the 9th Airwing and includes approximately 40 F-15s. In 2017 the ASDF also established the Southwestern Air Defense Force and the

---

[54] *Defense of Japan 2023*, p. 313.

[55] "Japan's GSDF to Procure Transport Vessels Amid China's Rise," *Japan Times*, February 14, 2021, as accessed August 11, 2023, at https://www.japantimes.co.jp/news/2021/02/14/national/ground-self-defense-vessels/; and Christopher W. Hughes, *Japan as a Global Military Power* (Cambridge: Cambridge University Press, 2022), p. 26; *Defense of Japan*, p. 314.

[56] Newsham, "How Japan got an Amphibious Rapid Deployment Brigade;" Eldridge, "Organization and Structure of the Contemporary Ground Self-Defense Force," p. 29.

[57] Pugliese speculates that this Marine regiment could be deployed to the Sakishima islands to launch attacks on Chinese forces invading Taiwan. See Pugliese, "In It Together," p. 41. Making a similar argument is Cooper and Eric Sayers, "Japan's Shift to a War Footing." However, given the risks that allowing this Littoral Regiment to deploy to the Southwest islands for offensive operations beyond Japanese territory would have for the residents of these islands (Chinese counterstrikes), it appears unlikely that Japan would allow this, especially as MOD has promised the residents of Yonaguni, the island closest to Taiwan, that no offensive missiles would be deployed there. "Missaru butai haibi, Yonaguni jūmin ni setsumei kai, 'hangenki nōryoku ni naranu,' kyōchō," *Asahi Shimbun*, May 16, 2023, as accessed May 17, 2023 at https://www.asahi.com/articles/DA3S15636698.html?iref=pc_ss_date_article.

Southwestern Aircraft Control and Warning Wing, both based in Naha, with responsibility for the entire southwest region.[58] From early 2019 the ASDF adopted a more forceful reaction to People's Liberation Air Force (PLAAF) aircraft flying over the East China Sea even at some distance from the Senkakus: it started a standing air patrol and scrambled four, rather than the previous two jets, when Chinese PLAAF combat aircraft were detected heading east from a base in Fujian province that is closer to the Senkakus (380 km) than the ASDF base at Naha (410 km).[59]

Challenges

While the SDF buildup in the Ryukyu islands and Kyushu during the ten years following the start of the new status quo of constant confrontation around the Senkakus significantly reenforced Japan's military capabilities for defending the Senkaku and the Sakishima islands from China, the SDF's new defense strategy for these islands has faced significant challenges. Heginbotham and Samuels had a modest evaluation of Japan's new capabilities: "Japanese forces are currently best suited for low-end military conflict, such as a localized skirmish or set-piece battle in the skies or waters immediately around the Senkaku Islands."[60]

Lack of Jointness. The biggest shortcomings in Japan's buildup concern inadequate intelligence-gathering resources, a lack of jointness and even data networks between the SDF services and the JCG, community relations and protection. The SDF has been promoting "jointness" in operations between the three SDF services, but so far, the results have been modest, and jointness remains a problem, in significant part due to bureaucratic resistance.[61] Nowhere was this issue more apparent than with the new GSDF amphibious brigade, which relies on cooperation

[58] Heginbotham & Samuels, "Active Denial," p. 148, note 77; Japanese Ministry of Defense, *Heisei 28 Boei Hakusho* (Tokyo: Nikkei Insatsu, 2016), p. 181; *Defense of Japan 2023*, p. 313. Le, *Japan's Aging Peace*, p. 111.

[59] Mulloy, *Defenders of Japan*, p. 257; "Japan Now Instantly Scrambles Jets against China's from Fujian," *Kyodo*, July 19, 2020, as accessed October 1, 2023, at https://english.kyodonews.net/news/2020/07/c0f33e803562-japan-now-instantly-scrambles-jets-against-chinas-from-fujian.html.

[60] Heginbotham and Samuels, "Active Denial," p. 149.

[61] Heginbotham and Samuels, "Active Denial," pp. 163–164; Mulloy, *Defenders of Japan*, pp. 252–253; Jeffrey W. Hornung, "Japan's Amphibious Joint Pain," *US-Japan Rand Conference* (Santa Monica: Rand Corporation, 2018), pp. 25–46.

from the other SDF services, especially on the MSDF for sea lift and the ASDF for air support, but the GSDF has not had the Link-16 data system or other data systems for communicating with the MSDF and ASDF; the JCG has also lacked access to Link-16. In 2021 the GSDF obtained the Link-16 data system for its T-12 anti-ship missiles but lacked access for its other units. Moreover, access to this expensive system has been limited even within the ASDF and MSDF where many combat units have lacked it.[62] Additionally, the three SDF services have had little experience with joint command and each service appears reluctant to be commanded by an officer from another service. An attempt was made to form a joint command in 2016, but that failed apparently due to inter-service rivalry. A related problem is the dominance of the GSDF in budget and leadership of the joint staff, with approximately half of the chiefs of staff from the three services coming from the GSDF.[63]

Paucity of Intelligence Assets. A scarcity of intelligence-gathering assets is another limitation. Japan lacks a human intelligence service (i.e., agents deployed overseas to gather intelligence).[64] Despite the establishment of a GSDF maritime surveillance base on Yonaguni in 2015 and an SDF SIGNET base on Miyako in 2008, the SDF and the GSDF in particular continue to lack sufficient intelligence-gathering assets around the Sakishima and Senkaku islands, lack integration of coordinated fire control (merely deconfliction of fire) with other services, and suffers from "poor fire support doctrine." Although the SDF demonstrated the ability to rapidly mobilize and deploy on a large scale (over 100,000 troops within a week) following the Great East Japan Earthquake triple disaster (earthquake, tsunami, and nuclear meltdown) of March 11, 2011, and even with the acquisition of tilt-rotor Osprey aircraft, questions persist in the

[62] Jefffrey W. Hornung, *Japan's Potential Contributions in an East China Sea Contingency* (Santa Monica, CA: Rand Corporation, 2020), p. 81; Mulloy, *Defenders of Japan*, pp. 252–253; and Desmond Ball and Richard Tanter, "The Transformation of the JASDF's Intelligence and Surveillance Capabilities for Air and Missile Defence," *Security Challenges* 8, no. 3 (Spring 2012), pp. 37–38.

[63] Heginbotham & Samuels, "Active Denial," p. 163; Hornung, *Japan's Potential Contributions*, pp. 80–83; Jiji, "Japan Eyes Permanent Joint HQ for SDF," *Japan Times*, March 14, 2016, p. 2. The plan to establish a Permanent Joint Headquarters for the SDF was resurrected in the 2022 NDPG, although no timeline for establishing it was provided. See Chapter 6.

[64] Richard J. Samuels, *Special Duty: A History of the Japanese Intelligence Community* (Ithaca: Cornell University Press, 2019), pp. 181–183.

southwest over "how quickly its forces can assemble, integrate, match troops with logistics and deploy once conflict commences, as well as concerns over how well it can move from its bases to battle space."[65] Similarly, although the MSDF only possesses a small number of comparatively older oilers and, with only three Osumi Landing Ship Tank (LST) transport ships, lacks sufficient sealift capabilities for supporting oversized transport and amphibious operations. Obviously, these logistical challenges make it even harder to envisage the SDF playing a military role beyond the defense of Japanese territory.[66]

Paucity of Bases. The relative paucity and small size of bases, especially in the Sakishima islands, exacerbates logistical challenges for the SDF in defending the Senkakus and Sakishima islands (much more so in the case of participating in regional conflicts). This situation is not unique to the Ryukyus or Japan, as obtaining land for new military bases is a struggle in any liberal democracy.[67] Nonetheless, this problem is especially acute in the case of the Ryukyus. Hornung observes that there are "no plans to further build out its presence on any additional islands, despite the strategic benefits that an expanded footprint would bring," a result that he attributes "to strong public opposition to expanding the SDF's footprint in the region."[68]

A recent notable example involves an effort by Tokyo to facilitate an expansion of the GSDF presence on Okinawa by expanding the GSDF's 15th Brigade into a Division. This sparked opposition over plans to build a new training area and ammunition depot in the central Okinawan town of Uruma, which is near residential areas and public facilities. Residents' associations have called for the plan to be scrapped over concerns about noise and potential accidents; Okinawa Governor Tamaki Denny also

---

[65] Hornung, *Japan's Potential Contributions*, p. 20.

[66] Hornung, *Japan's Potential Contributions*, pp. x–xii, 29, 52–53.

[67] Le, *Japan's Aging Peace*, pp. 111.

[68] Cite: Hornung, *Japan's Potential Contributions*, pp. x, 29, 30, and more generally see pp. 107–108. Also see *Japan's Aging Peace*, p. 135.

came out in opposition to the plan.[69] In mid-March 2024 a large demonstration against this base was held in Uruma that was reportedly attended by 1200 people including the town's mayor.[70] Even if this and similar opposition movements are ultimately unsuccessful (though this one was eventually successful), they at least slow down the creation of new bases while increasing base construction costs. They may also have implications for the effective operation of these bases (see Chapter 4).

Pace of Scrambles. Another challenge for Japan's attempts to reenforce its control of the Senkaku islands and its airspace is that despite the buildup of ASDF combat aircraft in Naha, frequent scrambles around the Senkakus are imposing costs on the ASDF, taking resources away from training pilots and imposing heavier maintenance and asset depreciation costs.[71] This has especially been the case since Japan picked up the pace of intercepts of Chinese military aircraft flying east from an airbase in Fujian from 2019, demonstrating the limits of the new Naha Airwing. This raises questions about the sustainability of Japan's current pace of interceptions, especially given the age of its planes and growing difficulty maintaining them.[72]

Community-Base Relations. Community-base relations are an issue impinging on SDF operations throughout Japan, but nowhere more so than in the Ryukyus, given the experience of Okinawa and other islands during World War II, and the fraught relations between local communities in Okinawa and the many large US bases present there over eight decades. The current conflict regarding the relocation of a US base on Okinawa island between the Okinawan prefectural government and Okinawan public opinion (with 72% voting against the relocation plan

---

[69] "Editorial: Government Must not Rush to Boost SDF Forces in Okinawa," February 20, 2024, *Asahi Shimbun,* as accessed February 29, 2024, at https://www.asahi.com/ajw/articles/15172569 MOD subsequently canceled the plan to expand the Uruma base because of this local opposition, highlighting the challenges of expanding bases in Okinawa prefecture. See "Okinawa SDF Training Site Plan Shelved Following Local Opposition," *Asahi Shimbun,* March 1, 2024 as accessed May 1, 2024 at https://www.asahi.com/ajw/articles/15184655

[70] Kaigo Narisawa, Taro Ono and Satsuki Tanahashi, "1st GSDF Missile Battery on Main Island of Okinawa Set up," *Asahi Shimbun,* March 22, 2024, as accessed February 29, 2024 at https://www.asahi.com/ajw/articles/15207076.

[71] Burke et al., *China's Military Activities in the East China Sea,* p. 18; Mulloy, *Defenders of Japan,* p. 257.

[72] Mulloy, *Defenders of Japan,* p. 257.

in a prefectural referendum),[73] on the one hand, and the government in Tokyo, on the other, have, by extension, made SDF-Ryukyu relations, and possible plans for further SDF base expansion, even more fraught.[74]

However, the anti-base activism of Okinawa has been somewhat less evident in the Sakishima islands, with Yonaguni agreeing to host a GSDF maritime observation base consisting of 160 GSDF members in exchange for economic benefits (after some bargaining over the terms). Ishigaki also agreed to host a GSDF base there, with support based more on local politics driven by nationalism and a desire to defend Japanese control of the Senkaku islands, which are a part of Ishigaki city. However, the prospect of deploying long-range stand-off or counterstrike missiles to Okinawa that could potentially hit targets in China has provoked a rise in opposition to the SDF base on Ishigaki (see Chapters 4 and 6). Often difficult SDF base-community relations not only make SDF expansion in the Ryukyus difficult, they also potentially significantly complicate base operations, including during a conflict (see Chapter 4).[75]

Demographic Challenges. The SDF's broader and longer-term problems exacerbate these challenges. The biggest of these is arguably its growing recruitment challenges. Japan has rapidly become one of the oldest societies in the world with a shrinking population. The population eligible to serve in the SDF has dropped 40% since 1994 and is expected to drop another 30% over the next 40 years,[76] although demographic decline in the early 2020s is exceeding projections from just a few

---

[73] Paul Midford, "Okinawa Casts a Decisive Vote Against the Relocation of a US Base," *Australian Outlook*, March 13, 2019, accessible at the website of the Australian Institute of International Affairs: https://www.internationalaffairs.org.au/australianou tlook/okinawa-decisive-vote-against-relocation-us-base/?fbclid=IwAR0V17C1h4nNnJsx vdt9ZIA8dGK6VZCbtBWtU5C-D2vPZ6BDFK35MSMjt0k.

[74] Brad Williams, "Militarizing Japan's Southwest Islands: Subnational Involvement and Insecurities in the Maritime Frontier Zone," *Asian Security* 11, no. 2 (2015), pp. 136–153, at pp. 139–140; Mulloy, *Defending Japan*, p. 249; Lyle Goldstein, "Bad Idea: Turning A2/AD against China with "Archipelagic Defense," *Defense 360 CSIS*, December 21, 2021, as accessed November 24, 2023 at https://defense360.csis.org/bad-idea-turning-a2-ad-against-china-with-archipelagic-defense/ Goldstein notes similar community opposition facing plans US bases in Guam.

[75] Williams, "Militarizing Japan's Southwest Islands," pp. 142–147.

[76] Le, *Japan's Aging Peace*, p. 82. More generally, see Oros, *Japan's Security Renaissance*, pp. 72–75.

70 P. MIDFORD

years earlier.[77] While this reality not only significantly shrinks the pool of potential applicants, it also means the SDF faces fiercer competition from other prospective employers as Japan's labor shortage becomes increasingly severe.[78] The paucity of housing and other facilities for female SDF members, and the notorious lack of other amenities for SDF members at bases that they must obtain out-of-pocket, most notoriously toilet paper,[79] handicaps the SDF in its recruitment efforts. Japan's security isolationism also exacerbates Japan's shortage of SDF members, as no legal framework has been created to allow foreign nationals (even permanent residents) to serve in the SDF, and there still has not been any serious national debate on this issue.

The MSDF has been responding to personnel short-falls by developing a new class of frigates that require only two-thirds the number of sailors as older models, but sometimes experiences trouble sufficiently manning even these ships.[80] More generally, some ships have been undermanned by up to 30%, while some frontline GSDF units have been as much as 20% short on personnel.[81] On the other hand, the MSDF's new maritime patrol plane, the P-1, is no less labor intensive than its predecessor, the P-3C.[82]

---

[77] In 2023 births in Japan fell below the 760,000 level (to 758,631), twelve years earlier than the National Institute of Population and Social Security Research had forecast (by 2035). The decline in marriages, which fellow below 500,000 in 2023 for the first time in 90 years, is a leading indicator of continued decline in births. See "Japan births at record low, population down by largest margin in 2023," *Kyodo*, February 27, 2024 as accessed February 29, 2024 at https://english.kyodonews.net/news/2024/02/2a0a266e13cd-urgent-japans-population-declines-by-largest-margin-of-831872-in-2023.html; Masaki Ishihara, "Japan Heads for 'Marriage Ice Age' with Lowest Number in 90 Years," *Nikkei Asia*, February 17, 2024, as accessed February 29, 2024 at https://asia.nikkei.com/Spotlight/Society/Japan-heads-for-marriage-ice-age-with-lowest-number-in-90-years).

[78] Le, *Japan's Aging Peace*, p. 84.

[79] Rie Ogasawara, *Jieitai-in wa kichi no toirettopēpā o 'jibara' de kau* (Tokyo: Fusōsha, 2019).

[80] Motoko Rich, Hikari Hida and Chang W. Lee, "Japan Wants a Stronger Military. Can It Find Enough Troops?" *New York Times*, December 13, 2023, as accessed December 14, 2023, at https://www.nytimes.com/2023/12/13/world/asia/japan-military.html.

[81] Susan Yoshihara, "The Setting Sun? Strategic Implications of Japan's Demographic Transition," in Susan Yoshihara and Douglas A. Sylvia, eds., *Population Decline and the Remaking of Great Power Politics* (Washington, DC: Potomac, 2012), as cited by Le, *Japan's Aging Peace*, p. 86.

[82] MSDF 4th Air Wing briefing, March 8, 2024.

One way the SDF has responded is by raising recruitment and retirement ages, and the average age in each of the three services has risen by a year or more since 2009, but that results in an older and potentially less capable force. Older recruits might experience more difficulty responding to rapidly changing military technology. As Hornung notes, "recruitment problems coupled with an aging force are likely to negatively affect Japan's ability to support a regional contingency, particularly as these trends continue over time."[83] On the other hand, as Le notes, "an older armed forces in and of itself is not problematic for a defense-oriented security posture."[84] This idea appears to have gained currency in Japanese defense circles. According to one defense official interviewed by Le, "A declining birthrate encourages the tendency to preserve the status quo. Our mindset of national security is overly defensive. Very defensive. We just want to preserve our territory."[85]

[83] Hornung, *Japan's Potential Contributions*, pp. xii, 86.

[84] Le, *Japan's Aging Peace*, p. 85.

[85] Le, *Japan's Aging Peace*, p. 68, quoting a government official in June 2020.

CHAPTER 4

Japan's Emerging A2/AD Strategy in the East China Sea

Abstract This chapter maps Japan's emerging Anti-access and Area Denial (A2/AD) strategy as a response to China's continual threat to Japan's control of the Senkaku islands, consistent with a focus on territorial defense and deterrence by denial. Japan's A2/AD strategy was inspired by China's original A2/AD strategy. Japan's A2/AD strategy covers the Senkaku islands and the Ryukyu islands, and has developed during the decade following the emergence of the new status quo of confrontation around the Senkakus. This chapter analyzes how Japan began by deploying anti-ship and anti-aircraft missiles to the Ryukyu islands and how it is building out these deployments with projects to develop longer-range and more versatile missiles, including a new ground-launched Hyper-Velocity Gliding Projectile (HVGP) missile.

Keywords Anti-access Area Denial (A2/AD) · defense by denial · Senkaku islands · Ryukyu islands · Hyper-velocity gliding projectile (HVGP) · T-12 surface to ship missile (SSM)

© The Author(s), under exclusive license to Springer Nature Switzerland AG 2025
P. Midford, *The Senkaku Islands Confrontation and the Transformation of Japan's Defense*, Palgrave Studies in Maritime Politics and Security, https://doi.org/10.1007/978-3-031-77727-1_4

73

Introduction

This chapter maps out Japan's emerging Anti-access and Area Denial (A2/AD) strategy as a response to China's continual threat to Japan's territorial control of the Senkaku islands. It reveals a defensive realist focus on territorial defense and deterrence by denial. Japan's A2/AD strategy has been inspired by China's original A2/AD strategy that is based on long-range anti-ship and anti-aircraft missiles, and that is designed to prevent the US military from operating near China's shores in the case of a conflict in the East or South China Seas. Japan's A2/AD strategy covers the Senkaku islands and the Ryukyu islands and has developed during the ten years following the emergence of the new status quo of constant confrontation around the Senkakus. This chapter analyzes how Japan began this strategy by deploying anti-ship and anti-aircraft missiles to several islands in the Ryukyu chain, especially in the Sakishima islands southwest of Okinawa[1] and how it is building out this strategy with projects to develop longer-range and more versatile missiles, including a new ground-launched Hyper-Velocity Gliding Projectile (HVGP) missile for targeting ships and protecting remote islands. This chapter also considers the challenges Japan faces in fully developing this A2/AD strategy, including limited land area and the difficulty of moving mobile missile units around populated areas, especially in view of difficult relations with local communities characterized by high levels of mistrust.

What Is an Anti-Access/Area Denial (A2/AD) Strategy?

Anti-Access and Area Denial (A2/AD, in Japanese 接近阻止/領域拒否) capabilities, as the term suggests, refers to two types of capabilities. First, it refers to long-range kinetic capabilities, generally longer-range precision guided munitions, anti-aircraft missiles and anti-ship missiles, designed

---

[1] The term Yaeyama Islands is sometimes used, but that term excludes Miyako and Tarama islands. Yonaguni island is the western most of these islands, while Ishigaki is the eastern most of the principle Yaeyama islands. The Sakishima islands includes all the Ryukyu islands on the southwestern side of the Miyako Strait (including Miyako and Tarama islands as well as the Yaeyama islands) opposite of Okinawa. See Brad Williams, "Militarizing Japan's Southwest Islands: Subnational Involvement, and Insecurities in the Maritime Frontier Zone," *Asian Security* 11, no. 2 (2015), p. 138.

to block an adversary's military from entering an operating zone. Area Denial or AD capabilities refer to shorter-range kinetic capabilities, generally precision guided munitions, intended to deny or limit adversaries' freedom of action within an operating zone. A2/AD relies on highly accurate surveillance capabilities for precisely tracking opposing forces so they can be effectively targeted with precision guided munitions, creating what is often called an "A2/AD umbrella." So far, the concept has only been applied to maritime space. China originally developed this strategy to deny US aircraft carriers and other naval assets access to the East and South China Seas, and even western Pacific Ocean waters near Taiwan.[2]

In recent years East Asian security analysts have been recommending that other countries copy (or steal) China's A2/AD strategy for use against China itself. In 2016 US and Japanese military analysts recommended that Japan adopt just such a strategy in the East China Sea to deter and defend against Chinese military attacks on the Senkaku and Ryukyu islands.[3] In a 2020 Rand Corporation report Jeffrey W. Hornung highlighted Japan's "recent acquisitions that support an A2/AD strategy."[4] Similarly, Eric Heginbotham and Richard J. Samuels observe in a 2018 article in *International Security* that Tokyo, by moving to create and deploy new classes of anti-ship missiles in the Ryukyus, is "creating Japan's own miniature A2/AD zone."[5] Finally, it should be

---

[2] Grant Newsham, Ryo Hinata-Yamaguchi and Koh Swee Lean Collin, "Japan Should Steal a Strategy from China's Playbook: How Tokyo Can Build Its Own A2/AD Network in the East China Sea," *National Interest*, May 11, 2016 as accessed August 8, 2023 at https://nationalinterest.org/feature/japan-should-steal-strategy-chinas-playbook-16159. For a more recent critique of this concept of an island based A2/AD strategy, see Lyle Goldstein, "Bad Idea: Turning A2/AD against China with "Archipelagic Defense," Defense 360 CSIS, as accessed November 24, 2023 at https://defense360.csis.org/bad-idea-turning-a2-ad-against-china-with-archipelagic-defense/

[3] Newsham, Hinata-Yamaguchi and Collin, "Japan Should Steal a Strategy from China's Playbook."

[4] Jeffrey W. Hornung, *Japan's Potential Contributions in an East China Sea Contingency* (Santa Monica: Rand Corporation, 2020), p. 14.

[5] Eric Heginbotham and Richard J. Samuels, "Active Denial: Redesigning Japan's Response to China's Military Challenge," *International Security* 42, no. 4 (Spring 2018), p. 158. These authors also cite an early Reuters story on Japan building its own A2/AD

76   P. MIDFORD

noted that military analysts have also advocated that other states near China adopt their own A2/AD strategy, most notably Taiwan.[6]

EMERGENCE OF JAPAN'S A2/AD STRATEGY

Conceptual Emergence of A2/AD. Japan has in fact been developing its own version of China's Anti-Access/Area Denial (A2/AD) strategy, with the ongoing deployment of anti-ship and other missile systems throughout the Ryukyu chain not only creating a missile umbrella designed to deny China access to the Senkaku islands, but also to deny access to the Western Pacific through the Miyako Strait and other Ryukyu-island straits.[7] This strategy is centered on the Ryukyu islands nearest to the Senkakus, specifically the Sakishima islands of Miyako Island, Ishigaki Island, and Yonaguni Island, although SSM and SAM missiles have also been deployed further to the northeast on Okinawa island, and between Okinawa and Kyushu on Amami Oshima.

No mention of Japan pursuing an A2/AD strategy or deploying its major components appeared in the 2013 NDPG, which instead focused on establishing air and naval superiority to prevent attacks on remote islands and developing the GSDF's Amphibious Rapid Deployment Brigade (ARDB) to provide amphibious assault capabilities in case the GSDF needed to retake remote island, e.g. the Senkakus, that had

---

zone from 2015. See "Higashi Shinakai de Nihonban 'A2AD' senryaku, Chugoku shinshutsu fūjikome," *Reuters*, December 17, 2015, as cited by Heginbotham and Samuels, p. 158.

[6] See Lt Col Julian Thomas, USAF, "Bold and Unprecedented Moves: Building a US-Taiwan Defense Strategy in the Strait of Taiwan and South China Sea," *Journal of Indo-Pacific Affairs*, May 5, 2022, as accessed November 19, 2023 at https://www.airuniversity.af.edu/JIPA/Display/Article/3019529/bold-and-unprecedented-moves-building-a-us-taiwan-defense-strategy-in-the-strai/; and Pei-Shiue Hsieh, "Building Taiwan's Own Area Denial Capabilities: Taiwan Can Use Long-Range Anti-Ship Missiles to Create Its Own A2/AD Strategy," *The Diplomat*, September 21, 2022, as accessed November 19, 2023 at https://thediplomat.com/2022/09/building-taiwans-own-area-denial-capabilities/

[7] Senior Japanese Ministry of Defense Officials to whom the author presented the argument that Japan is developing its own A2/AD strategy covering the Senkaku and Ryukyu islands in mid-March 2022 did not disagree with this characterization. Also see Xavier Vavasseur, "Japan's Type 12 SSM Deployed to Keep Watch On Miyako Strait," *Naval News*, April 3, 2020, and SSM missiles in the Sakishima islands is also closing a "security vacuum."

been seized.[8] Nonetheless, already a month before the 2013 NDPG was published Japan had already conducted its first SSM exercise in the Sakishima islands, specifically on Miyako Island, where a T-88[9] SSM launcher and two T-88 missiles were deployed, two T-88 launchers and four T-88 missiles were also deployed to the Naha airbase on Okinawa, on the other side of the Miyako Strait. This was part of a larger exercise involving 34,000 SDF personnel that focused on remote island defense, and for the first time practiced retaking a remote island that had been seized by an unspecified enemy. This exercise also featured the deployment of SAM units to Ishigaki Island and Kume Island for anti-aircraft and missile defense exercises.[10] SSM and SAM systems are the key components of an A2/AD strategy.

The first mention of developing stand-off missile capabilities in an NDPG appeared in the 2018 edition in the context of remote island defense. According to the *2018 NDPG*: "SDF will acquire stand-off firepower and other requisite capabilities to deal with ships and landing forces attempting to invade Japan including remote islands from the outside of their threat envelopes."[11] Following Japan's initial reaction to the

---

[8] Cabinet of Japan, *National Defense Program Guidelines for FY 2014 and Beyond* (*2013 NDPG*) pp. 14, 19–20.

[9] Also known as Type-88 SSMs, throughout this book this will be rendered as T-88, or in the case of its successor missile, as the T-12, rather than as Type-12.

[10] "Ritō bōei wo sōtei, Okinawa de tōgō enshū chitaikan misairu tenkai," *Asahi Shimbun*, November 12, 2013 (chōkan, seibu), p. 38; Heginbotham and Samuels, "Active Denial," p. 145; and Desmond Ball and Richard Tanter, *The Tools of Owatatsumi: Japan's Ocean Surveillance and Coastal Defence Capabilities* (Canberra: Australian National University, 2015), pp. 11–12, who also report that the Chinese media saw the deployment of these anti-ship missiles as aimed at blocking and posing a real threat to the Chinese navy.

[11] Cabinet of the Government of Japan, *National Defense Program Guidelines for FY 2019 and beyond* (*2018 NDPG*), December 19, 2018, p. 21. Some hints were dropped as early as November 2017 that the Abe administration was studying acquiring stand-off missiles, with an MOD official stating: "Our main target will be ships at sea." Nonetheless, in the lead up to the issuance of the NDPG there was some discussion about targeting North Korean missile bases as well. See Kyodo, "Japan Eyes Budget for Long Range Cruise Missiles amid North Korean threat, *Mainichi*, December 6, 2017, p. 2. Yet, the North Korean enemy base argument was not politically persuasive, and provoked push back from Komeito as well as the Constitutional Democratic Party. See "Justification shaky for Japanese government's cruise missile plans," *Mainichi*, December 22, 2017, as accessed August 11, 2024 at https://mainichi.jp/english/articles/20171222/p2a/00m/0na/021000c; and Mulloy, *Defenders of Japan*, pp. 199–200; 352.

78 P. MIDFORD

new status quo of China continuously challenging Japan's control of the Senkaku islands, Tokyo focused on building up its JCG deployments and capabilities, ASDF deployments on Okinawa and GSDF deployments on the Sakishima islands focusing on maritime surveillance (better maritime radar, signals intelligence on Yonaguni) and deploying troops near (Miyako Island) to the Senkaku islands to defend Japan's control there in a crisis (as explained in Chapter 3).

Emergence of A2/AD in Hardware. Beginning in 2019 Japan launched a new phase in its response to China's challenge to Japanese control of the Senkaku islands: the beginning of a nascent A2/AD strategy. In March 2019 Japan opened new GSDF bases in Amami Oshima Island between Kyushu and Okinawa that had been under construction since 2016: Camp Amami and Camp Setouchi. Camp Amami received a T-3 Chu-SAM unit and 350 GSDF members, while Camp Setouchi received a T-12 SSM unit and 210 troops. Also, in March 2019 another GSDF base was opened on Miyako Island with the deployment of 380 troops as a Sakishima islands guard unit. A year later in March 2020 a T-12 SSM unit was deployed there, although the deployment of the missiles was delayed (see below).[12] In March 2023 another T-12 and SAM base that had been under construction since 2019 at the site of a defunct golf course opened on Ishigaki Island. This base hosts T-3 SAM missiles and T-12 SSM missiles (with no delay in the arrival of missiles or other ammunition unlike the Miyako base), with an expected personnel strength of 500–600 GSDF soldiers. The Ishigaki GSDF base is key as it is the only one that covers all the Senkaku islands and Yonaguni with T-12 missiles in their current 200 km notional range configuration.[13] Thus, this base

---

[12] Asian Maritime Transparency Initiative (AMTI), "Remote Control: Japan's Evolving Senkakus Strategy," (July 29, 2020), as accessed April 7, 2022 at https://amti.csis.org/remote-control-japans-evolving-senkakus-strategy/; and Xavier Vavasseur, "Japan's Type-12 SSM Deployed to Keep Watch on Miyako Strait," *Naval News*, April 3, 2020, https://www.navalnews.com/naval-news/2020/04/japans-type-12-ssm-deployed-to-keep-watch-on-miyako-strait/; and Naohito Toki, *Nanseishotō wo Jieitai misairu kichika* (Kamogawa Shuppan, 2022), Chapter 1.

[13] AMTI, "Remote Control;" Jiji, "GSDF begins moving vehicles to new base on Okinawa's Ishigaki Island," *Japan Times*, March 5, 2023, as accessed February 14, 2024 at https://www.japantimes.co.jp/news/2023/03/05/national/ishigaki-okinawa-sdf-base/; Gale Alastair and Austin Ramzy, "In Beijing Japan's Foreign Minister Warns Over Russia-China Military Ties; Top diplomats joust while Tokyo opens a missile base on a southern island," *The Wall Street Journal*, April 2, 2023, p. 2; "Ishigakijima ni misairu butai haibi e... Chūgoku ni taikō suru nerai, Nanseishotō wa 4 kyoten taisei ni,"

plays the key role in putting Chinese surface ships operating around the Senkaku islands at risk.

At the same time Japan developed and deployed an air-launched supersonic anti-ship missile, the ASM-3A, as an additional capability against Chinese ships threatening Japanese control of the Senkakus or even the Sakishima islands. Japan is also purchasing long-range air-launched anti-ship JSM missiles from Norway.[14] The acquisition of these missiles for the ASDF extended the range of Japan's A2/AD umbrella, which only the Ishigaki-based T-12 SSMs barely covered (and the Chu-SAM missiles do not cover at all). Nonetheless, the ASM-3A and other air launched anti-ship missiles gave the SDF only modestly more long-range strike beyond ground-based T-12s, given the strains on the ASDF especially in Okinawa. Despite its much-noted acquisition of in-air-refueling capabilities just after the turn of the century, Japan's inventory of tankers is few, and they are vulnerable.[15] "The ASDF," according to Hornung, "does not appear to have adequate logistical support capabilities to perform in a contingency that is likely to require operations in airspace far from Japan's mainland."[16] The ASDF would be hard pressed to operate effectively in defense of the Senkakus and Sakishima islands, and would effectively lack the capability to go beyond territorial defense (Fig. 4.1).

Yomiuri Shimbun, August 2, 2021, as accessed February 2, 2024 at https://www.yomiuri. co.jp/politics/20210802-OYT1T50230/; Kyodo, "Japan Sends Missile Units to Southwestern Island to Face China Threat," *Japan Times*, March 16, 2023, as accessed March 2, 2024 at https://www.japantimes.co.jp/news/2023/03/16/national/gsdf-ishigaki-dep loyment/. For this 200 km range to be effective rather than merely notional, effective Command, Control, Communications, Computers (C4) Intelligence, Surveillance and Reconnaissance (ISR, or C4ISR) is required. Thanks to Garren Mulloy for his detailed comments on this point.

[14] AMTI, "Remote Control;" Yoshihiro Inaba, "Extended Range Version of ASM-3 is being Mass Produced in Response to China's Maritime Expansion," *Naval News*, December 30, 2020, at https://www.navalnews.com/naval-news/2020/12/japan-to-field-new-asm-3a-long-range-supersonic-anti-ship-missile/; and "'Kokusan tomahōku' kaihatsu he shatei 2 sen kiro no shingata taikandan 12 shiki wa 1500 kiro ni enshin," *Sankei Shimbun*, December 29, 2020, https://www.sankei.com/politics/news/201229/ plt2012290001-n1.html; and Franz-Stefan Gady, "Japan Places Follow-on Order for Joint Strike Missiles, *The Diplomat*, as accessed August 11, 2024 at https://thediplomat.com/ 2019/11/japan-places-follow-on-order-for-joint-strike-missiles/

[15] Thanks to Garren Mulloy for his discussion on this point.

[16] Hornung, *Japan's Potential Contributions in an East China Sea Contingency*, pp. xi, 66.

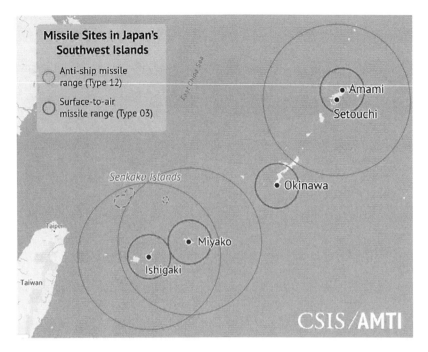

Fig. 4.1 Map of Japan's Nascent A2/AD Umbrella As of April 2023 (*Source* Asia Maritime Transparency Initiative (AMTI), "Remote Control: Japan's Evolving Senkaku Strategy," July 29, 2020, as accessed February 29, 2024, at https://amti.csis.org/remote-control-japans-evolving-senkakus-strategy/)

A2/AD Rationale. Why, after 2016 has Japan progressively placed greater emphasis on a stand-off missile response relative to dispatching the SDF to defend the Senkakus and other remote islands? Although the 2013 NDPG insisted that Japan would be able to maintain air and sea superiority, doubts about Japan's ability to do so were already creeping into the 2018 NDPG, which identified long-range stand-off missiles as the solution to this problem. In case of an attack on Japan, "including its remote islands," "even when maintaining maritime and air superiority becomes untenable, SDF will block invading forces' access and landing from outside their threat envelopes."[17] The reference to "outside their threat envelopes" refers to the ability to target enemy forces with long-range missiles that are out of range of enemy weapons. While implausible in a literal sense as China and North Korea have their own long-range missiles that can target all of Japan, the reference here is to more numerous shorter-range systems, and the rationale is clear: the SDF can defend the Senkakus and other remote islands without having to put SDF units in harm's way by dispatching them, especially in situations where Japan does not maintain air or naval superiority. Nonetheless, conventional military capabilities beyond stand-off missiles remain important, as the 2018 NDPG also notes that "Should any part of the territory be occupied, SDF will retake it by employing all necessary measures."[18] This passage also appears to reflect growing pessimism about Japan's previously undoubted ability to defeat an enemy's assault before it even reached its shores.

Geographical realities make stand-off missiles especially important for defense of the Senkakus. The Senkakus are closer to mainland China than were the Falkland islands from mainland Argentina (550 km), and further away from Okinawa and Kyushu (although not further away from the Sakishima islands), creating in this respect a militarily more difficult challenge for Japan than the UK faced during the Falklands war in 1982. Heginbotham and Samuels argue that for Japan "sustaining forces would be progressively more difficult farther southwest."[19] Moreover, the Senkaku (Diaoyu) Islands, although close to Yonaguni (170 km), are closer to China (approximately 350 km) than they are to Okinawa Island, at 410 km, or Kyushu at just over 900 km. This geography poses challenges to any attempt to send the SDF to defend or recapture the Senkakus. Moreover, these islands, and to a lesser extent the Sakishima islands, are within China's A2/AD umbrella. "The Senkakus in particular are vulnerable to most of China's short-range missiles, and to a lesser extent so are Yonaguni, Ishigaki, Miyako and smaller Sakishima islands."[20]

---

[17] *2018 NDPG*, pp. 11, 12.

[18] *2018 NDPG*, p. 12.

[19] Heginbotham and Samuels, "Active Denial," p. 152.

[20] Ibid., pp. 152, 157.

82   P. MIDFORD

This geography combined with China's own A2/AD umbrella is what makes Japan's A2/AD strategy attractive. It potentially allows Japan to avoid putting the SDF in a highly vulnerable position by deploying it to the Senkakus and simultaneously defend Japanese control of those islands by building its own A2/AD umbrella with anti-ship, anti-air and anti-missile systems that can hold at risk any Chinese forces that might attempt to seize the Senkakus or the Sakishima islands. For either China or Japan, seizing an island under an opposing side's A2/AD umbrella is risky at best. As Heginbotham and Samuels argue: "Opposed landings require not just the finely orchestrated application of force, but also the protracted maintenance of air and sea control in the immediate vicinity— turning mobile assets into fixed or semi-fixed targets for the adversary's submarines, aircraft, and ground-launched missiles."[21]

As such, Japan's emerging A2/AD strategy is seen by close analysts as a retreat from the forward defense strategy (which involves defeating an attack on the seas or in the air just beyond Japanese territory with superior military forces) that emerged at the end of the Cold War and represents a turn back toward a deterrence by denial strategy. Heginbotham and Samuels argue that while a forward defense strategy had become dominant by the 1990s, after 2010, the year the Senkaku conflict management regime began decisively breaking down, elements of deterrence by denial began to (re)appear. This started with Japan's decision to significantly increase its submarine fleet from 16 to 22.[22] Stronger elements of a deterrence by denial strategy, or what they call "active denial," had emerged around 2020 with Japan's stationing of SSM and SAM systems in the Ryukyu, and especially the Sakishima, islands. Beyond identifying recent trends in Japan's military strategy, they recommend that "maintaining the ability to survive, fight, and ultimately prevail in a general conflict...should be the focus of Japanese military strategy...A strategy with a heavy denial component offers the most promising means to this end."[23] They further note that as long as China's A2/AD capabilities for precision strike are intact, "a premature Japanese counterattack against Chinese

---

[21] Ibid., "Active Denial," p. 157. Also see Newsham, Hinata-Yamaguchi and Collin, "Japan Should Steal a Strategy from China's Playbook."

[22] Cabinet of Japan, *National Defense Program Guidelines for FY 2011 and beyond*, p. 20.

[23] Heginbotham and Samuels, "Active Denial," p. 153.

forces on the Senkaku Islands" with a forward defense posture "would court military disaster."[24]

These changes essentially represent a return to the Cold War equilibrium in Japanese strategy,[25] based on the reality of again being located next to a military superpower: "In some ways, those circumstances resemble early Cold War ones more than those of the early post–Cold War, a shift that brings new relevance to the concept of denial."[26] However, Heginbotham and Samuels see active denial as a step beyond Japan's Cold War era territorial defense strategy in that its A2/AD strategy gives Japan some stand-off options: "Japanese defense would more closely resemble a porcupine, able to inflict painful and costly wounds at limited distances, than the more purely defensive hedgehog."[27]

Jeffrey Hornung agrees that Japan is edging away from the forward defense strategy that emerged at the end of the Cold War and is to some extent moving back toward a strategy of denial focused more squarely on territorial defense, and Japan's emerging A2/AD strategy is a key indicator of this. According to Hornung, "While the bulk of Japan's defense capabilities today remain consistent with a forward defense strategy, such as fighter aircraft and destroyers, recent acquisitions that support an A2/AD strategy show that elements of a denial strategy are reemerging."[28] The move away from forward defense in new procurements and back toward a hedgehog or porcupine strategy of deterrence by denial or active deterrence reflect and reenforce Japan's priority on territorial defense, but this also translates into less ability to project force beyond Japan's borders. This is especially the case given the difficulty Japan has competing with China in air and naval power, and the still nascent nature of Japan's A2/AD capabilities covering the Senkakus and Ryukyu islands, which are still very much being built out. Contributing SDF forces to a regional military contingency, such as defending Taiwan, looks even more unrealistic

---

[24] Ibid., p. 156.

[25] For an argument that Japan's defense strategy is returning toward its Cold War era "equilibrium" focus on territorial defense, see Paul Midford, "Japan's Approach to Maritime Conflicts with China in the East China Sea and Prospects for Renewed Conflict Management and Resolution," *International Security Studies* 12 (2021), p. 80.

[26] Ibid., p 168.

[27] Heginbotham and Samuels, "Active Denial," pp. 168–69.

[28] Hornung, *Japan's Potential Contributions in an East China Sea Contingency*, p. 14. Also see pp. 23, 46.

84   P. MIDFORD

given that the SDF remains hard pressed to defense the Senkakus, if not the Sakishima islands.

Building Out Japan's AD/A2 Strategy

Range Extension. Beyond the initial deployment of Japan's nascent A2/AD umbrella covering the Senkaku and Ryukyu islands in the form of T-12 SSM and SAM bases that were completed in 2023 and following the development and deployment of the hypersonic air-launched ASM 3A missile developed for the ASDF, Japan was already preparing to further build out its A2/AD umbrella by 2017. Although not yet using the term stand-off missiles, from 2017 the defense budget added funds for extending the range and capabilities of Chu-SAM-3 and T-12 SSM systems, plus developing an air-launched version of the T-12. The 2017 budget mandated 11.5 billion Yen for developing an extended range and more capable T-12 ground to ship missile, and for developing an air to ship version of this missile in an attempt to make the T-12 the common platform for anti-ship missiles.[29] The 2017 budget also added 1.7 billion Yen for upgrading the Chu-SAM-3 surface-to-air missile to better deal with fast and low altitude targets, 9 billion Yen for creating a new ship-launched version of this missile, and 9.2 billion Yen for upgrading early warning radars in the Southwest, including the early warning radar on Miyako Island, to provide ballistic missile targeting capabilities for missile defense.[30]

Subsequently it became clear that Japan was aiming to extend the range of the T-12 SSM from 200 km to nearly 1000 km.[31] Japan also

---

[29] Bōeisho, *Waga kuni no bōei to yosan-Heisei 29 nendo no gaiyō* (Tokyo: Bōeisho, December 2016), pp. 8, 34, 42. The term used in the budget is *famirika*, or familization: creating a family of commonly based missiles. In the previous 2016 budget the focus was on gradually increasing the number of existing technology T-12 missiles, with nearly 10.2 billion Yen allocated for an additional T-12 battery. See Bōeisho, *Waga kuni no bōei to yosan-Heisei 28 nendo gaisan yōkyū no gaiyō* (Tokyo: Bōeisho, August 2015), pp. 35.

[30] Bōeisho, *Waga kuni no bōei to yosan-Heisei 29 nendo*, pp. 6, 7, 34, 42.

[31] Yoshihiro Inaba, "Japan to Greatly Extend Range of Type 12 Anti-ship Missiles, Modify It for F-15 J," *Naval News*, January 21, 2021, https://www.navalnews.com/naval-news/2021/01/japan-to-greatly-extend-range-of-type-12-anti-ship-missiles-modify-it-for-f-15j; Jun Aoki, "'Sono ki ni nareba dekiru,' kokusan nagashatei misairu ni komerareta 'kakureta nerai' to ha," *Mainichi Shimbun*, January 18, 2021, https://mainichi.jp/articles/20210117/k00/00m/040/147000c; and "'Kokusan tomahōku' kaihatsu he.

decided to develop an extended range version of its hypersonic air-launched anti-ship missile, the ASM-3A, and started importing other ASMs from Norway and the US.[32] Japan also launched a development program for a new ground-launched Hyper-Velocity Gliding Projectile (HVGP) missile for targeting ships and remote islands, with deployment expected from 2026 or later. According to *Mainichi Shimbun*, Ministry of Defense officials stated that "behind the ministry's move" to develop HVGP, "lies China's intensifying maritime moves in waters near the Senkaku Islands in Okinawa Prefecture and other parts of Japan," and HVGP missiles "would make it possible for Japan to respond to China's activities" around the Senkaku Islands "without deploying the Maritime Self-Defense Force's vessels and aircraft."[33] This rationale clearly represents deterrence by denial logic, and especially "active denial," as it would in theory negate the need to forward deploy the SDF to the Senkaku islands where they would be highly vulnerable to precision strikes under China's own A2/AD umbrella.

One notable gap in the initial deployment of T-12 SSMs was evident in the Miyako Strait between Miyako Island and Okinawa Island. The current T-12 SSM has a range of 200 km, but this strait is 250 km wide, hence the T-12 SSM base on Miyako could not fully cover the strait. Japan has moved to close this gap with the deployment of T-12 missiles at Katsuren on Okinawa Island, which is the first SSM deployment to the main island. This deployment was completed in mid-March 2024 at the GSDF's existing sub-camp Katsuren at a cost of $19 million. This latest deployment thus completes the A2/AD umbrella over the Miyako Strait by deploying the T-12 on both sides of the strait to put at risk any Chinese surface naval vessel attempting to transit the strait in

---

[32] AMTI, "Remote Control;" Inaba, "Extended Range Version of ASM-3 is being Mass Produced in Response to China's Maritime Expansion;" and "'Kokusan tomahōku' kaihatsu he;" Hornung, *Japan's Potential Contributions in an East China Sea Contingency*, p. 66.

[33] Yusuke Tanabe, "Ritō bōei yō 'kōsoku kakkūdan' tai kūbo mo kentō-Boueishō, sokudo ya shatei kōjō e," *Mainichi Shimbun*, February 25, 2020, https://mainichi. jp/articles/20200224/k00/00m/010/219000c; and "Japan Mulls Anti-aircraft Carrier Gliding Missiles for Remote Island Defense," *The Mainichi*, February 25, 2020, https:// mainichi.jp/english/articles/20200225/p2a/00m/0na/012000c; and Yoshihiro Inaba, "Japan to Develop and Deploy Supersonic Glide Weapons that can Target Ships, *Naval News*, March 4, 2020, https://www.navalnews.com/naval-news/2020/03/japan-to-dev elop-and-deploy-supersonic-glide-weapons-that-can-target-ships/

wartime. The Katsuren base will also have command over the SSM units deployed to Amami Oshima, Miyako and Ishigaki. Although blocking Chinese naval access to the Pacific via the Miyako Strait is one purpose of Japan's A2/AD strategy, the primary objective is to protect the Senkakus and other remote islands. As *Asahi Shimbun* notes, the SSM deployments in the Ryukyu islands are "intended to allow the GSDF to prevent enemy landings on outlying islands, including the disputed Senkaku Islands in the East China Sea."[34]

ASW Strengths. Japan is complementing its developing A2/AD strategy with buildups of its Anti-Submarine (ASW) and electronic warfare capabilities, effectively an underwater version of its A2/AD strategy. During the Cold War Japan built the most robust ASW capabilities after those of the US. As mentioned earlier Japan initiated a large expansion of its own very quiet submarine fleet under the DPJ in 2010 by extending the service life of its subs from 20 to 25 years, matching the NATO standard.[35] In 2021 Japan added a third ship to its dedicated submarine surveillance flotilla, marking the first time since the early 1990s that Japan had built a new ship of this kind. This appears to be a reaction to the detection of a Chinese sub intrusion into contiguous waters around the Senkakus in 2018, as well as another Chinese sub entering contiguous waters around Amami Oshima Island north of Okinawa in June 2020.[36] Both buildups appear to be attempts by Japan to preserve its underwater dominance.

Japan also deploys an impressive array of underwater sensors, notably sound surveillance system (SOSUS) sensors for detecting foreign submarines (and more recently foreign undersea unmanned vehicles), complemented by airborne surveillance mostly provided by P-1 and

[34] Daizo Teramoto and Kaigo Narisawa, "Missile Battery in Okinawa to Give Miyako Strait Full Protection," *Asahi Shimbun*, September 2, 2021, as accessed September 5, 2021, at https://www.asahi.com/ajw/articles/14431815; and Kaigo Narisawa, Taro Ono and Satsuki Tanahashi, "1st GSDF Missile Battery on Main Island of Okinawa Set up," *Asahi Shimbun*, March 22, 2024, as accessed February 29, 2024 at https://www.asahi.com/ajw/articles/15207076.

[35] Cabinet of Japan, *National Defense Program Guidelines for FY 2014 and Beyond*, p. 20; and "Japan's Defense Policy under the Democratic Party of Japan (DPJ)," Paul Midford, *ISPI Analysis* (Istituto per gli Studi di Politica Internazionale) 81 (December 2011), p. 3.

[36] Yoshitaka Ito, "MSDF Adds 3rd Surveillance Ship to Listen Carefully for Chinese Subs," *Asahi Shimbun*, March 5, 2021, as accessed September 27, 2021, at https://www.asahi.com/ajw/articles/14242991; and Mulloy, *Defenders of Japan*, p. 256.

P-3C long-range maritime patrol craft and a variety of short-range helicopters. In proximity to the Senkaku islands Japan has a long-range hydrophone listening station at White Beach in Okinawa, a signals intelligence (SIGNET) facility on Miyako Island, and a GSDF maritime observation unit on Yonaguni completed in 2015, plus a hydrophone on that island that was reportedly installed around 2010 as the Senkaku conflict management regime was breaking down.[37]

Desmond Ball and Richard Tanter characterize Japan's hydrophones as "the most advanced submarine detection system in the world"[38] In addition, Japan together with the US constructed a line of undersea surveillance sensors from Kyushu through the full extent of the Ryukyu islands (with the US extending the line past Taiwan and through the Bashi Strait), which Ball and Tanter refer to as the "Fish Hook Undersea Defense Line," that is clearly primarily targeted at monitoring and excluding Chinese submarines from the Miyako and other Japanese straits and waters during wartime.[39]

Challenges to Japan's Emerging A2/AD Umbrella

ASW Vulnerabilities. While Japan's strengthening A2/AD umbrella has already made it significantly more difficult for Chinese air and naval forces to operate around the Senkakus and Ryukyus during a military conflict, significant weaknesses and challenges remain, many of which will not soon or easily be remedied. Starting with the immediately preceding analysis of Japan's attempt to deny Chinese subs access and maneuver around its islands or straits in the case of a conflict, as Ball and Tanter note, much of the ASW infrastructure, including electronic intelligence (ELINT), electronic support and measures (ESM) stations, and communications between these stations and analysis facilities are vulnerable to electronic jamming. Moreover, Japan's hydrophones and other undersea sensors are vulnerable to kinetic attack, as is the White Beach MSDF Ocean Observation Station, which "is the key station for processing and analyzing data collected by underwater arrays strung from along the Ryukyu archipelago, and hence for detecting submarine movements within and from the East

---

[37] Ball and Tanter, *The Tools of Owatatsumi*, pp. 3, 57, 103.

[38] Ball and Tanter, *The Tools of Owatatsumi*, p. 103.

[39] Ibid., pp. 78, 103.

China Sea."[40] Moreover, the MSDF Fleet Wing 5, which is based at Naha in Okinawa, with approximately 20 P-3Cs, is the busiest Fleet Wing as it makes "daily flights" "over the Senkaku and surrounding waters."[41] Yet, the MSDF Fleet Wing 5 is the only major wing that does not yet deploy the more modern and capable P-1, despite its superior capabilities relative to the P-3C, including faster patrolling speeds, greater range and longer patrol periods. Despite the frontline location of the MSDF 5th Fleet Wing in Okinawa, no timetable has been decided for when P-1s will be deployed there.[42] Relatedly, although Japan possesses impressive minesweeping capabilities, it lacks significant minelaying capabilities that could greatly hinder a Chinese amphibious landing on the Senkakus or any Sakishima islands. Japan previously had some minelaying assets, but decided after the end of the Cold War that this capability was no longer needed.[43]

Electronic Warfare. Electronic warfare (EW) is an area where Japan now lags China, as Tokyo has not invested much in updating its capabilities since the 1980s, when the GSDF's single electronic warfare unit was established in Hokkaido in 1981 as part of preparations to defend Japan's main northern island from a Soviet attack. Today the SDF's electronic warfare protection measures capability appears inadequate. Many of the ASDF's radars are single frequency and hence vulnerable to jamming. Moreover, the SDF lacks electronic attack assets. Only some ASDF planes have counter EW jamming pods. The ASDF lacks usable electronic attack assets. Although Japan is attempting to upgrade its EW capabilities, the "fruits of this effort are years away" and there are no efforts to develop dedicated electronic attack capabilities.[44] Hornung finds the SDF

[40] Ball and Tanter, *The Tools of Owatatsumi*, pp. 103–104.

[41] Ball and Tanter, *The Tools of Owatatsumi*, p. 81.

[42] MSDF 4th Fleet Wing briefing, Atsugi MSDF airbase, March 8, 2024.

[43] Hornung, *Japan's Potential Contributions*, pp. xii, 78, 108.

[44] Hornung, *Japan's Potential Contributions*, pp. xii–xiii, 26, 36, 73, 78–79. Japan has recently budgeted funding for developing an electronic warfare aircraft by 2034 to replace its aging five signals intelligence EP-3 Orion aircraft. However, this aircraft will only have defensive electronic warfare capabilities, as it is intended to gather information on electromagnetic waves necessary for electronic protection and jamming. It will not have offensive or attack capabilities. See Kosuke Takahashi, "Japan pushes ahead with plans to develop a new EW aircraft based on the Kawasaki P-1," *Naval News*, September 20, 2024, as accessed February 14, 2025 at https://www.navalnews.com/naval-news/2024/09/japan-pushes-ahead-with-plans-to-develop-a-new-ew-aircraft-based-on-the-kawasaki-p-1/

has "no EA [electronic attack] capabilities aside from those used for training purposes." Overall, he concludes that "Japan's electromagnetic capability focuses on sensors, and its capability for conducting electromagnetic warfare is relatively weak."[45] Similarly, Heginbotham and Samuels conclude that in "electronic warfare, the PLA has moved ahead of Japan in both equipment and technique."[46]

In contrast to Japan, China is deploying a Wild Weasel type aircraft, the J-16D, which like that Cold War era plane or the more modern E/A-18 Growler that the US deploys is designed to jam and target enemy radars. The J-16D carries CM-102 supersonic anti-radiation missiles with a range of 100 km that home in on radars and other electronic signals. Japan by contrast has not developed or deployed comparable offensive electronic warfare planes with anti-radiation homing missiles for targeting enemy radars. Jeffrey Lin and P.W. Singer's analysis of the implications of China's wild weasel offensive electronic warfare capability applies to Japan in the negative: "China's increasing ability to protect its power projection capabilities shows that its advances in military technology are just as much focused on taking action abroad to advance its interests, as opposed to the A2AD narrative of hunkering down against enemy threats."[47] In contrast, the fact that Japan is not acquiring this capability clearly indicates that Tokyo is hunkering down to defend against enemy threats rather than shape its forces for military operations beyond Japanese territory.

During 2021 and early 2022, in an attempt to start catching up, the GSDF established several new electronic warfare units for the first time since the original unit was established in Hokkaido in 1981. These units have been stationed throughout Japan, but most have been placed in the Ryukyu islands, including Okinawa, and Yonaguni from March 2024, and nearby areas of Kyushu. These are mobile truck-mounted units that use the Network Electronic Warfare System (NEWS) that Japan developed between 2010 and 2016. In March 2022 a headquarters for deployed units was established near Tokyo. Yet, the effort remains relatively small,

---

[45] Hornung, *Japan's Potential Contributions*, pp. 72, 78–79. The ASDF operates five EA trainer aircraft, but they are only designed to jam SDF radios for training purposes.

[46] Heginbotham & Samuels, "Active Denial," p. 149.

[47] Jeffrey Lin and P.W. Singer, "China Builds Its Own 'Wild Weasel' To Suppress Air Defenses J-16D brings hammer down on SAMs, *Popular Science*, December 29, 2015, as accessed March 11, 2024 at https://www.popsci.com/china-builds-its-own-wild-weasel-to-suppress-air-defenses/

this unit (the 301st GSDF Electronic Warfare Company) having only 180 personnel nationwide.[48]

Also, although mobile, these ground-based NEWS units are not easily usable for regional conflicts, including Taiwan. Air or sea-based units would be more suitable for regional conflicts. Rather, these truck-mounted NEWS units are "designed for island defense."[49] The fact Japan is focusing on ground-based units again shows how it is shaping its military for territorial defense, starting with the Senkakus, rather than regional contingencies. Nonetheless, it is not clear that these NEWS units would be effective in foiling attacks on SSM and SAM systems deployed on Ishigaki, Miyako and Okinawa by China's J-16D and its anti-radiation homing missiles. Overall, electronic warfare assets, like its recently deployed NEWS system, are designed for island defense and are less useful for supporting longer-range stand-off missile strikes beyond Japanese territory.

Paucity of Bases. Another weakness with Japan's A2/AD strategy is the paucity of bases for deploying anti-ship missiles and even anti-aircraft missiles (see the more general discussion on this problem in Chapter 3). As Heginbotham and Samuels note, "to some extent, assets on the southern Ryukyu islands of Ishigaki or Miyako could support operations around the Senkaku Islands, but the former islands are small and are themselves distant from the more substantial bases on Okinawa Island. Their size would limit the ability of surface-to-air missile (SAM) and anti-ship missile (ASM) systems to maneuver and would greatly ease the Chinese ISR burden in supporting attacks on them."[50] Similarly, Hornung notes "not being able to further distribute Japan's defenses simplifies targeting objectives for China during a contingency to a small number of bases."[51]

---

[48] Yoshitake Matsuura, "Japan Ground Self-Defense Force Unveils New Electronic Warfare Unit in Kumamoto," *Mainichi*, March 30, 2021, as accessed April 11, 2022 at https://mainichi.jp/english/articles/20210330/p2a/00m/0na/018000c; Kyodo, "Japan's GSDF Marks Launch of New Electronic Warfare Unit," *Mainichi*, March 28, 2022, as accessed March 11, 2022 at https://mainichi.jp/english/articles/20220328/p2g/00m/0na/030000c; Narisawa, Ono and Tanahashi, "1st GSDF Missile Battery on Main Island of Okinawa Set up;" and *Defense of Japan 2023*, pp. 313.

[49] Hornung, *Japan's Potential Contributions*, pp. 26, 73.

[50] Heginbotham & Samuels, "Active Denial," p. 152.

[51] Hornung, *Japan's Potential Contributions*, p. 30.

Yet, it is especially difficult to obtain new bases in the Sakishima or Ryukyu islands for historical reasons.[52] According to Tokuchi Hideshi, former Vice Defense Minister for International Affairs, "the biggest obstacles" to building new SDF bases "are local politics and getting the support and understanding of the local community."[53] Moreover, Japan's Constitution, specifically Articles 92–95, guarantee significant local autonomy, making it hard in practice for the central government to force local governments to accept military bases. Rather than expanding bases, the priority over the next decade or more will likely be on building SDF housing to ensure the smooth stationing of SDF members in the existing bases, hardening these bases to make them more survivable in a conflict, and retrofitting older bases to reduce the impact of bases on local communities in the Ryukyus and address recruitment problems by building more female-only facilities. These base improvements will consume a significant portion of Japan's growing defense budget.[54]

Potentially compensating for this vulnerability is Japan's well-developed two-layers of missile defense, with Aegis missile defense destroyers and Patriot Pac III terminal missile defense layers, Japan has good prospects to at least significantly complicate and delay Chinese efforts to target Japan's A2/AD assets, a result that might be enhanced if Japan's new electronic warfare units were to prove effective at interfering with Chinese surveillance and targeting, and could overcome China's counter-measures and targeting of the NEWS system. Although Japan does not currently deploy Patriot batteries to the Ryukyus, it did set a precedent for temporary deployments over a decade ago in response to North Korean missile tests over the East China Sea (though these Patriot batteries were slow to deploy). That precedent, plus the mission of these missiles to prevent missile strikes on the Ryukyus might reduce the potential for political controversy, especially in a crisis. Nonetheless, in the face of potentially several large-scale waves of missile attacks it would probably be more a matter of "when" rather than "if" Japan's new A2/AD assets in the Ryukyus and Amami Oshima would be taken out and missile defense exhausted. These assets would at least make it significantly more costly for

---

[52] Williams, "Militarizing Japan's Southwest Islands," pp. 139–140.

[53] As quoted by Tom Phuong Le, interview of December 2018, *Japan's Aging Peace*, p. 111.

[54] Ibid., pp. 111–112.

China to operate in and around the Senkaku and Ryukyu islands, perhaps prohibitively so if the assets needed to neutralize Japan's SSMs, SAMS, and affiliated infrastructure were needed elsewhere.

Community-Base Relations. Difficult community-base and community-SDF relations on the Sakishima islands as well as Okinawa[55] pose significant challenges for the effective employment of the two main components of Japan's A2/AD strategy, namely SSM and SAM systems, both in the context of peacetime exercises and wartime operations. Problematic community relations make it difficult for the GSDF to deploy either type of missile system outside of their bases and in civilian areas, even for peacetime exercises. Such deployments would be even more difficult during a military conflict as nearby civilians might be (or at least feel) put at risk. This is especially true for the "frontline" islands of Ishigaki and Miyako Islands, and potentially on Yonaguni, if such missiles were to be deployed there (though that appears unlikely, see below), which are small, and offer these mobile missile units limited scope to roam even outside bases due to geographic limits in addition to those related to community relations.

To be sure, these problems are not confined to the Ryukyus, but are a more general phenomenon throughout most of Japan. According to data from the Ministry of Defense as reported by *Asahi Shimbun*, between 2009 and April 2022 Patriot Advanced Capability 3 (Pac 3) missile units were only deployed for exercises outside of SDF and US military bases five times. Yet, such exercises are crucial for ensuring that these missile defense units can deploy quickly and effectively in the event of a crisis. According to MOD anonymous sources summarized by *Asahi Shimbun*, "Local opposition to carrying out deeply unpopular anti-missile drills in urban areas is preventing it [the SDF] from being adequately prepared to carry out defensive measures in the event of an actual crisis because of the scant training taking place." As a result, local governments have been reluctant to allow Patriot missile drills in areas outside of bases. According to one MOD official quoted by *Asahi*, "we can sympathize with local governments' worries about complaints from citizens, but gaining experience in stationing interceptors in urban districts plays a major role in protecting these very citizens in the event of an emergency. We want them to know how essential it is." As a local government official in the Tokyo

---

[55] For an overview of these problems, see Toki, *Nanseishotō wo Jieitai misairu kichika*, Chapter 2.

region that does not allow the SDF to conduct missile defense exercises there explained: "We do not want to see ourselves bear the brunt of criticism from residents." *Asahi* summarized that the SDF "is waging a battle of public opinion here at home to keep its missile defense system ready to deploy" in a crisis."[56]

The deployment of Patriot PAC III missile defense systems to civilian areas can be considered a relatively easy case as these systems are not offensive weapons and are directly connected to protecting the locality where they are deployed. Stand-off and counterstrike missile systems on the other hand would likely be a much harder sell for municipal governments and citizens as they could be expected to attract counterstrikes. This is especially true in the case in the Ryukyus, where the SDF, except for the island of Okinawa, has only been deployed relatively recently (since 2015), and where a lack of trust and significant opposition to these new bases exist. Local political sensitivity if not opposition to these bases, especially in the Ryukyus, has slowed the speed at which these bases have been built and can be expanded. Internal SDF documents on remote island defense have made clear that building confidence with communities hosting bases and exercises is a priority.[57]

Problems at the Miyako Island base have come under critical scrutiny. The base is located in a central and relatively populated part of the island and is home to a 380-personnel guard unit, available for deployment to the Senkakus, and 320 personnel who operate the truck-mounted T-12 SSM batteries and the SAM batteries. Ammunition is not stored at the base but is supposed to be stored at an ammunition depot 10 km away in a relatively unpopulated area. This has created concern about possible enemy strikes on roads linking the depot and the base during a conflict. Moreover, the building of that depot was delayed by local opposition, and a lack of transparency from the Ministry of Defense in briefing residents about what sorts of weapons would initially be deployed at the base versus the depot, specifically missiles and heavy mortars, which created a public backlash that alienated even supporters of the base and led to the temporary removal of all SDF weapons from Miyako Island. When the T-12

---

[56] Kaigo Narisawa and Yoshitaka Ito, "SDF Faces 'High Hurdles' on Missile Defense System Training," *Asahi Shimbun*, April 29, 2022, as accessed April 30, 2022, at https://www.asahi.com/ajw/articles/14598622.

[57] Makoto Konishi, Jieitai no tōsho senso: Shiryoshu, rikuji "kyō han" de yomu sono sakusen (Tokyo: Shakai Hihyosha, 2017), pp. 284–285.

anti-ship missile battery was deployed to the island in 2020 it was initially deployed without any missiles.[58] That the Ministry of Defense initially had to take these dramatic steps illustrate the sensitivity and difficulty of community-SDF relations in the Sakishima islands. It is also worth noting that the currently deployed T-12 anti-ship missiles do not have counterstrike capabilities and are only useful for territorial defense, with a range from Ishigaki that just covers the Senkakus. The deployment of longer-range missiles, especially if perceived by local communities as being intended for possible defense of Taiwan instead of territorial defense, would attract more opposition in Okinawa prefecture, especially in the Sakishima islands.

The GSDF SSM and SAM base that opened on Ishigaki Island in March 2023, much closer to the Senkakus, has also generated opposition locally due to fears that it would result in China targeting the island in the event of a conflict over Taiwan. By contrast, there has been a notable absence of opposition over concerns that the island might be targeted in the context of defending Japan's control of the Senkakus.[59] Nonetheless, local opposition is a major reason why base building was slow on Ishigaki and especially on Miyako. The Miyako base took nearly ten years to construct, plus the additional time needed for the ammunition depot, while Ishigaki took just over five years (Fig. 4.2).

Strong opposition began to emerge even on Ishigaki as the possibility that this base might host long-range stand-off or even counterstrike missiles came to light. The Ministry of Defense had sold the base to Ishigaki city as for the sake of defending the Senkakus and other Sakishima islands. In reaction to reports that long-range strike missiles might be deployed to Ishigaki, the city council adopted a resolution by majority vote "flatly refusing" to accept the deployment of such long-range missiles. The controversy also provoked a lawsuit and a petition to

---

[58] Shinichi Fujiwara, "Clumsy Strategy Weakening Bid to Shore up Remote Island Defenses," *Asahi Shimbun*, April 29, 2020, as accessed February 14, 2022, at https://www.asahi.com/ajw/articles/13300444.

[59] Dooley & Ueno, "The Island Paradise Near the Front Line of Tensions Over Taiwan."

Fig. 4.2 The Japanese Ground Self-Defense Forces Base on Ishigaki Island (*Source* Author's photograph)

hold a referendum on the issue, a petition that gained the signatures of approximately 40% of voters in the city.[60]

Another problem regarding these concerns over the bases and especially the ammunition depot that has not received much attention is whether these deployed truck-mounted T-12 missile launchers have any scope for deploying beyond their small bases? In the absence of any debate, and given the political sensitivities regarding these deployments locally the answer would seem to be no, especially if territorial defense of the Senkakus or other Sakishima islands was not the mission. It should

---

[60] "EDITORIAL: Biggest Threat to Japan is a Government that Ignores Public," *Asahi Shimbun*, May 3, 2023, as accessed March 11, 2024 at https://www.asahi.com/ajw/articles/14899630. This prospect also led to local demonstrations when the base opened in March 2023. See Taro Ono, "Protest held as Possible Missiles Taken to New SDF Camp in Okinawa," *Asahi Shimbun*, March 19, 2023, at https://www.asahi.com/ajw/articles/14864918

be noted that similar controversies over a lack of transparency slowed basing decisions for the missile defense system Aegis Ashore, while the US contractor's inability to ensure that Aegis Ashore booster rockets would not fall on residential areas led to the program's cancellation.[61] The Aegis ashore cancellation demonstrates the power that local safety concerns can exert over SDF deployment decisions.

All things considered, it seems unlikely that GSDF missile batteries would be allowed to deploy near residential areas or shopping centers, or perhaps even around remote farm fields or forests. Even if these SSM trucks did have some range for roaming, the small land areas of Ishigaki, Miyako Island, and even Okinawa Island would make them very vulnerable to Chinese missile strikes. The absence of any range to roam beyond their bases would make the T-12 and other mobile missile batteries even more vulnerable to counterstrikes. Even if one argues that in an actual crisis urgent military necessity might trump local opposition, the fact that extra-base exercises in peacetime appear nearly impossible reduces the military effectiveness of any such sudden deployments. Moreover, even in the case of a military conflict deploying T-12 and other mobile missiles near civilian areas on these relatively densely populated islands would be difficult, as counterstrikes on those mobile units could produce significant civilian casualties. Indeed, international human rights and just war norms preclude such deployments.[62]

One option would be evacuating the civilian population before a conflict, an option that the LDP's Policy Affairs Research Council's Defense Committee endorsed as a response to missile attacks in general in its recommendations for the 2018 NDPG.[63] However, that option would

---

[61] Ankit Panda, "Japan Suspends Aegis Ashore Missile Defense Plans: What Happens Now?" *The Diplomat*, June 23, 2020, as accessed April 11, 2022 at https://thediplomat.com/2020/06/japan-suspends-aegis-ashore-missile-defense-plans-what-happens-now/; "What's Behind the Sudden Decision to Cancel Aegis Ashore Deployment?" *Genron NPO*, August 12, 2020, as accessed April 1, 2022, at https://www.genron-npo.net/en/issues/archives/5561.html.

[62] Ukraine was criticized by Amnesty International for deploying military assets in civilian areas, and launching attacks from those areas, placing civilians at risk. See Amnesty International, "Ukraine: Ukrainian Fighting Tactics Endanger Civilians," August 4, 2022, as accessed March 11, 2024 at https://www.amnesty.org/en/latest/news/2022/08/ukraine-ukrainian-fighting-tactics-endanger-civilians/.

[63] Jimintō seisaku chōsakai, "Aratana bōei keikaku no taikō oyobi chūki bōeiryoku seibi keikaku no sakutei ni muketa teigen," May 29, 2018, p. 11.

be difficult, uncertain, and risky. It would be a difficult undertaking logistically as the Sakishima islands have nearly 110,000 residents (1700 on Yonaguni, 53,000 on Ishigaki and Iriomote, and 55,000 on Miyako),[64] meaning that any such evacuation would be a massive undertaking, and especially challenging and risky in the context of a military conflict and the need to use available lift capabilities to move SDF forces and supplies forward to these islands.

Another option would be to invest in building bomb shelters on the Sakishima islands, which local leaders and some residents have called for.[65] Nonetheless, shelters would presumably only be a short-term solution during a prolonged conflict.[66] A government plan released in spring 2024 calls for building deep and robust bomb shelters in five Sakishima municipalities, but the plan specifies that they will only be capable of accommodating residents for up to two weeks.[67] On the other hand, evacuation would also be difficult as many residents would likely be reluctant to leave, a sentiment that would be exacerbated by mistrust and poor base-community relations. And such an undertaking would be uncertain and risky if a military conflict had already begun before the civilian population had been evacuated. The local population recalls evacuations of the islands during the closing days of World War II that resulted in evacuation ships being attacked from the air by US fighters, with a large number of evacuees dying, and many others ending up as castaways (ironically) on the barren main Senkaku island of Uotsuri for 45 days.[68]

---

[64] Yurika Ishii, "Japanese Legal Challenges in Rescuing Nationals Abroad," International Law Studies 100 (2023), p. 665.

[65] Shohei Sasagawa and Nobuhiko Tajima, "Island Leaders Call for Shelters to Prepare for Taiwan Crisis," *Asahi Shimbun*, July 25, 2023, as accessed February 2, 2024 at https://www.asahi.com/ajw/articles/14965358.

[66] See the discussion in Chapter 6.

[67] "Evacuation Shelters to Be Built in 5 Municipalities of Sakishima Islands; Okinawa Gov. Denny Tamaki Expresses Caution," *Japan News*, April 2, 2024, as accessed August 11, 2024 at https://japannews.yomiuri.co.jp/politics/defense-security/20240402-178136/

[68] Williams, "Militarizing Japan's Southwest Islands, p. 139. Also well remembered is the case of the Tsushima-maru, which evacuated school children, women and the elderly from the main island of Okinawa, and was torpedoed by a US submarine, resulting in the deaths of approximately 80% of the 1788 aboard. This memory is preserved by the Tsushima-maru Memorial Museum in Naha. See https://www.tsushimamaru.or.jp/english.

CHAPTER 5

Japan's Emerging A2/AD Strategy and Its Offensive Missile Debate

Abstract This chapter briefly analyzes how the continuing Senkaku islands confrontation shifted the debate about acquiring offensive missiles in Japan between 2012 and 2022. Under its defensive defense strategy Japan has avoided acquiring offensive weapons, including long-range missiles. This chapter outlines how decisions to acquire long-range anti-ship missiles to defend the Senkakus and avoid the need to deploy the SDF to those islands effectively eroded the prohibition on obtaining long-range missiles that could attack enemy bases on foreign territory, paving the way for the Kishida cabinet's decision to acquire such missiles in December 2022. The deployment of such long-range missiles could be justified for the first time as a defensive response to a concrete threat to Japan's territorial integrity.

Keywords Senkaku islands · Counterstrike capability · Tomahawk cruise missiles · Kishida cabinet · LDP National Defense Sub-Committee · Public opinion

© The Author(s), under exclusive license to Springer Nature Switzerland AG 2025
P. Midford, *The Senkaku Islands Confrontation and the Transformation of Japan's Defense*, Palgrave Studies in Maritime Politics and Security, https://doi.org/10.1007/978-3-031-77727-1_5

Introduction

This chapter briefly examines how the continuing Senkaku confrontation significantly shifted the defense debate in Japan between 2012 and 2022. Under its defensive defense strategy Japan has avoided acquiring offensive weapons, including long-range missiles, although this strategy had already been eroding in some respects, as Japan for example acquired in-air-refueling capabilities for the ASDF during the first decade of this century. This chapter outlines how decisions to acquire long-range anti-ship missiles to defend the Senkakus, in order to avoid the need to deploy the SDF to those islands, effectively eroded the prohibition on obtaining long-range missiles that could attack enemy bases on foreign territory, paving the way for the Kishida cabinet's decision to acquire such missiles in December 2022. The deployment of long-range missiles could be justified for the first time as a defensive response to a concrete threat to the country's territorial integrity.

Counterstrike Debate Emerges

As developed in Chapters 3 and 4, the continuing Senkaku confrontation has significantly shifted the defense debate in Japan. Under its defensive defense strategy (*senshu bōei* 専守防衛) Japan has avoided deploying offensive weapons. However, this policy has been gradually eroding over the years as Japan has acquired small aircraft carriers and in-air-refueling capabilities.[1] Japan's very quiet submarines have always been an exception to its aversion to acquiring offensive capabilities.

Starting in March 2017 hawks in the LDP began publicly calling for Japan to acquire offensive missiles, starting with cruise missiles, that can target enemy bases. Specifically, the LDP's Security Affairs Research Committee issued a policy report that stated "Japan's must have the capability to counterattack on enemy territory, including cruise missiles." This report was developed by a team lead by former Defense Minister Onodera

---

[1] Garren Mulloy, *Defenders of Japan: The Post-Imperial Armed Forces 1946–2016* (London: Hurst & Company, 2021), p. 255. Japan has arguably had helicopter carriers since the 1970s (Shirane class), and in 2018 decided to retrofit 2 Izumo flat-top helicopter carriers to accommodate up to 8 F-35B vertical take-off fighter jets. However, that small number would only translate into an extremely limited capability. Indeed, Mulloy suggests that the two Izumo class carriers "would only seem tenable as a training carrier" (p. 255).

Itsunori and was approved by a joint meeting of the LDP's Policy Research Council and its National Defense Subcommittee.[2] However, this was not enough to convince Komeito, with a party executive reportedly telling an MOD official in early December 2017 "the explanation that this is for the minimal defense of the Japanese islands can't convince members of our party."[3]

More than a year later, in May 2018, the full Policy Research Affairs Council (PARC) of the LDP issued recommendations for what should be included in the 2018 NDPG that was then being drafted, and repeated the recommendation that Japan acquire offensive missiles for striking enemy bases.[4] Although the threat of China's offensive missiles was in the background of these calls, the threat from North Korean missiles was the main focus as the enemy base attack capability was framed as a way to suppress new missile attacks once an initial attack had been launched. Nonetheless, the North Korean missile threat was insufficient to legitimate the idea of developing a counterstrike capability in 2018.

However, even absent an explicit decision to acquire missiles capable of attacking enemy bases the Abe administration already included funds in the 2017 budget (11.5 billion Yen) for developing a new extended range version (from 200 km to approximately 1000 km) of the T-12 ground to ship cruise missile, and for developing an extended range air to ship version of this missile.[5] Although the T-12 is not optimized to attack large land targets such as enemy bases, it nonetheless has at least a residual capability to do so. This acquisition effectively eroded the prohibition on acquiring offensive enemy base counterstrike weapons without making a decision to acquire such missiles. This can be seen as a case, unintentionally, or perhaps intentionally, of de facto eroding a precedent without formally breaking a precedent.

---

[2] Akihara Hara, Yuki Isabel Reynolds, "Teki kichi hangeki nōryoku hoyū e, seifu wa kentō kaishi o - Jimin chōsakai teigen," *Bloomberg*, March 29, 2017, as accessed March 11, 2024, at https://www.bloomberg.co.jp/news/articles/2017-03-29/ONK9D76K50XS01.

[3] "Justification Shaky for Japanese Government's Cruise Missile Plans," *Mainichi*, December 22, 2017 as accessed August 11, 2024 at https://mainichi.jp/english/articles/20171222/p2a/00m/0na/021000c.

[4] Jiyūminshutō seisaku chōsakai, "Aratana bōei keikaku no taikō oyobi chūki bōei-ryoku seibi keikaku no sakutei ni muketa teigen ~ 'tajigen ōdan (kurosu domein) bōei kōsō' no jitsugen ni mukete," May 29, 2018.

[5] Bōeisho, *Waga kuni no bōei to yosan-Heisei 29 nendo no gaiyō* (Tokyo: Bōeisho, December 2016), pp. 8, 34, 42.

Nonetheless, in 2018 the Abe administration, possibly because of opposition from Komeito, did not heed the LDP PARC and decided against including the acquisition of a counterstrike capability against enemy bases in the 2018 NDPG. This reflected the relatively recent nature of the debate on acquiring such a capability, with the LDP only beginning to call for such a capability a little over a year before, and the lack of any national consensus on the idea. Nonetheless, a senior Ministry of Defense (MOD) official emphasized to *Nikkei* that the extended range T-12 would in fact provide Japan with some ability to attack enemy bases on land.[6]

STAND-OFF CAPABILITIES

Reflecting the consensus around remote island defense and the lack of a national consensus around attacking enemy bases, the 2018 NDPG mentioned stand-off missile capabilities for the first time as a way to ensure remote island defense: "SDF will acquire stand-off firepower and other requisite capabilities to deal with ships and landing forces attempting to invade Japan including remote islands from the outside of their threat envelopes."[7]

Nonetheless, calls from the LDP and among defense hawks for Japan to acquire counterstrike systems optimized for attacking enemy bases, especially enemy missile bases escalated after the cancelation of the Aegis Ashore missile defense system in 2019. Aegis Ashore was canceled in large part due to the US contractor's inability to ensure that Aegis Ashore booster rockets would not fall on residential areas without a costly and decade-long delay to allow for a redesign of the system. Local fears about falling boosters and the possibility that nearby residents could be hit by enemy counterstrikes stoked opposition.[8] Local opposition in Akita

---

[6] Masaya Kato, "Japan Defense Plan to Omit Mention of Strike Capability," *Nikkei Asia*, October 21, 2018, as accessed February 29, 2024, at https://asia.nikkei.com/Pol itics/Japan-defense-plan-to-omit-mention-of-strike-capability.

[7] Cabinet of the Government of Japan, *National Defense Program Guidelines for FY 2019 and Beyond (2018 Guidelines)*, December 19, 2018, pp. 21–22.

[8] Two other factors were MOD errors in surveying the proposed Aegis-ashore site and mismanagement in communicating with the host community (including a MOD official falling asleep during a public hearing). I thank Garren Mulloy for his insights on these latter two points.

Prefecture effectively cost the LDP a safe Upper House seat in the 2019 election, which may have been an additional factor behind the cancelation.[9] Defense hawks in the LDP who had seen counterstrike capability as a supplement to missile defense doubled down on their calls for offensive missiles capable of striking enemy bases that could launch missile strikes again Japan. The LDP's PARC issued a report in early August 2020 calling for acquiring missiles that could attack enemy bases.[10] Nonetheless, it was not North Korea, but rather legitimization of stand-off missiles with extended ranges for defending the Senkakus and other remote islands that eroded the prohibition against obtaining offensive missiles and tipped the balance in favor of obtaining such missiles.

LONG-RANGE MISSILES SURFACE IN DOMESTIC POLITICS

According to *Mainichi Shimbun*, in response to the Abe administration's plan to develop a long-range HVGP missile, some Diet members argued that such missiles "make it possible for the SDF to directly attack other countries' territories" and would "deviate from Japan's exclusively defense-oriented policy." However, a MOD official responded that this missile is "intended for homeland defense and are not considered attacking weapons."[11] With the ongoing confrontation around the Senkaku islands, this kind of homeland defense argument from the government no longer appears to be an abstract hypothetical scenario but has gained credibility as a concrete scenario.

[9] Ankit Panda, "Japan Suspends Aegis Ashore Missile Defense Plans," *The Diplomat*, June 23, 2020, as accessed April 11, 2022 at https://thediplomat.com/2020/06/japan-suspends-aegis-ashore-missile-defense-plans-what-happens-now/; "What's Behind the Sudden Decision to Cancel Aegis Ashore Deployment?" *Genron NPO*, August 12, 2020, as accessed April 1, 2022, at https://www.genron-npo.net/en/issues/archives/5561.html. See "Opposition Candidate's Assured Victory in Akita a Possible Blow to Missile Defense Plan," *Mainichi Shimbun*, July 21, as accessed July 23, 2019, at 20 https://mainichi.jp/english/articles/20190721/p2a/00m/0na/015000c.

[10] Jiyūminshutō seimu chōsa-kai, "Kokumin o mamoru tame no yokushi-ryoku kōjō ni kansuru teigen," August 4, 2020, as accessed at https://news.yahoo.co.jp/expert/articles/ecc60025eb46d6e6b69df0e0b5b.

[11] Yusuke Tanabe, "Rittō bōei yō 'kōsoku kakkūdan' tai kūbo mo kentō: Bōeishō, sokudo ya shatei kōjō e," *Mainichi Shimbun*, February 25, 2020, https://mainichi.jp/articles/20200224/k00/00m/010/219000c; and "Japan Mulls Anti-Aircraft Carrier Gliding Missiles for Remote Island Defense," *The Mainichi*, February 25, 2020, https://mainichi.jp/english/articles/20200225/p2a/00m/0na/012000c.

A poll conducted by Jiji press in February 2022 found 34.3% favored Japan acquiring enemy base attack capabilities, which in practice mostly means ground-launched ballistic or cruise missiles, although this question did not specify the means. By contrast 26.1% opposed this acquisition and 39.5% were unsure. Even among LDP supporters, only 45.7% favored acquiring this capability.[12] A poll conducted in early April 2022 by *Yomiuri Shimbun* asked respondents whether they supported Japan possessing "the ability to attack enemy bases," which it defined as "being able to destroy enemy bases before Japan was attacked." The response was evenly divided with 46% supporting and 46% opposing Japan obtaining this capability (8% did not answer), indicating that even after the start of the Ukraine conflict no public consensus in favor of obtaining this capability has emerged, even though the poll presented this option in an excessively optimistic light.[13] Specifically, the wording of this poll implies that Japan could obtain the capability to destroy enemy missile bases before they could attack Japan, when in reality such a capability would at best be partial and unpredictable.

Moreover, this question also assumed a preemptive strike on enemy bases, which the Japanese government subsequently made clear it does not deem as legal under international law.[14] Nonetheless, Japan's developing capabilities to defend the Senkakus with longer-range stand-off missiles has already provided it with at least some capability to attack land targets in China and perhaps North Korea even without Japan adopting a policy of developing dedicated capabilities to attack such targets.

Whereas the LDP's PARC and its National Defense subcommittee had been calling for Japan to acquire counterstrike capabilities, this call had been notably absent from LDP election manifestos from 2017, when the issue was first raised in the party, through the Lower House election of 2021. Nonetheless, with public opinion becoming less opposed, the LDP's election manifesto for the 2022 Upper House election became the

---

[12] Jiji, "Poll Suggests More Details Needed on Enemy Base Attack Capabilities," *Japan Times*, February 22, 2022, p. 2.

[13] "Honsha zenkoku yoron chōsa kekka," *Yomiuri Shimbun*, April 4, 2022, p. 16. The same poll found nearly two-thirds (64%) of Japanese favored strengthening the country's defense, versus 27% who were opposed, although the poll did not ask by how much or in what way.

[14] This reversed a Japanese government position stated by Prime Minister Hatoyama Ichirō in the Diet in 1956. See the next chapter and Mulloy, *Defenders of Japan*, p. 199.

first one to state that Japan should have counterstrike capabilities to deter and respond to an attack on Japan itself. However, no mention was made of using this capability to defend any other country, including Taiwan.[15]

Nonetheless, Komeito, the LDP's long-term anti-militarist leaning coalition partner in government and "brake" on the LDP's more hawkish policies, publicly criticized the LDP's 2021 Lower House election platform where it proposed that Japan increase its defense spending to 2% of GDP and criticized Defense Minister Kishi Nobuo for calling for Japan to acquire missiles that could attack enemy bases .[16] On the other hand, the acquisition and development of increasingly long-range anti-ship missiles for defense of the Senkakus has not proven to be very controversial domestically, including for Komeito, as it is clearly tied to defense of the Senkakus and Japan's other outlying islands.

CONCLUSIONS

The emergence of a serious debate around deploying ground-launched long-range missiles from 2017 reflected a growing perception that the traditional "shield-spear" (*tate to yari*) division of labor between the two allies,[17] with Japan serving as the shield and the US as the spear, was no longer adequate. There was a growing chorus, especially in the LDP that called on Japan to acquire its own spear. It is also notable that the US was no longer openly complaining about Japan acquiring offensive capabilities, which it once routinely derided as "unnecessary duplication of effort." A MOD official told *Asahi Shimbun* that although the US government had turned down previous inquiries from Japan about possibly purchasing Tomahawk missiles, the "the Biden administration

[15] Jimintō, *Reiwa 4 nen sangiin senkyo kōyaku: Ketsudan to jikkō* (Jiyū Minshutō honbu, 2022), p. 4, as accessed at November 10, 2022 at https://storage.jimin.jp/pdf/pamphlet/202206_manifest.pdf.

[16] Tobias Harris and Levi McLaughlin, "The Small Pacifist Party That Could Shape Japan's Future," *Foreign Policy*, November 4, 2021, as accessed on April 26, 2022, at https://foreignpolicy.com/2021/11/04/komeito-ldp-japan-elections-defense-policy-china/.

[17] Jeffrey W. Hornung and Scott W. Harold, "Japan's Potential Acquisition of Ground-Launched Land-Attack Missiles: Implications for the US-Japan Alliance," *War On The Rocks*, September 9, 2021, as accessed April 26, 2022, at https://warontherocks.com/2021/09/japans-potential-acquisition-of-ground-launched-land-attack-missiles-implications-for-the-u-s-japanese-alliance/.

might be more willing to allow Japan to purchase Tomahawks as.... the United States may feel it is no longer able to deal with China by itself."[18]

Acquiring long-range stand-off weapons, and especially counterstrike missiles, have broader implications for Japanese security and far-reaching implications for the Japan-US alliance, including multiple entrapment risks for Japan that need to be managed.[19] Nonetheless, it is clear for Japan that the acquisition of stand-off missiles is intended for territorial defense, while the acquisition of counterstrike capabilities is intended to deter strikes, especially missile strikes, on Japan itself, as explained in the next two chapters.

[18] Naoki Matsuyama, "Japan Trying to Run Before It Can Walk on Missile Purchase Choice," *Asahi Shimbun*, October 29, 2022, as accessed February 29, 2024, at https://www.asahi.com/ajw/articles/14755399.

[19] Hornung and Harold, "Japan's Potential Acquisition of Ground-Launched Land-Attack Missiles."

CHAPTER 6

The Culmination: Japan's New Security and Defense Strategies of 2022

Abstract This chapter analyzes new versions of Japan's three fundamental security documents, referred to in Japanese as *Anpo San Bunsho*, that the Kishida administration issued in December 2022. It argues that the three new security documents represent a major pivot in Japan's defense posture, as they mandate a large increase of approximately 60% in defense spending up to 2% of GDP (based on NATO accounting standards) and the acquisition of offensive missiles for counterstrikes against military bases on foreign territory. This milestone represents the culmination of Japan's defense transformation resulting from the materialization in the Senkakus of the first direct threat to Japan's territorial integrity since 1945. The focus of the three new security documents is thus on territorial defense and does not indicate any intention to use military power beyond Japan's borders.

Keywords Senkaku islands · *Anpo San Bunsho* · 2% of GDP defense spending goal · Counterstrike capability · National Security Strategy · Taiwan · Preemption

© The Author(s), under exclusive license to Springer Nature
Switzerland AG 2025
P. Midford, *The Senkaku Islands Confrontation and the Transformation of Japan's Defense*, Palgrave Studies in Maritime Politics and Security,
https://doi.org/10.1007/978-3-031-77727-1_6

Introduction

This chapter analyzes the latest versions of Japan's three fundamental security documents, referred to in Japanese as *Anpo San Bunsho*,[1] that the Kishida administration issued in December 2022. In declining level of importance, but increasing level of specificity, these are the National Security Strategy (NSS), the National Defense Strategy (NDS), and the Defense Buildup Program (DBP). This chapter argues that these three new security documents represent a major pivot in Japan's defense posture, as they mandate a large 60% increase in defense spending up to 2% of GDP (based on NATO accounting standards) and the acquisition of offensive missiles for counterstrikes against military bases on foreign territory.

This milestone represents the culmination of Japan's defense transformation resulting from the materialization in the Senkakus of the first direct threat to Japan's territorial integrity since 1945. The focus of the three new security documents is thus on territorial defense and does not indicate any intention to use military power beyond Japan's borders. The *Anpo San Bunsho* does not signal a willingness to help the US defend Taiwan in case of a conflict with China, although recent Chinese military exercises around Taiwan have caused Japan to start perceiving a potential threat to Yonaguni island (which is only 110 km from Taiwan), if not the other Sakishima islands, a perception that is also reflected in the policies outlined in the 2022 NSS and NDS. This chapter analyzes these documents and their implications for Japanese defense. It focuses on the decision to acquire counterstrike missiles, possible implications for a Taiwan conflict, the large-planned increase in defense spending, and its link to a reenforced emphasis on territorial defense and defense autonomy.

Counterstrike Capability

As discussed in the previous chapter, the acquisition of long-range stand-off missiles to defend the Senkakus effectively undermined Japan's ban on acquiring offensive missiles and helped ignite a debate over acquiring "so-called counter-strike missiles," especially when the Aegis Ashore missile defense system was cancelled. The decision to acquire "counter-strike

---

[1] 安保三文書.

capabilities" that can attack enemy bases is only one step beyond the *2018 NDPG*'s focus on acquiring "stand-off capabilities" for the purpose of defending Japan's remote islands such as the Senkakus.[2] Japan first signaled its interest in developing something along the lines of counterstrike capability as early as the 2013 NDPG, which stated "in order to strengthen the deterrent of the Japan-U.S. Alliance as a whole through enhancement of Japan's own deterrent and response capability, Japan will study a potential form of response capability to address the means of ballistic missile launches and related facilities, and take means as necessary."[3]

Counterstrikes are justified as a response to an attack on Japan, not an attack on another country. According to the *National Security Strategy* (*NSS*) issued in December 2022, "a key to deterring invasion against Japan is counterstrike capabilities that leverage stand-off defense capability and other capabilities.... Missile attacks against Japan have become a palpable threat."[4] The NSS defines counterstrike capabilities as "the SDF's capabilities that leverage stand-off defense capability and other capabilities. In cases where armed attack against Japan has occurred, and as part of that attack ballistic missiles and other means have been used, counterstrike capabilities enable Japan to mount effective counterstrikes against the opponent's territory. Counterstrikes are done as a minimum necessary measure for self- defense and in accordance with the Three New Conditions for Use of Force."[5] In short, counterstrike capabilities are justified only as a way to deter or respond to the use of ballistic missiles and similar weapons against Japan.

The *National Defense Strategy* (*NDS*), issued at the same time as the NSS in December 2022, similarly defined counterstrike capabilities in the context of defending Japan: "A key to deterring invasion

---

[2] Cabinet of the Government of Japan, *National Defense Program Guidelines for FY 2019 and beyond* (*2018 NDPG*), December 19, 2018, pp. 21–22.

[3] Cabinet of the Government of Japan, *National Defense Program Guidelines for FY 2014 and Beyond* (*2013 NDPG*), December 17, 2013, p. 20.

[4] In the Japanese version of the NSS, see p. 9.

[5] Ibid., p. 19. The Japanese version also specifies that counter-strike capabilities are for defense against attacks on Japan itself: "この「反撃能力とは、我が国に対する武力攻撃が発生し、その手段として弾 道ミサイル等による攻撃が行われた場合、武力の行使の三要件に基づき、そのような攻撃を防ぐのにやむを得ない必要最小限度の自衛の措置として、相 手の領域において、我が国が有効な反撃を加えることを可能とする、スタンド・オフ防衛能力等を活用した自衛隊の能力をいう。」," p. 10.

against Japan is counterstrike capabilities that leverage stand-off defense capability and other capabilities."[6] Like the NSS, the NDS argues counterstrike capabilities are a complement to missile defense that is unable to keep up with advances in offensive missile technology: "Looking ahead, however, if Japan continues to rely solely upon ballistic missile defenses, it will become increasingly difficult to fully address missile threats with the existing missile defense network alone."[7] The *DBP*, issued at the same time as the *NSS* and the *NDS*, contains similar, and even stronger language limiting the use of counterstrike capabilities to cases where Japan is attacked first. "In cases where armed attack against Japan has occurred, and as part of that attack ballistic missiles and other means have been used, counterstrike capabilities enable Japan to mount effective counterstrikes against the opponent's territory."[8] The use of this counterstrike capability for missions other than deterrence and to respond to attacks on Japan itself is not discussed at all in any of the three defense documents.[9] Japan subsequently announced that it would seek to purchase approximately 400 US-made Tomahawk Land Attack Missiles (TLAMs) missiles with a range of 1000 miles to provide it with a counterstrike capability between 2025 and the early 2030s when the extended range T-12 missile was expected to be fully deployed.[10]

Even while demonstrating a sober realism about the limits of missile defense, the NDS and NSS optimistically oversell the potential of counterstrike capabilities. According to the NDS, "By possessing such capabilities to mount effective counterstrikes, Japan will deter armed attack itself. If an opponent ever launches missiles, it will be able to prevent the opponent's further armed attacks by counterstrike capabilities, while protecting

[6] Cabinet Secretariat, Government of Japan, *National Defense Strategy* (*NDS*), December 16, 2022, p. 13, as accessed April 11, 2023, at https://www.mod.go.jp/j/policy/agenda/guideline/strategy/pdf/strategy_en.pdf.

[7] Ibid.

[8] *NDB*, p. 8.

[9] This is not surprising given that even the US may be reluctant to launch missile strikes on the mainland of China, even in retaliation, in defense of Taiwan. See Chapter 7.

[10] Michelle Ye Hee Lee and Ellen Nakashima, "Japan to Buy Tomahawk Missiles in Defense Buildup Amid Fears of War," *Washington Post*, December 12, 2022, as accessed January 5, 2023 at https://www.washingtonpost.com/world/2022/12/12/japan-tomahawk-missiles-ukraine-war/; Reuters, "U.S. Gives nod to Potential Sale of 400 Tomahawk Missiles to Japan," *Asahi Shimbun*, November 18, 2023, as accessed February 29, 2024 at https://www.asahi.com/ajw/articles/15060461.

itself against incoming missiles by the missile defense network, thereby defending the lives and peaceful livelihoods of Japanese nationals."[11] Most analysts would not agree with such optimism (see the discussion in the previous chapter). Moreover, this optimism is entirely presented in the context of territorial defense, there is no attempt to justify the acquisition of counterstrike missiles for the sake of defending other countries beyond Japan's borders.

EXPLICIT PROHIBITION ON PREEMPTIVE STRIKES

The *NSS* and *NDS* explicitly prohibit preemptive strikes[12] against another country, while the NDB does not discuss the issue. The NSS states this prohibition in unambiguous terms: "Needless to say, preemptive strikes, namely striking first at a stage when no armed attack has occurred, remain impermissible."[13] The same language appears on p. 20 of NDS.[14] In his press conference announcing the three new security documents Prime Minister Kishida went further in renouncing the possibility of preemption, claiming "a preemptive attack" would "violate international law."[15] This is in contrast to media and pundit speculation before the adoption of these three defense documents that preemption would be allowed.[16] It also stands in contrast to a statement Prime Minister Hatoyama Ichirō

[11] Ibid., p. 14.

[12] 先制攻撃.

[13] *NSS*, p. 19.

[14] For the same statement in the Japanese version of the NDS, see *Kokka bōei senryaku* (December 2022), p. 10. This prohibition is repeated in the 2023 defense white paper. See Ministry of Defense, *Defense of Japan*, pp. 234, 235.

[15] Fumio Kishida, "Kisha Kaiken," Shusho Kantei, December 16, 2022, p. 13, in answer to a question by an *Asahi Shimbun* journalist, as accessed September 3, 2023, at https://www.kantei.go.jp/jp/101_kishida/statement/2022/1216kaiken.html.

[16] EDITORIAL: Japan must not rush to gut its purely defensive security policy, *Asahi Shimbun*, December 2, 2022, as accessed September 3, 2023 at https://www.asahi.com/ajw/articles/14782504 *Yomiuri Shimbun* even asked a polling question about acquiring counterstrike capabilities that implied preemption (i.e. attacking enemy missile bases before they could attack Japan) in April 2022. See "Honsha zenkoku yoron chōsa kekka," *Yomiuri Shimbun*, April 4, 2022, p. 16.

112 P. MIDFORD

made before the Diet in 1956, which stated that preemptive strikes against enemy missile bases would be constitutional.[17]

SENKAKU ISLANDS

The NSS explicitly mentions China's ongoing challenge to Japan's territorial integrity around the Senkaku islands and claims that this challenge is intensifying. "China has intensified its attempts to unilaterally change the status quo by force in the maritime and air domains including in the East and South China Seas, such as its intrusions into the territorial waters and airspace around the Senkaku Islands."[18]

The Senkakus are discussed again several pages later, where defense of the Senkakus and Japanese territory more generally is given as the reason for greatly strengthening the JCG:

> The role played by the JCG, Japan's maritime law enforcement agency, is essential to its national security. In order to ensure the security of Japan's territory, including the areas surrounding the Senkaku Islands, and to respond effectively in the event of multiple major incidents, Japan's maritime law enforcement capabilities will be significantly reinforced, in conjunction with efforts to strengthen its organization.... the JCG will promptly increase assets and introduce new technologies, secure sufficient operational expenses, renew degraded vessels, and secure and train personnel.[19]

The emphasis placed on building up the JCG again points to the focus on territorial defense as opposed to defending other countries or partners. In the case of a military conflict between China and Taiwan, the JCG would have little role to play as its capabilities and training are limited to maritime policing, it does not possess military capabilities. On the other hand, the JCG is the first line of defense for the Senkakus and Japan's other remote islands.

---

[17] Defense Minister Ishiba Shigeru (who became prime minister in October 2024) made a similar statement in the Diet in 2003. See Mulloy, *Defenders of Japan*, pp. 199, 352.

[18] Ibid., p. 8.

[19] Ibid., pp. 24–25.

Reflecting on the changes announced in the 2022 NSS and NDS, RAND Corporation analyst Jeffrey Hornung referred to the changes in Japanese security set in motion by China's constant challenging of Japan's territorial control over the Senkaku islands since 2012. "China's behavior over the last 10 years has really put Japan on a trajectory of thinking more seriously about its defense."[20]

NO COMMITMENT TO DEFEND TAIWAN

Strikingly, the December 2022 defense documents have little discussion about Taiwan, and no content at all about what, if anything, Japan would do to help defend Taiwan. The NSS mentions China's possible use of force to achieve their goal of Taiwan's reunification with mainland China: "While maintaining its policy of peaceful reunification of Taiwan, China has not denied the possibility of using military force."[21] The same paragraph warns that "regarding peace and stability across the Taiwan Strait, concerns are mounting rapidly, not only in the Indo-Pacific region including Japan, but also in the entire international community."[22] However, nothing is mentioned about what Japan or the "international community" intend to do to ensure peace and stability in the Taiwan Strait, and peace in the Taiwan Strait is not identified as essential for Japan's security.

Even when discussing Taiwan the focus quickly returns to defense of Japan, especially China's military exercises around Taiwan in the wake of US House Speaker Nancy Pelosi's visit to that island in August 2022 that resulted in large-scale Chinese military exercises around the island, and specifically five Chinese missiles that landed in Japan's EEZ: "In addition, China has been intensifying its military activities in the sea and airspace surrounding Taiwan, including the launch of ballistic missiles into the waters around Japan."[23] Although the landing of these missiles in Japan's EEZ is arguably legal according to UNCLOS and especially freedom of

---

[20] Quoted in Hee Lee and Nakashima, "Japan to Buy Tomahawk Missiles in Defense Buildup Amid Fears of War."

[21] NSS, p. 8.

[22] Ibid. Similar language appears in the NDS, p. 6. There is only a single paragraph about Taiwan in the entire NDS.

[23] Ibid. Regarding the ballistic missiles landing in Japan's EEZ, see NDS, p. 6.

navigation norms promoted (ironically) by the US Navy,[24] this incident appeared to exacerbate Japanese perceptions of Chinese aggressiveness, as did several Chinese military drones that flew roundtrip to areas east of Taiwan through the Miyako Strait (again, legal under international law, but viewed as threatening by Japan).[25]

On the following page of the *NSS* there is a more general statement of Japan's desire to respond to China's military and foreign policies when they threaten peace and security, although there is no mention of a military response, and no mention of Taiwan or even the Taiwan Strait. According to the *NSS*:

> China's current external stance, military activities, and other activities have become a matter of serious concern for Japan and the international community, and present an unprecedented and the greatest strategic challenge in ensuring the peace and security Japan and the peace and stability of the international community, as well as in strengthening the international order based on the rule of law, to which Japan should respond with its comprehensive national power and in cooperation with its ally, like-minded countries and others.[26]

The only other mention of Taiwan in the *NSS* is on page 14, where Japan's relationship with Taiwan is described in between descriptions of its bilateral ties with China and South Korea. This NSS description starts by reaffirming Japan's fifty-year-old policy of non-recognition of Taiwan as a sovereign state: "Japan's relationship with Taiwan has been maintained as a non-governmental working relationship based on the Japan–China Joint Communique in 1972. Japan's basic position regarding Taiwan remains

---

[24] The US has been the most extreme in rejecting any restrictions on military operations in EEZs, by arguing: "'Freedom of navigation' is clear and easy to understand. 'Freedom of navigation in some circumstances' is more problematic, and leaves ships open to selective enforcement by the coastal state." Edward Schwarck, E., "Freedom of Navigation and China: What Should Europe Do?" *PacNet* 68 (August 18, 2014), p. 3, as accessed February 29, 2024 at https://csis-website-prod.s3.amazonaws.com/s3fspublic/legacy_files/files/publication/Pac1468.pdf.

[25] "Maps: Tracking Tensions Between China and Taiwan: Shows of Force Near Taiwan and Japanese Islands," *New York Times*, August 7, 2022, as accessed August 15, 2022, at https://www.nytimes.com/interactive/2022/world/asia/taiwan-china-maps.html.

[26] Ibid., p. 9. A similar statement appears in the *NDS*, p. 7.

unchanged."[27] The NSS then describes Japan's informal ties with Taiwan: "Taiwan is an extremely important partner and a precious friend of Japan, with whom Japan shares fundamental values, including democracy, and has close economic and personal ties."[28] That description is followed by a passage that does mention the importance of peace and stability in the Taiwan Strait but says nothing about Japan potentially defending Taiwan. "Peace and stability across the Taiwan Strait is an indispensable element for the security and prosperity of the international community, and Japan will continue to make various efforts based on its position that the cross-strait issues are expected to be resolved peacefully."[29]

Overall, the NSS, NDS, and NDB contain no mention of potentially defending any other country, either by name, or even theoretically. Remarkably, none of these documents even mention Japan's right to exercise the right of collective self-defense to defend another country that comes under attack, despite the fact that asserting this right had been a major priority and the single biggest security policy accomplishment of Prime Minister Abe. This can be considered a surprising omission, in that emphasizing Japan's right to exercise collective self-defense could have signaled to both international and domestic audiences that Japan was willing to use force to defend Taiwan without explicitly identifying this island polity as the entity Japan intended to defend (and thereby sharply provoking China).

While the 2022 NSS and NDS do not contain any reference to collective self-defense, a reference to the enabling legislation for collective self-defense was included in the 2018 NDPG in the context of regional contingencies.[30] Moreover, the 2022 NDS does not contain any discussion of how Japan would respond to "an armed attack against a country

---

[27] Ibid., p. 14.

[28] Ibid. Notably, Taiwan is described as a "partner," not a "country" like South Korea. Not recognizing Taiwan as a country creates a domestic legal barrier to defending Taiwan as Japan's exercise of collective self-defense is limited to defending another "country."

[29] Ibid.

[30] According to the 2018 NDPG, "While the Japan-U.S. Alliance has been reinforced through activities including those that were made possible by the Legislation for Peace and Security, Japan needs to further enhance the Alliance through efforts under the "Guidelines for Japan-US Defense Cooperation" in order to achieve its national defense objective as security environment surrounding Japan becomes more testing and uncertain at remarkably fast speeds." Cabinet of the Government of Japan, *National Defense Program Guidelines for FY 2019 and beyond (2018 NDPG)*, December 19, 2018, p. 13.

other than Japan," language that was included in the 2015 Japan-US Defense Guidelines. It is also worth noting, however, that even the 2015 Japan-US Defense Guidelines, although mentioning the possibility of Japan using force to defend another country, only included examples of non-combat and rear area support operations for the US military, except for interdicting civilian shipping carrying war supplies (which could also be seen as a non-combat maritime police action).[31] Although the right to Collective Self-Defense of course remains a legal option for Japan, the decision to omit any mention of this right from the NSS and NDS reflects the shift in policy priorities toward doubling down on territorial defense.

Strikingly, Prime Minister Kishida's press conference announcing the three new defense documents included no mention of Taiwan whatsoever, nor of collective self-defense. Nonetheless, Kishida does make clear that the resort to military force will only start after Japan has been attacked: "Japan will only use force after being attacked by another country."[32] Although Kishida has often been described as continuing and deepening Abe's hawkish defense legacy,[33] at least when it comes to emphasizing the right of collective self-defense, Kishida has effectively deemphasized, if not attempted to politically bury, this right in favor of doubling down on territorial defense, whether in the case of Taiwan or more generally.

Retired GSDF Lt. General Banshō Kōichirō, former commander of the GSDF's Western Army, who played a key role in developing the GSDF's amphibious assault unit, and developed the "southwestern wall" concept surrounding the Sakishima and Senkaku islands, has emphasized that if China launches an invasion of Taiwan, Japan will play a role similar to the role that Poland plays in the Ukraine War, as a logistical hub for

---

[31] *The Guidelines for Japan–U.S. Defense Cooperation*, April 27, 2015, pp. 15–16, as accessed at as accessed August 11, 2023, at https://www.mofa.go.jp/files/000078188. pdf. Also see Mark F. Cancian, Matthew Cancian and Eric Higenbotham, *The First Battle of the Next War: Wargaming a Chinese Invasion of Taiwan* (Washington, DC: Center for Strategic and International Studies, 2023), p. 58.

[32] The original passage in Japanese: 「相手から武力攻撃を受けたとき初めて防衛力を行使し」 Kishida, "Kisha Kaiken," p. 8, in response to a question by a reporter from *The Japan Times*. Also see Adam P. Liff, "Kishida the Accelerator: Japan's Defense Evolution After Abe," *The Washington Quarterly* 46, no. 1 (Spring 2023), p. 74.

[33] Ibid., pp. 78–79.

international assistance for Taiwan, but like Poland, will not play a direct military role in combat.[34]

INCREASED DEFENSE SPENDING AND AUTONOMOUS DEFENSE

The New NSS and NDS mandate increasing defense spending to 2% of GDP by 2027.[35] As Japan's defense spending had previously been calculated at 1%, this appeared to many media commentators to represent a doubling of Japan's defense spending. However, by effectively committing to meet the NATO goal of spending 2% of its GDP on defense, Japan also adopted the NATO accounting standard for defense spending, an accounting method far broader than Japan's previous standard of only including spending on the Defense Ministry and the SDF. According to the NATO standard Japan was already spending around 1.3% to 1.4% of its GDP on defense. Adopting the NATO standard involved including the JCG budget, the budget for maintaining US bases in Japan including host nation support, pensions for retired SDF members, and civilian infrastructure construction that can have dual use for the SDF (e.g. extending airport runways and expanding ports in the Sakishima islands). Consequently, Japan's sustained increase in defense spending is closer to a 60% increase (from $40 billion or 5.4 trillion Yen to up to $66 billion or 8.9 trillion Yen), which represents a huge increase, but is significantly less than a doubling of the defense budget.

In the first year of the new plan Japan increased its defense budget by 26% for Fiscal Year 2023 as compared with 2022.[36] For 2024 the

[34] Ken Moriyasu, "In Taiwan Crisis, Japan to Play Role Like Poland to Ukraine: Ex-general," *Nikkei*, December 1, 2023, as accessed January 11, 2023, at https://asia.nikkei.com/Editor-s-Picks/Interview/In-Taiwan-crisis-Japan-to-play-role-like-Poland-to-Ukraine-ex-general. Banshō "Southwestern Wall" concept, that he developed after retiring from the GSDF, has yet to be implemented in important aspects, notably his call for a joint southwest regional command of the three SDF services.

[35] *NSS*, p. 20.

[36] Adam P. Liff, "No, Japan Is Not Planning to "Double Its Defense Budget," *Brookings Commentary*, May 23, 2023, as accessed September 3, 2023, at https://www.brookings.edu/articles/no-japan-is-not-planning-to-double-its-defense-budget/.

118   P. MIDFORD

Ministry of Defense (MOD) requested an increase of nearly 12%,[37] but the cabinet eventually approved a 16.5% increase.[38] However, funding a permanent 60% increase over 5 years, and sustaining that spending level thereafter, remains a challenge, with little agreement on how to pay for the increase. Tax increases to pay for this defense spending increase have proved very unpopular, and Prime Minister Kishida reneged on his pledge to implement tax increases in 2024, delaying any such increases until at least 2025.[39] The scale of the buildup may be reduced due to the weakening of the Yen that significantly reduces Japan's buying power and has already caused a scaling back of the equipment purchases envisaged in the 2022 Defense Buildup Plan.[40]

Strikingly, this increase in defense spending is justified as a means for achieving defense autonomy. According to the *NSS*, "by FY 2027, five years after the formulation of the Strategy, Japan will strengthen its defense capabilities to the point at which Japan is able to take the primary responsibility for dealing with invasions against its nation and disrupt and defeat such threats while gaining the support of its ally and others."[41] Achieving primary responsibility for dealing with invasions of Japan "will entail unprecedented undertakings in terms of size and content. The

[37] AP, "Defense Ministry Requests Nearly 12% Budget Increase to Bolster Strike Capability," *Asahi Shimbun*, August 31, 2023, as accessed September 3, 2023, at https://www.asahi.com/ajw/articles/14994155.

[38] Takahashi Kosuke, "Japan Approves 16.5% Increase in Defense Spending for FY2024," *Diplomat*, December 22, 2023, as accessed August 11, 2024 at https://thediplomat.com/2023/12/japan-approves-16-5-increase-in-defense-spending-for-fy2024/.

[39] Liff, "Kishida the Accelerator," p. 76; Michael MacArthur Bosack "Kishida's Proposed Tax Cuts put Higher Defense Spending on Hold," *Japan Times*, October 23, 2023, as accessed March 1, 2023 at https://www.japantimes.co.jp/commentary/2023/10/23/japan/kishida-tax-cuts-defense-budget/.

[40] River Akira Davis and Hisako Ueno, "The Yen Is Plunging, so Is Japan's Defense Budget," *New York Times*, July 9, 2024, as accessed August 11, 2024 at https://www.nytimes.com/2024/07/08/business/japan-yen-defense-spending.html; and Nobuhiro Kubo, Takaya Yamaguchi and Tim Kelly, "Exclusive: Weak yen forces Japan to shrink historic military spending plan," *Reuters*, November 3, 2023 as accessed March 11, 2024 at https://www.reuters.com/markets/currencies/weak-yen-forces-japan-shrink-historic-military-spending-plan-2023-11-03/. In late July 2024 the Bank of Japan partially reversed the decline of the Yen, at least temporarily, by increasing interest rates. However, that poses another problem for Japan's plans to increase defense spending: the rising cost of interest payments on the budget deficit and national debt.

[41] *NSS*, p. 20. Also see the *NDS*, pp. 11, 12.

fundamental reinforcement of defense capabilities will not be achieved by a temporary increase in spending."[42] By 2033 the NSS envisages Japan having an even more autonomous defense. "by approximately ten years from now, Japan will reinforce its defense capabilities to the point at which it will be possible to disrupt and defeat invasions against its nation much earlier and at a further distance."[43] The *NDS* has even stronger language, as it states that "Japan will defend our own country to the end from all situations through the combination of Japan's own efforts," with the only exception being nuclear deterrence, where Japan relies on the US.[44]

This new emphasis on autonomous defense appears to be driven by fear of abandonment, starting with a conflict over the Senkaku islands, but more recently extending to the Sakishima islands.[45] The cause for Japan's new emphasis on autonomous defense can be traced back to the first tumultuous first Trump administration, when the US came to be viewed increasingly as an increasingly unreliable ally, with subsequent concerns that Trump or a similar politician might return to the White House in 2025, a concern that came to be realized.[46] It can also be viewed as a result of China's growing military prowess and declining or eclipsed US military hegemony. The late Prime Minister Abe, in the context of evaluating the US policy of strategic ambiguity toward Taiwan, made clear

---

[42] NSS, p. 20.

[43] Ibid.

[44] *NDS*, p. 10. The same passage does mention the expectation that Japan would receive "support from its ally and others" in the case of invasion, while stressing that "disrupting and defeating an invasion" is Japan's "primary responsibility." On page 11 the goal that Japan must be able to disrupt and defeat an invasion on its own is restated but adds that Japan having the capability to defend itself will enable the US to be able to deter unilateral changes to the status quo in the broader Indo-Pacific. The same goal is reiterated in the 2023 defense white paper. See MOD, *Defense of Japan 2023*, pp. 8, 17, 18, 219, 233, 246, 257, 261, 296, 310.

[45] Arguing for the importance of fear of abandonment vis a vis China in pushing Japan toward autonomous defense, see Lionel P. Fatton, "A New Spear in Asia: Why Is Japan Moving Toward Autonomous Defense?" *International Relations of Asia Pacific* 19, no. 2 (2019), pp. 297–325. Fatton also argues that growing fear of entrapment in a war with North Korea is a another a motivator for a more autonomous defense, although in this author's view that is not currently a strong motivating factor in Japan' move toward a more autonomous defense.

[46] Sheila Smith, *Japan Rearmed* (Cambridge: Harvard University Press, 2019), pp. 4, 233; and Tobias Harris, *Iconoclast: Shinzō Abe and the New Japan* (London: Hurst, 2020), pp. 271–272. Also see the next chapter.

his view that the US no longer had unquestioned regional military hegemony. "The policy of ambiguity worked extremely well as long as the U.S. was strong enough to maintain it and as long as China was far inferior to the U.S. in military power. But those days are over."[47]

Notably, since 2012 some Japanese defense analysts suggest that something close to a doubling of Japan's defense spending would be necessary just to achieve autonomous defense.[48] Although the mandated increase is only approximately 60%, it does support the observation that Japan is moving in the direction of defense autonomy, as it is turning to stand-off weapons and deemphasizing forward defense to achieve a variation of defense by denial. This is what Heginbotham and Samuels call "active denial," a shift they recommend, and which would require smaller defense spending increases than forward defense.[49]

Whatever the reason, Japan aims to achieve autonomy in territorial defense, perhaps only continuing to rely on the US for its nuclear umbrella. Tokyo will consequently double down even more on territorial defense as the strategic imperative shaping the SDF. Japan will thereby be even less able and willing to defend others, including Taiwan, as this would divert resources from territorial defense and require an SDF with more power projection capabilities. Japan might have the resources to hold off a Chinese attack on its own territory, but it does not have the resources to do that and defend Taiwan or project military force into the South China Sea. Creating a credible defense and deterrence by denial posture will require devoting its entire buildup to territorial defense. At the same time, Japan will be less dependent on the US and hence less subject to pressure to commit the SDF to defending others such as Taiwan. Japan's rapid increase in defense spending thus appears to be focused on doubling down on territorial defense, not preparing for a region-wide military role.

Base Hardening and Recruitment. While pundits and media headlines have focused on Japan's acquisition of a modest counterstrike capability

---

[47] Shinzo Abe, "U.S. 'Strategic Ambiguity' over Taiwan Must End," *Japan Times*, April 19, 2022, p. 6.

[48] See Takeda Yasuhiro, *Kosuto wo Shisan! "Nichibei Domei Kaitai": Kuni wo Mamoru no ni, Ikura Kakaru no ka?* (Tokyo: Mainichi Shimbun, 2012). Also see Eric Heginbotham and Richard J. Samuels, "Active Denial: Redesigning Japan's Response to China's Military Challenge," *International Security* 42, no. 4 (Spring 2018), p. 156.

[49] Heginbotham and Samuels, "Active Denial," p. 156.

and the large increase in Japan's defense spending, often overlooked is that a large portion of that defense increase will be dedicated to hardening SDF bases, ammunition depots and other defense facilities to make them more survivable and resilient in the face of missile and other attacks, a task the NSS describes as a "top priority."[50] Although base hardening is advantageous even for non-territorial defense missions, it is especially important for territorial defense operations where the SDF will be operating on Japanese soil to defend Japanese territory. Another large portion of the increase in defense spending is being allocated to extending airports and expanding ports to make them dual use for the SDF, especially in the Sakishima islands.[51] Japan subsequently identified 14 airports and 24 seaports that should be upgraded to make them usable for the SDF. Fourteen of these airports and 14 of these seaports are located in Okinawa prefecture and Kyushu and include building a new port on Yonaguni and upgrading an airport on Hateruma Island, the southern most of the Sakishima islands (and the southernmost inhabited point in Japan).[52]

In late March 2024 the Japanese government also announced plans to support the construction of shelters on the Sakishima islands of Miyako, Ishigaki, Taketomi, Tarama, and Yonaguni, with the shelters able to store enough food and water to last for two weeks. Nonetheless, questions remain about whether each shelter (below a new city hall on Yonaguni or a municipal gym on Miyako) could accommodate the entire local population, and what would happen after two weeks if transportation links were disrupted. With planning just beginning, these shelters will likely take at least several years to build.[53]

Another large share of Japan's increased defense spending needs to be spent on increasing salaries to recruit enough military personnel in an era of rapid decline in the number of SDF eligible age cohorts. Living conditions for SDF troops also need substantial improvement (see the

---

[50] *NSS*, p. 18. Also see *NDS*, pp. 13, 17.

[51] *NSS*, pp. 27–28.

[52] "Japan Identifies 38 Airports, Ports for SDF Use After Upgrades Made," *Asahi Shimbun*, November 27, 2023, as accessed December 14, 2023, at https://www.asahi.com/ajw/articles/15067912.

[53] Shohei Sasagawa, Nen Satomi, and Taro Ono, "Japan to Build Shelters on Isles Near Taiwan in case of Attack," *Asahi Shimbun*, March 30, 2024, as accessed April 1, 2024 at https://www.asahi.com/ajw/articles/15215063.

122   P. MIDFORD

discussion in Chapter 3), with troops often forced to buy daily necessities for their bases out of their own pocket.[54] SDF housing and other facilities also need to be upgraded, both to accommodate more female soldiers and to catch up with years of delayed maintenance.[55] Nonetheless, there is little content in the *Anpo San bunsho* on how to sustain SDF personnel numbers or even reduce staffing requirements through automation. Reflecting Japan's security isolationism, these security documents are also silent on the possibility of creating a legal framework for recruiting foreign nationals (starting with permanent residents) to serve in the SDF, a framework that could help reduce the SDF's short-fall of personnel.

PUBLIC REACTION TO THE NEW SECURITY DOCUMENTS

Opinion polling in the leadup to the issuance of the three new security documents in December 2022 indicated that a clear majority favored strengthening the SDF. A *Yomiuri Shimbun* poll published in early April 2022 found nearly two-thirds (64%) of Japanese favored strengthening the country's defense, versus 27% who were opposed, and 8% who did not answer. However, the poll did not ask by how much or in what way respondents favored strengthening Japan's defense. The same poll found that 46% of respondents favored acquiring a counterstrike capability to destroy enemy missile bases, versus 46% who opposed Japan acquiring such a capability, and 8% who did not answer.[56]

However, polling following the issuance of the new *Anpo San Bunsho* security documents in December 2022 found greater ambivalence, especially about the large-envisaged increases in defense spending. A *Yomiuri Shimbun* poll conducted January 2023 that asked specifically about the decision mandated in the three defense documents to increase total defense spending by 43 trillion Yen (US$284 billion as of March 2024)

---

[54] Beyond the need for improved housing, former Defense Minister Kōno Tarō has noted that often SDF members are forced to buy basic comforts for military bases out of their own pockets, such as toilet paper. Also see Rie Ogasawara, *Jieitai-in wa kichi no toirettopēpā o 'jibara' de kau* (Tokyo: Fusōsha, 2019); and Motoko Rich, Hikari Hida and Chang W. Lee, "Japan Wants a Stronger Military. Can It Find Enough Troops?" *New York Times*, December 13, 2023, as accessed December 14, 2023, at https://www.nytimes.com/2023/12/13/world/asia/japan-military.html.

[55] I thank Tom Phuong Le for sharing insights from his research on this issue.

[56] "Honsha zenkoku yoron chōsa kekka," *Yomiuri Shimbun*, April 4, 2022, p. 16.

over 5 years found a large plurality of 49% opposed, versus only 43% who approved. Likewise, the same poll found 63% opposed to the government's plan to increase income, corporate, and other taxes to pay for this increase in defense spending, versus only 28% who supported this proposal.[57] Similarly, an *Asahi Shimbun* poll taken at approximately the same time produced very similar results: 49% opposed increasing defense spending by 43 trillion Yen, while only 44% approved. When asked about 1 trillion Yen in tax increases (over $6.6 billion) to pay for increased defense spending, 71% opposed, versus 24% who approved.[58]

Opposition to increasing defense spending appears to have grown over the course of 2023, with a Japan Press Research Institute (JRI) poll conducted in July–August 2023 finding a clear majority of 55.5% opposed to increasing defense spending, versus 42.8% who approved increased defense spending. In terms of spending priorities, rather than prioritizing defense spending 74.1% of respondents prioritized increasing spending on measures to raise the birthrate, another very expensive policy priority of the Kishida administration. By contrast, only 23.4% prioritized defense spending over birthrate raising measures.[59] These poll results foreshadowed a decision by the Kishida administration in late 2023 to delay its plan to increase taxes to pay for the increase in defense spending, if not delay the full defense spending increase itself in the face of rising public opposition, the collapse of the hawkish Abe faction, and the weakening of the Kishida administration itself and the LDP in the face of a massive funding scandal.[60]

---

[57] "Shōshika taisaku kakujū 'hyōka' 58%, futan-zō wa 'hantai' 56-pāsento, Yomiuri yoron chōsa," *Yomiuri Shimbun*, January 15, 2023, p. 1.

[58] "Shitsumon to kaitō," *Asahi Shimbun*, January 24, 2023 (chōkan), p. 4. Even some current and retired SDF officers have opposed the large increase in defense spending, arguing that it reflects a domestic political logic rather than a coherent and sustainable security strategy, and could even degrade capabilities if it is wasted on the wrong capabilities and technologies. See Kazuki Iwamoto, "Japan MSDF Regional Chief Concerned about Proposed Rise in Defense Spending," *Mainichi*, July 6, 2022 as accessed July 6, 2022 at https://mainichi.jp/english/articles/20220706/p2a/00m/0na/008000c?fb; and Kuniaki Nishio, "INTERVIEW/ Yoji Koda: Rush defense programs look like wish list of greedy children," *Asahi Shimbun*, January 11, 2023, as accessed February 29, 2024, at https://www.asahi.com/ajw/articles/14800076.

[59] *Dai-16 kai media ni kansuru zenkoku yoron chōsa (2023 nen)* (Tokyo: Kōeki zaidanhōjin shimbun tsūshin chōsakai, 2023), pp. 16–17.

[60] Bosack, "Kishida's Proposed Tax Cuts put Higher Defense Spending on Hold;" "Japan's LDP demands Abe faction leaders leave party or resign over slush fund scandal,"

124   P. MIDFORD

Nonetheless, strengthening Japan's defenses remained well supported, at least in principle. An *Asahi Shimbun* poll conducted in March–April 2023, asked respondents: "In February last year Russia invaded Ukraine. Following this invasion have you started to think that Japan should strengthen its defense capabilities? Or do you think you think there should not be any change in particular?" In answer to this question, 57% answered that Japan should strengthen its defense, versus 39% who answered that there is no need for change.[61] Framing the question of a defense build-up in the context of Russia's invasion of Ukraine probably boosted the numbers who favored increasing Japan's defense spending. However, this question framing and the response it generated highlights the tendency of the Japanese public to see Japan itself as a potential victim of an invasion, rather than as a savior of another country that comes under attack, a perception that politically empowers the doubling down on territorial defense (but not involvement of the SDF in conflicts beyond Japanese territory) that was evident in the three defense documents. Supporting this perception is a November 2022 Genron NPO poll that found the number of Japanese respondents who felt Russia posed a

Mainichi, January 25, 2024, as accessed February 2, 2024, at https://mainichi.jp/english/articles/20240125/p2a/00m/0na/012000c; Jiji, "Kishida Cabinet's Approval Rate Falls, Below 20% for First Time," *Japan Times*, December 15, 2023, as accessed February 29, 2024 at https://www.japantimes.co.jp/news/2023/12/15/japan/politics/kishida-cabinet-approval-rate-sinks/#:~:text=The%20approval%20rate%20for%20Prime,Jiji%20Press%20survey%20showed%20Thursday; Daizo Teramoto, "Survey: 72% Say Dissolving LDP Factions Will Not Restore Trust," *Asahi Shimbun*, January 22, 2024, as accessed March 11, 2024 at https://www.asahi.com/ajw/articles/15123687; and Yomiuri Shimbun, "Support for Kishida Cabinet Falls Back to Its All-time Low; Worst Showing since LDP's Return to Power," *Japan News*, January 22, 2024, as accessed February 29, 2024 at https://japannews.yomiuri.co.jp/politics/politics-government/20240122-163803/; and Tobias Harris, "Three Questions about the State of Japan's Politics: Making Sense of a Turbulent Moment," *Observing Japan*, January 26, 2024, as accessed February 2, 2024 at https://observingjapan.substack.com/p/three-questions-about-the-state-of?utm_source=post-email-title&publication_id=868206&post_id=141062 207&utm_campaign=email-post-title&isFreemail=true&r=18g5cy&triedRedirect=true.

[61] "Shitsumon to kaitō," *Asahi Shimbun*, May 3, 2023 (chōkan), p. 6. In English see Taizo Teramoto, "Asahi poll: 56% want only SDF rear support to U.S. in event of Taiwan crisis," *Asahi Shimbun*, May 1, 2023, as accessed May 3, 2023, at https://www.asahi.com/ajw/articles/14898395.

military threat to Japan itself nearly doubled from 32.1% in 2021 to 62.2% in 2022.[62]

Further evidence of this pattern can be seen in the same *Asahi Shimbun* opinion poll conducted in spring 2023, which found that 80% of respondents worried (28% were greatly worried and 52% were somewhat worried) about Japan becoming entrapped in an armed conflict between China and the US over Taiwan. When asked how Japan should use the SDF to respond to possible Sino-US military conflict over Taiwan, 56% answered that the SDF's response should be limited to rear area support for the US military, and 27% replied that the SDF should not cooperate with the US military at all. Only 11% replied that the SDF should join the US military in using force,[63] which is a similar portion of the public to those who have been in favor of Japan arming itself with nuclear weapons.[64] A Japan Press Research Institute poll conducted in July 2023 reached similar results. When asked how Japan should respond in case of a Chinese attack on Taiwan, and given four choices to choose from, a small plurality of 31.2% chose "have the SDF provide logistical support to the US military," the second largest group of 23.3% chose only to "allow

---

[62] Genron NPO, *Dai 18-kai nitchū kyōdō yoronchōsa (2022-nen) kekka* (November 2022), pp. 22/57, as accessed August 3, 2023, at https://www.genron-npo.net/world/archives/13950-2.html. For an argument that Russia's invasion of Ukraine strengthens the case for Japan's traditional strategy of defensive defense, see Sugawa Kiyoshi, "Taichu bōei senryaku no yōtei wa 'senshu bōei no jūjitsu' ni ari: Ukuraina sensō ni manabu Nihon no bōei-ryoku seibi," Alternative Viewpoint number 45, *Sekai yuai Fo-ramu*, November 5, 2022, as accessed February 29, 2024, at https://www.eaci.or.jp/archives/avp/758.

[63] "Shitsumon to kaitō;" Teramoto, "Asahi poll." This poll did not specify by how much respondents wanted Japan to strengthen its defense or how much that should cost. Also noting is a *Nihon Keizai Shimbun* poll from April 2021 that found 74% of Japanese supported the Japanese government being "engaged" in the pursuit of peace and stability in the Taiwan Strait, which was interpreted by some western commentators as meaning that the Japanese public broadly supports using military force to prevent a Chinese invasion of Taiwan. However, unless the polling question asks explicitly about the involvement of the SDF in a military conflict, as did the spring 2023 *Asahi Shimbun* poll, it should not be assumed that a neutral term like "engagement" (*kanyo* 関与) implies the use of military force. Rather engagement in the *Nikkei* poll has a stronger implication of diplomacy. See "Taiwan kaikyō ni kanyo '74%,'" *Nihon Keizai Shimbun* April 26, 2021 (chōkan), p. 2; and Ryo Nemoto and Natsumi Iwata, "74% in Japan support engagement in Taiwan Strait: Nikkei poll," *Nikkei Asia*, April 26, 2021, as accessed February 29, 2024, at https://asia.nikkei.com/Politics/International-relations/74-in-Japan-support-engagement-in-Taiwan-Strait-Nikkei-poll.

[64] See Paul Midford, *Rethinking Japanese Public Opinion and Security: From Pacifism to Realism?* (Stanford University Press, 2011), pp. 37–38.

the US to use its bases in Japan for combat operations, but without any SDF involvement," whereas 26.9% chose "not to be involved in the military aspect of the conflict at all, including the non-use of US bases in Japan." Only 13.3%, the smallest group, chose fight alongside the US; 5.2% had no answer.[65]

These results again indicate that the Japanese public favors strengthening the SDF for territorial defense, not for defending others, including friends and fellow democracies. Addressing the latter point, Mori Satoru, a Keio University professor of politics observed, "if you ask the question of whether you are willing to risk your life to defend Taiwan, I think 90% of Japanese people would say 'no.'"[66]

The same *Asahi Shimbun* poll also asked respondents which of two options should be prioritized in Japan's national security, deepening relations with China through diplomacy and economic means, or by strengthening Japan's defense capabilities: 70% chose strengthening relations with China through diplomacy and economic means, versus 26% who favored strengthening defense capabilities.[67] Although more than two-thirds wanted to strengthen relations with China rather than build up Japan's defense capabilities, this result should not be taken as an indicator that the Japanese public does not see a potential military threat from China or opposes a military buildup. Rather this result indicates skepticism about getting involved in a Sino-US military conflict over

---

[65] *Dai-16 kai media ni kansuru zenkoku yoron chōsa (2023 nen)* (Tokyo: Kōeki zaidanhōjin shimbun tsūshin chōsakai, 2023), p. 15. The JRI poll from 2022 asked the same question using a different question methodology, separating each of these four answer options into separate questions, and produced rather different results. A larger (although still small) 22.5% favored the SDF fighting alongside the US military to defend Taiwan, versus 74.2% who opposed this policy option. However, a small majority of 51.8% opposed having the SDF provide logistical support for the US military, whereas only 44.8% supported this option. Likewise, only a very narrow plurality of 48.4% supported allowing the US to use its bases in Japan for launching combat operations to defend Taiwan, whereas 47.1% opposed this option (a difference likely within the margin of error). Likewise, only a narrow plurality opposed Japan's non-involvement in any military response to a Chinese attack on Taiwan, 48.7%, versus 46.8% who supported complete non-involvement. See *Dai-15 kai media ni kansuru zenkoku yoron chōsa (2022 nen)* (Tokyo: Kōeki zaidanhōjin shimbun tsūshin chōsakai, 2022), p. 15.

[66] Quoted by Alastair Gale, "Would Allies Fight With U.S. for Taiwan? Japan Is Wary," *Wall Street Journal*, July 15, 2023, as accessed February 29, 2024, at https://www.wsj.com/articles/would-allies-fight-with-u-s-for-taiwan-japan-is-wary-d90dd924.

[67] "Shitsumon to kaitō," May 1, 2023, p. 6; and Teramoto, "Asahi poll."

Taiwan. A November 2022 Genron NPO opinion poll found that 79.8% of Japanese respondents saw China as a military threat, with the largest share, 64.7%, pointing to "intrusions into Japanese territorial waters," almost all of which happen in the territorial waters of the Senkakus, as the reason for identifying China as a threat. This same poll found that another 50% answered "the existence of confrontation over the Senkaku islands and maritime resources" as the reason for seeing a military threat from China (multiple answers allowed). A *Yomiuri Shimbun* poll conducted in spring 2024 similarly found that 93% of respondents saw China's military buildup and intrusions into Japan's territorial waters as greatly (59%) or somewhat (34%) threatening national security.[68]

The same *Asahi Shimbun* poll from spring 2023 poll found support for the Kishida administration's decision to acquire a modest counter-strike capability, with 52% of survey participants responding that they supported Japan acquiring a counterstrike capability against missile bases in an adversary's country, versus 40% who opposed Japan acquiring such a capability. At the same time 59% supported Japan maintaining its policy of "Defensive Defense" (*Senshu bōei*, 専守防衛), which the question defined as not counter-attacking an adversary until first being attacked, and then only defending with the smallest amount of force necessary. On the other hand, 37% thought Japan should revise its policy of Defensive Defense.[69] The answers to these two questions also suggest that the Japanese public only supports acquiring a counterstrike capability for deterrence and defense of Japanese territory, not for the defense of other countries.

[68] Genron NPO, *Dai 18-kai nitchū kyōdō yoronchōsa (2022-nen) kekka*, p. 20–21/57; "Poll: 63% Support Constitutional Revision Amid Japan's Changing Security Environment; 93% Cite National Security Risk from China," *Japan News*, May 3, 2024, as accessed on February 14, 2025 at https://japannews.yomiuri.co.jp/politics/politics-government/202 40503-183778/ Also see Chapter 3.

[69] "Shitsumon to kaitō," May 1, 2023, p. 6; and Teramoto, "Asahi poll." For a detailed description and critique of *Senshu Bōei*, see Yumi Hiwatari, *Senshu Bōei kokufuku no senryaku: Nihon no anzenhoshō wo dō toraeru ka* (Kyōto: Mineruva Shobō, 2012).

Counterstrike Missiles and Ryukyuan Public Opinion

Echoing strong nationwide concern about becoming entrapped in a Sino-US conflict over Taiwan, but at an even higher level because of their location closer to Taiwan, concern and opposition to counterstrike missiles has been significantly greater in Okinawa, especially the Sakishima islands, than elsewhere in Japan. Local opposition in the Ryukyus to SDF bases since the release of the three new security documents in 2022 centers on their potential use in a wider regional conflict beyond defending the Senkakus, especially for defending Taiwan. Although the new security documents do not discuss the use of counterstrike capabilities to defend Taiwan or participate in a wider regional conflict at all, as discussed above, that has not stopped media speculation and fear of such scenarios from taking hold in Okinawa.

The building of new bases and deployment of anti-ship and anti-aircraft missiles on Miyako and Ishigaki had initially been relatively uncontroversial, but these bases became more controversial after the Kishida administration decided to acquire counterstrike capabilities, even though it is not clear if counterstrike missiles (initially Tomahawk cruise missiles) would ever be deployed to these bases. The Ishigaki City Assembly, which has been a hotbed of sentiment favoring strong measures to defend Japan's control of the Senkakus islands,[70] and even nationalist sentiment, nonetheless approved by a majority vote a motion refusing the deployment of long-range offensive missiles at the new GSDF base on that island. In Spring 2023 a movement for a citizens' referendum opposing the possible deployment of counterstrike missiles to the Ishigaki base was launched. Approximately 40% of voters reportedly signed a petition in support of such a referendum. Many supporters of the referendum support the base but have become concerned since December 2022 that long-range counterstrike missiles might deployed at the Ishigaki base.

---

[70] Brad Williams, "Militarizing Japan's Southwest Islands: Subnational Involvement, and Insecurities in the Maritime Frontier Zone," *Asian Security* 11, no. 2 (2015), p. 147. For example, in December 2010 the Ishigaki city assembly enacted an ordinance declaring January 14th as "Senkaku Pioneering Day," commemorating Japan's annexation of the Senkakus on that day in 1895. This ordinance was modeled on the Shimane Prefectural Assembly's enactment of a Takeshima Day in 2005 to commemorate Japan's annexation of those islands (South Korea now occupies those islands, which it calls Dokdo, and claims them as its sovereign territory).

Originally the bases had been justified as important for the defense of the Senkakus, which are a part of the City of Ishigaki.[71]

Concern about the deployment of counterstrike missiles apparently spurred the growth of local opposition to the opening of this base on Ishigaki in Spring of 2023. The base hosts 570 GSDF members, and they operate SAM and T-12 SSM batteries, the latter being tasked with the mission of defending the Senkakus. The opening of the base was obstructed by local protestors who tried to block the movement of GSDF vehicles to the base. They had to be removed by prefectural police. Although the protest participant numbers were small, they are another indication of local concern and mistrust regarding the base, mistrust that could obstruct the operation of the base in a conflict, and especially peacetime exercises to prepare for a conflict.[72]

In the prefectural capital of Naha, the prospect of deploying counterstrike missiles for scenarios beyond defending the Senkakus provoked a demonstration against involvement in a possible conflict over Taiwan in late February 2023, a demonstration reportedly attended by over 1000 protestors (organizers claimed 1600). Some protestors also called for building shelters[73] for civilians and formulating evacuation plans from the Sakishima islands. Complicating the new Miyako Island GSDF base's operations and especially the relationship with a suspicious and worried local community is the proximity of the base and its ammunition depot to civilian residential areas. According to Shimoji Hiromori, the cohead of a residential association opposing the deployment of missiles to that base, "The GSDF camp is in an area close to residential homes, and the ammunition depot is also near the community. If something happens, residents would not be able to survive it."[74]

---

[71] "EDITORIAL: Biggest Threat to Japan Is a Government That Ignores Public," *Asahi shimbun*, May 3, 2023, as accessed May 4, 2023, at https://www.asahi.com/ajw/articles/14899630.

[72] Jiji, "GSDF Begins Moving Vehicles to New Base on Okinawa's Ishigaki Island," *Japan Times*, March 5, 2023, as accessed April 11, 2023, at https://www.japantimes.co.jp/news/2023/03/05/national/ishigaki-okinawa-sdf-base/and Kyodo, "Japan Sends Missile Units to Southwestern Island to Face China Threat, *Japan Times*, March 16, 2023, as accessed March 17, 2023, at https://www.japantimes.co.jp/news/2023/03/16/national/gsdf-ishigaki-deployment.

[73] Also see the previous discussion.

[74] Shinnosuke Kyan, "1,600 People March Through Naha Protesting Japan's Defense Buildup in Okinawa," *The Mainichi*, February 27, 2023, as accessed February 27, 2023 at

Okinawa Governor Tamaki Denny also voiced his opposition. Reflecting the attitudinal defensive realism of the Japanese public, especially regarding the use of force overseas,[75] Tamaki has supported the establishment of the GSDF bases on Miyako, Ishigaki and Yonaguni, and the deployment of anti-aircraft and anti-ship missiles there but has strongly opposed the deployment of counterstrike missiles for attacking enemy bases anywhere in Okinawa prefecture. "If equipment with the capability to attack enemy bases were placed in Japan's southwest area, I would definitely object."[76]

In the face of local opposition to deploying long-range and counterstrike missiles, MOD, in a briefing to residents promised that no counterstrike or long-range missiles would be deployed on Yonaguni. This illustrates the strength of local opposition and its impact on military strategy and deployments.[77]

---

https://mainichi.jp/english/articles/20230227/p2a/00m/0na/009000c. Also see Mika Kuniyoshi, "1,600 Rally in Naha to Protest SDF Missile Deployments," *Asahi Shimbun*, February 27, 2023, as accessed February 27, 2023 at https://www.asahi.com/ajw/articles/14849145.

[75] On the attitudinal defensive realism of the Japanese public, see Paul Midford, *Rethinking Japanese Public Opinion and Security: From Pacifism to Realism?* (Stanford: Stanford University Press, 2011), pp. 36–37.

[76] Kenji Kimura, "Okinawa governor objects to Japan's possession of 'counterstrike capabilities,'" *Mainichi*, February 9, 2023, as accessed February 10, 2023 at https://mainichi.jp/english/articles/20230209/p2a/00m/0na/017000c; and Kaigo Narisawa, Taro Ono and Satsuki Tanahashi, "1st GSDF Missile Battery on Main Island of Okinawa Set Up," *Asahi Shimbun*, March 22, 2024, as accessed February 29, 2024 at https://www.asahi.com/ajw/articles/15207076; and "Tamaki Denny Okinawa-ken chiji, hageki nōryoku hoyū ni 'meikaku ni hantai,'" *Mainichi Shimbun*, February 9, 2023, as accessed February 10, 2023 at https://mainichi.jp/articles/20230209/k00/00m/010/086000c.

[77] "Missaru butai haibi, Yonaguni jūmin ni setsumei kai, 'hangeki nōryoku ni naranu,' kyōchō," *Asahi Shimbun*, May 16, 2023, as accessed May 17, 2023 at https://www.asahi.com/articles/DA3S15636698.html?iref=pc_ss_date_article.

CHAPTER 7

Conclusions: The Senkaku Islands, Japan's Defense Transformation and Regional Security

Abstract This chapter summarizes the argument of this book, demonstrating how the new status quo of continuous threat to Japan's control of the Senkaku islands has had a transformative impact on Japanese defense politics and strategy. As per balance-of-threat logic, this threat to Japan's bedrock value of territorial integrity caused the country to reevaluate China's intentions, and Tokyo has come to see China as having aggressive if not malevolent intentions. The focus on territorial defense means that Japan is not planning to use the SDF to help defend Taiwan or participate in other regional conflicts beyond Japanese territory. If Japan nonetheless finds itself embroiled in a conflict over Taiwan, its military role will remain focused on territorial defense. It will use its limited counterstrike capability only to maintain or reestablish deterrence.

Keywords Taiwan · Senkaku Islands · Counterstrike · US bases · Ryukyu Islands · Miyako Strait · Ukraine war

This book began by observing that the decade of 2012–2022 witnessed two major developments in Japan's security. The first has been the emergence of a new status quo of continuous confrontation between China and Japan over the Senkaku (known in China as the Diaoyu) islands as

© The Author(s), under exclusive license to Springer Nature
Switzerland AG 2025
P. Midford, *The Senkaku Islands Confrontation and the Transformation of Japan's Defense*, Palgrave Studies in Maritime Politics and Security,
https://doi.org/10.1007/978-3-031-77727-1_7

131

132   P. MIDFORD

China began continuously challenging Japan's control of these islands by regularly sending Chinese Coast Guard (CCG) vessels into the territorial waters around these islands, something it had almost never done before.

The second major development has been the transformation of Japan's defense policy overall. The main milestones in this transformation include establishing a National Security Council and secretariat (2013), reinterpreting the constitution to allow for the right to collective self-defense (2014) enacting enabling security legislation for collective self-defense (2015), the withdrawal from unit-level participation in UN peacekeeping (2017), and by the end of this period, in December 2022, new versions of the three fundamental defense documents (*Anpo San Bunsho*) that committed Japan to acquire offensive counterstrike missiles and increase its defense budget by approximately 60%.

This book has shown how this ongoing challenge to Japan's territorial integrity and its defense transformation are not unrelated, but are in fact very much connected. The new status quo of continuous threat to Japan's control of the Senkakus has had a transformative impact on Japanese defense politics and strategy, triggering the major changes in Japan's defense seen during this decade. This book has argued that Japan's response to the first new and direct challenge to its territorial integrity since the end of the Pacific War has followed the defensive realist strategy that Japan has pursued since regaining independence in 1952. As per balance-of-threat logic, this threat to Japan's bedrock value of territorial integrity caused Japanese elites and the public to fundamentally reevaluate China's intentions, as they came to see China as having aggressive if not malevolent intentions.

For inquiring readers who wonder whether this change in Japanese perceptions of Chinese intentions stemming from Beijing's threat to Japanese territorial control over the Senkaku islands has been sincere or opportunistic on the part of hawkish elites, this book answers that the change in perceptions has been genuine, but this change has also empowered hawkish elites. Crucially, however, this book has argued that hawkish elites have been empowered to build up the SDF and strengthen the Japan-US alliance for the sake of territorial defense, but they have not been empowered to push for Japan to play a military role overseas or to defend other countries, not even nearby Taiwan. The limits to the 2014 reinterpretation of Japan's constitution and subsequent security legislation of 2015 illustrate this (see Chapter 3), as does the de facto political retreat from collective self-defense evident in the three new defense documents (*Anpo San Bunsho*) from 2022.

This concluding chapter argues that the transformation in Japan's military strategy in the East China Sea and its broader security strategy has large implications for regional security, implications that were spelled out in the latest iterations of the three fundamental defense documents that were enacted by the Kishida administration in December 2022. This chapter explains how the changes that were set in motion in Japan's defense since the beginning of the continual confrontation over the Senkaku islands are having a significant impact on US regional security strategy, but also the limits of that transformation and its impact. Specifically, it argues that while Japan's new A2/AD strategy has significant implications for regional security, including for a conflict over Taiwan, Tokyo is not preparing to participate in combat to defend Taiwan or militarily participate in other regional conflicts but is instead doubling down on territorial defense. If Japan does end up directly involved in combat during a conflict over Taiwan, it will be unintentional, even accidental, and will be an involvement for which Japan has not prepared. Moreover, Japan's military involvement will remain limited and focused on territorial defense and maintaining or reestablishing deterrence vis-à-vis China. Japan's degree of success in defending its territory and closing access for China's military to the Pacific through its straits, including in all likelihood the Miyako Strait,[1] will be its main contribution to US regional strategy beyond allowing the US to use its bases in Japan in the defense of Taiwan or for other regional contingencies.

---

[1] As the 250 km wide Miyako Strait is a high sea strait under the UN Convention of the Law of the Sea (UNCLOS), closing it to China's military could be regarded by Beijing as an act of war. On the other hand, despite UNCLOS, Japan nonetheless regards the Miyako Strait as not being an international strait due to territorial defense concerns. See Peter Dutton, "International Law and the November 2004 'Han Incident,'" *Asian Security* 2, no. 2 (2006), pp. 87–101.

Japan's East China Sea Strategy and a Taiwan Scenario

Japanese Leaders on a Taiwan Crisis. Increasing tensions between China and Taiwan, especially since 2017, have provoked growing speculation in the western media about a potential Chinese invasion of the island.[2] This speculation has been increasingly echoed in the Japanese media since the latter stages of the first Trump administration, and the question of what Japan might do in the case of a Chinese attack began to be discussed among specialists, some conservative politicians and in the media. In mid-2021 this issue surfaced at the level of Japanese cabinet ministers. Defense Minister Kishi Nobuo (who is the brother of late Prime Minister Abe Shinzō) stated "the peace and stability of Taiwan is directly connected to Japan."[3]

Shortly thereafter the 2021 version of Japan's annual defense white paper, *Defense of Japan* added a new section on Taiwan and included the statement that "stabilizing the situation surrounding Taiwan is important not only for Japan's security but also for the stability of the international community. Therefore, it is necessary that we pay close attention to the situation with a sense of crisis more than ever before." However, the white paper did not mention anything about Japan playing a military role in defending Taiwan or maintaining stability in the Taiwan Strait,[4] and Japan has made similar statements in the past, starting with the 1969 Nixon-Sato communique between US President Richard Nixon and Japanese Prime Minister Sato Eisaku. As Adam Liff shows, Japan has made similarly authoritative statements of concern regarding a potential military conflict between China and Taiwan going back to at least 1997.[5]

Around the same time Deputy Prime Minister and Finance Minister Asō Tarō, speaking unofficially before a group of LDP Diet members,

---

[2] See Chapter 1 and Adam P. Liff, "The U.S.-Japan Alliance and Taiwan," *Asia Policy* 17, no. 3 (July 2022), pp. 131–132.

[3] Reuters, "Tokyo says Taiwan Security Directly Connected to Japan—Bloomberg," *Asahi Shimbun*, June 25, 2021, as accessed April 11, 2022, at https://www.asahi.com/ajw/articles/14380849.

[4] Ministry of Defense, *Defense of Japan 2021* (Tokyo: Ministry of Defense, 2021), pp. 91–92, 325; and Isabel Reynold, "Japan Mentions Taiwan Stability in Defense Paper for First Time," *Japan Times*, July 13, 2021, as accessed February 2, 2024, at https://www.japantimes.co.jp/news/2021/07/13/national/japan-taiwan-defense-paper/.

[5] Liff, "The U.S.-Japan Alliance and Taiwan," pp. 139, 151.

claimed that if China attacked Taiwan Japan "would have to defend Taiwan" along with the US. He added that in the event of a Chinese invasion of Taiwan "it would not be too much to say that it could relate to a survival-threatening situation" for Japan,[6] a reference to Japan's reinterpretation of its constitution in 2014 to allow it to defend other countries when Japan's own survival is at stake. In January 2024 Asō gave a similar statement to a US audience in Washington, DC: "There is an extremely strong possibility that the government will conclude Japan's very existence is at stake (if a military conflict broke out in the Taiwan Strait)," and added "China must understand what steps Japan might take (if fighting breaks out over Taiwan)."[7] Nonetheless, Asō's more forward leaning comments do not appear to be indicative of government thinking, given the audiences to which these remarks were addressed, and in view of Asō's long history of gaffes. His statements have been isolated and not echoed by other LDP leaders or members of the cabinet.

During the LDP presidential race in September 2021 that was effectively choosing the next prime minister, former foreign minister Kishida Fumio made history by becoming the first contender to raise Taiwan's security as a campaign issue. Kishida stated: "I have a strong feeling that the Taiwan Strait will be the next big problem" in Japanese foreign policy.[8] Nonetheless, Kishida did not echo Asō in stating that Japan would defend Taiwan together with the US during the LDP presidential campaign, or upon becoming prime minister. Moreover, during the

---

[6] "Deputy PM Aso says Japan would defend Taiwan with U.S., irking China," *Kyodo*, July 6, 2021, as accessed April 11, 2022, at https://english.kyodonews.net/news/2021/07/4303060a680b-deputy-pm-aso-says-japan-would-defend-taiwan-with-us-irking-china.html; and Liff, "The U.S.-Japan Alliance and Taiwan," p. 130. A Ministry of Foreign Affairs (MOFA) spokesperson reportedly stated that Asō's comment only represented his personal opinion. See Zhuoran Li, "No, Japan Will Not Defend Taiwan," *Diplomat*, March 18, 2024 as accessed March 25, 2024 at https://thediplomat.com/2024/03/no-japan-will-not-defend-taiwan/.

[7] Ayako Nakada, "Aso: Fighting in Taiwan Strait could force SDF to defend Japan," *Asahi Shimbun*, January 12, 2024 as retrieved March 11, 2024 at https://www.asahi.com/ajw/articles/15109484.

[8] Isabel Reynolds and Emi Nobuhiro, "Fumio Kishida, Top Contender to Lead Japan, Warns Taiwan is 'Next Big Problem,'" *Japan Times*, September 3, 2021, p. 3.

Lower House election a few weeks later the LDP manifesto made no mention of defending Taiwan and barely mentioned the island.[9]

Rather, the Kishida administration decided to maintain the status quo in policy toward China with respect to Taiwan: a mixture of non-military cooperation with Taipei and continued support for US forward deployments, but combined with dialogue with Beijing. Japan's continued if not deepening economic stakes in China provided an incentive for Kishida to maintain the status quo. Despite the COVID-19 era political tensions, in 2020 China's share in Japan's total trade volume set a record, and growth has continued since then with China still Japan's largest trading partner.[10] Even before the NSS, NDS, and DBP were issued more than a year later in December 2022, it was already clear from its inception that the Kishida administration was not going to commit to fighting alongside the US to defend Taiwan, although it would have likely provided the US military with logistical support.

Nonetheless, some LDP backbenchers, including former senior leaders, continued to publicly discuss what a Taiwan crisis would mean for Japan, although they did not discuss the possibility of Japan militarily defending Taiwan together with the US as Asō had done. In early December 2021 former prime minister Abe was widely quoted as warning during an online presentation organized by a Taiwanese private think tank that a "Taiwan contingency is a contingency for Japan and the Japan-U.S. alliance." At the same time even Abe, who has been outspoken in calling for a strong response against a possible Chinese invasion of Taiwan did not go as far as Asō has gone a few months earlier. He did not state that Japan would or should deploy the SDF in combat together with the US to repel a Chinese attack on Taiwan or use language suggesting such an attack would be a case that would fall under collective self-defense. As this book has shown, involving the Japan-US alliance in the defense of Taiwan can simply mean

---

[9] Jimintō, *Atrashii jidai wo mina san to tomo ni* (Tokyo: Jimintō honbu, 2021), with brief mentions of Taiwan in the context of regional security on pp. 31–32.

[10] Madoka Fukuda, "Kishida Unlikely to Change Course on China and Taiwan," *East Asia Forum*, December 16, 2021, as accessed April 11, 2022, at https://www.eastasiaforum.org/2021/12/16/kishida-unlikely-to-change; and Ministry of Foreign Affairs, "Japan-China Economic Overview," as accessed March 1, 2025 at https://www.mofa.go.jp/files/100540401.pdf

allowing the US to use its bases in Japan for the defense of Taiwan. Moreover, Abe was more explicit in saying that a Chinese invasion of Taiwan would be "economic suicide" for China.[11]

A day after Abe's remarks, former defense and foreign minister, Kōno Tarō, who came in a strong second in the LDP presidential race for the premiership to Kishida in October 2021, placed greater emphasis on the economic consequences for China if it attacked Taiwan. Kōno asserted that "if China actually tries to use force against Taiwan, it will probably lead to a very dire situation that would probably include some kind of economic sanctions," although Kōno added that the consequences might "not be limited to economic sanctions only."[12]

These comments indicate that even within the LDP, much less among Japan's political elites and society more broadly, there is currently no consensus in Japan about participating in combat operations to defend Taiwan should it come under attack. As discussed in Chapter 6, the three fundamental defense documents issued in December 2022 did not discuss the use of the SDF to help defend Taiwan and instead focused on the use of military power for achieving autonomous territorial defense. It is also notable that although the LDP's Policy Affairs Research Council's (PARC's) defense subcommittee issued reports in 2017, 2018, and 2022 in anticipation of the 2018 NDPG and the 2022 NDS that called for adopting the NATO standard of spending 2% of GDP on defense and acquiring counterstrike capabilities, none of these documents included any mention of possibly defending Taiwan.[13]

---

[11] Taiwan yūji wa nichibei yūji, jimin-Abe shi, Chugoku wo kensei," *Jiji*, December 1, 2021, as accessed December 5, 2021, at https://www.jiji.com/jc/article?k=202112010 0874&g=pol.

[12] "China attack on Taiwan could draw economic sanctions: Japan's Kono," *Kyodo*, December 2, 2021, as accessed April 11, 2022, at https://english.kyodonews.net/news/2021/12/d66059529168-update1-china-attack-on-taiwan-could-draw-economic-sancti ons-japans-kono.html?phrase=aso&words=.

[13] See Akihara Hara, Yuki Isabel Reynolds, "Teki kichi hangeki nōryoku hoyū e, seifu wa kentō kaishi o - Jimin chōsa-kai teigen," *Bloomberg*, March 29, 2017, as accessed March 11, 2024, at https://www.bloomberg.co.jp/news/articles/2017-03-29/ONK9D7 6K50XS01; Jiyūminshutō, "Aratana kokka anzen hoshō senryaku-tō no sakutei ni muketa teigen: yori shinkoku-ka suru kokusai jōsei-ka ni okeru wagakuni oyobi kokusai shakai no heiwa to anzen o kakuho suru tame no bōei-ryoku no bappon-teki kyōka no jitsugen ni mukete," April 26, 2022; and Jiyūminshutō seisaku chōsakai, "Aratana bōei keikaku no taikō oyobi chūki bōei-ryoku seibi keikaku no sakutei ni muketa teigen ~ 'tajigen ōdan (kurosu domein) bōei kōsō' no jitsugen ni mukete," May 29, 2018.

No Commitment to Defending Taiwan. It would take an explicit debate about defending Taiwan, followed by the conclusions of that debate being authoritatively endorsed in a future NSS, NDS, or similarly clear cabinet decision for Japan to start planning for how to build the necessary capabilities and how to participate in combat to help defend Taiwan, even together with the US. Barring such a shift away from territorial defense, it will continue to be China's threat to the Senkakus, plus new concerns that emerged in the wake of China's large military exercises around Taiwan in August 2022, that a Taiwan conflict could pose a threat to Yonaguni and other the Sakishima islands that will continue to drive Japan's military strategy in the East China Sea, specifically Japan's defense of its "southwest." This strategy is symbolized by the continued building of what retired GSDF General Banshō Kōichirō figuratively called the "Southwestern Wall" around Japan's territory there.[14] Taiwan is outside of the "Southwestern Wall," and hence beyond Japan's defense plans. As Banshō himself recently argued, in a conflict over Taiwan "the main areas of the SDF's activity will be in Japanese territory and perhaps international waters to protect Japanese ships." Banshō added, "a scenario in which the SDF will go onto Taiwanese land and defend Taipei alongside the U.S., for instance, is not expected." Rather, Banshō argued that Japan would play the same role toward Taiwan that Poland plays with respect to Ukraine.[15]

An indication of how much more controversial defending Taiwan is in Japanese politics compared to defending the Senkakus is that opposition to deploying SSMs to Ishigaki has not focused on their role in defending the Senkakus, arguably because such a role is beyond reproach in Japanese politics. This opposition has instead focused on Ishigaki facing Chinese missile strikes as a result of a Taiwan conflict in which Japan participates in combat. Nonetheless, the reality is that the current configuration of the T-12 missile, with a range of only 200 km can barely cover the Senkakus from Ishigaki and lacks the capability to significantly cover areas around

[14] Mulloy, *Defenders of Japan*, p. 249; and Robert D. Eldridge, "Organization and Structure of the Contemporary Ground Self-Defense Force," in Robert D. Eldridge and Paul Midford, eds., *The Japanese Ground Self-Defense Force*, p. 29; Sheila Smith, *Japan Rearmed* (Cambridge: Harvard University Press, 2019), p. 119.

[15] Ken Moriyasu, "In Taiwan Crisis, Japan to Play Role Like Poland to Ukraine: Ex-general," *Nikkei Asia*, December 1, 2023, as accessed February 29, 2024, at https://asia.nikkei.com/Editor-s-Picks/Interview/In-Taiwan-crisis-Japan-to-play-role-like-Poland-to-Ukraine-ex-general.

Taiwan, except for waters well to the northeast of Taiwan. The deployment of the improved T-12 with a notional range of up to 1000 km will, however, give Japan significantly greater capability to attack ships around Taiwan, giving it a more meaningful ability to help defeat a Chinese attack there, but also raising the priority of the Ishigaki T-12 missile launchers as a target for Chinese strikes. The deployment of the extended range T-12 is still years away, and the deployment of Tomahawks to these island bases would prove very controversial domestically, as MOD's public statement to Yonaguni residents that it would not deploy counterstrike missiles there makes clear. Moreover, the SDF's ability to effectively target Chinese ships around Taiwan, and perhaps even around the Senkakus, is hampered by the lack of sufficient C4ISR capabilities need to track mobile targets at such distances.[16]

Several Japanese security scholars and officials told the author that in their view international specialists, and especially American-based experts, have tended to misperceive Japan's NSS and NDS and Japan's overall posture as meaning that Japan has committed to militarily defend Taiwan. One Japanese security scholar told the author that Japan would have to increase its defense spending not by 60%, but by 150% in order to build sufficient military resources to help defend Taiwan.[17] The difficulty the Kishida administration and now the administration of Ishiba Shigeru has experienced finding the revenue to pay for a permanent increase of 60% in defense spending, combined with the collapse of the hawkish Abe faction, make it even less likely that Japan will move toward a more ambitious strategy of military involvement beyond Japanese territory. With demands for tax reductions rather than increases gaining ground since the LDP and Komeito lost their lower house majority in October 2024, it remains to be seen whether Japan will in fact be able to sustain the planned 60% increase in defense spending.[18] Moreover, Japan is being forced to scale

---

[16] I am grateful to Garren Mulloy for his insights on this point.

[17] Comments received by the author during a seminar, Research Institute of Peace and Security, Tokyo June 24, 2023.

[18] Michael MacArthur Bosack "Kishida's Proposed Tax Cuts Put Higher Defense Spending on Hold," *Japan Times*, October 23, 2023, as accessed March 1, 2023 at https://www.japantimes.co.jp/commentary/2023/10/23/japan/kishida-tax-cuts-defense-budget/.

back its weapons purchases from overseas due to the weakening of the Yen.[19]

Likely US-Japan Cooperation. A lack of joint command and procedures for fighting together would hamper joint US-Japan combat operations to defend Taiwan. During Diet debate Kishida promised that no joint command with the US would be established, and command of the SDF would not be transferred to the US.[20] Since regaining its independence Japan has rebuffed any suggestion of joint or American command over the SDF,[21] a position that Kishida's statement makes clear remains entrenched. In part this appears to reflect Japan's security isolationism: although Tokyo is willing to engage in deep and comprehensive cooperation with the US, this is aimed at territorial defense. As during the Cold War, there remain limits to how far Japan is willing to pursue political and military integration with neighboring countries, or even with the US. Rather Japan jealously guards its distinct identity and defense autonomy,

[19] River Akira Davis and Hisako Ueno, "The Yen Is Plunging, so Is Japan's Defense Budget," *New York Times*, July 9, 2024, as accessed August 11, 2024 at https://www.nytimes.com/2024/07/08/business/japan-yen-defense-spending.html; Nobuhiro Kubo, Takaya Yamaguchi and Tim Kelly, Exclusive: Weak yen forces Japan to shrink historic military spending plan," *Reuters*, November 3, 2023 as accessed March 11, 2024 at https://www.reuters.com/markets/currencies/weak-yen-forces-japan-shrink-historic-military-spending-plan-2023-11-03/. The cost of an Aegis equipped destroyer, for example, has ballooned from 240 billion Yen in 2020 to 395 billion in 2024. See Gabriel Dominquez, "Japan defense spending goals hit by inflation, weak yen, and political uncertainty," *Japan Times*, December 29, 2024 as accessed at https://www.japantimes.co.jp/news/2024/12/29/japan/japan-defense-spending-inflation/. From early 2022 through February 2025 the Yen weakened from approximately 115 Yen to the US dollar to 155 Yen.

[20] "Will to Fight? America's Ally Nervous about Waging War to Defend Taiwan," *The Economist*, May 10, 2023, as accessed August 11, 2023, at https://www.economist.com/asia/2023/05/10/will-japan-fight.

[21] On this history of Japan's opposition to American command over the SDF in wartime, see Eiji Takemae, *The Allied Occupation of Japan* (New York: Continuum, 2003), p. 506.

7 CONCLUSIONS: THE SENKAKU ISLANDS, JAPAN'S DEFENSE …   141

despite its alliance with the US.[22] The three defense documents (*Anpo San Bunsho*) of 2022 mark a renewed focus on defense autonomy.

For the first time since the Nixon-Sato communique of 1969,[23] the April 2021 Japan-US summit communique between President Biden and Prime Minister Suga mentioned Taiwan: "We underscore the importance of peace and stability across the Taiwan Strait and encourage the peaceful resolution of cross-Strait issues."[24] This passage raised questions about whether Japan was committing to using the SDF to help defend Taiwan. In response to a question about this in the Diet, Suga responded that his joint statement with Biden "does not presuppose military involvement at all" by the SDF.[25] To date this is the clearest statement any Japanese prime minister has given about the possible involvement of the SDF in defense of Taiwan. Similarly, on the same day, in testimony in the Foreign Affairs Committee of the Lower House of the Diet, Foreign Minister Motegi Toshimitsu and Vice Defense Minister Nakayama Yasuhide denied

---

[22] Tracing this tendency back to Prime Minister Yoshida Shigeru is Hideo Ōtake, "Defense Controversies and One-Party Dominance: The Opposition in Japan and West Germany," in T. J. Pempel, ed., *Uncommon Democracies: The One-Party Dominant Regimes* (Ithaca: Cornell University Press, 1990), p. 139. Also see Pyle, *The Japanese Question*, pp. 24; and Welfield, *An Empire in Eclipse*, p. 24; and John Welfield, *An Empire in Eclipse: Japan in the Post-war American Alliance System* (London and Atlantic Highlands, NJ: The Athlone Press, 1988), p. 90.

[23] However, the Japan-US 2+2 Meeting of February 2005 did mention the importance of peace and stability in the Taiwan Strait for the bilateral alliance.

[24] The White House, "U.S.-Japan Joint Leaders' Statement: U.S.-Japan Global Partnership for a New Era," p. 3/6 as accessed at August 11, 2023 at https://www.whi tehouse.gov/briefing-room/statements-releases/2021/04/16/u-s-japan-joint-leaders-sta tement-u-s-japan-global-partnership-for-a-new-era/.

[25] Ralph Jennings, "US-Japan Statement Raises Issue of Taiwan Defense Against China," *VOA*, April 24, 2021, as accessed August 11, 2023, at https://www.voanews. com/a/east-asia-pacific_us-japan-statement-raises-issue-taiwan-defense-against-china/620 4998.html; and Julian Ryall, "Japan Troops Won't Get Involved if China Invades Taiwan, PM Yoshihide Suga Says," *South China Morning Post*, April 21, 2021, as accessed March 11, 2024 at https://www.scmp.com/week-asia/politics/article/3130423/japan-troops-wont-get-involved-if-china-invades-taiwan-pm.

that the reference to strengthening deterrence in the joint communique referred to Taiwan, rather the passage referred to strengthening deterrence in relation to the Senkaku islands.[26]

Rather than participating militarily in defending Taiwan, Japan's support for the US in a conflict with China over Taiwan is likely to be logistical and indirect. Although allowing the US to use its bases in Japan for combat operations in defense of Taiwan is not automatic, it is nonetheless very likely. To ensure that Tokyo agrees to unconditional use of US bases in Japan and to maintain the longer-term viability of the alliance, it is important for Washington to consult with Tokyo at the beginning of the crisis rather than presenting Japan with a fait accompli.[27] Japan would also defend US bases, planes and ships on Japanese territory, territorial airspace, and waters. The SDF would also likely offer rear-area logistical support for the US military in areas removed from combat, a mission Japan has accepted in principle since the 1997 Japan-US defense guidelines.[28]

It is also likely that Japan would block access to the straits through the Japanese islands from the East China Sea to the Western Pacific for Chinese ships and aircraft, including the Miyako Strait. For example, Japan would likely block (shoot down) Chinese drones that tried to fly over the Miyako Strait on their way to Taiwan, as Chinese drones did during large-scale military exercises in August 2022 in response to US House Speaker Nancy Pelosi's visit to Taiwan.[29] This would represent a large contribution to the emerging US strategy of locking China's navy inside the first island chain, specifically inside the East China and South China Seas, and denying China access to the Pacific Ocean or Indian

---

[26] Dai 204 kai kokkai, gaimu iinkai, dai 9 gou (Reiwa 3 nen, 4 gatsu 21 nichi (suiyōbi), as accessed August 17, 2023 at https://www.shugiin.go.jp/internet/itdb_k aigiroku.nsf/html/kaigiroku/000520420210421009.html; Also see The White House, U.S.-Japan Joint Leaders' Statement," p. 2/6.

[27] Jeffrey W. Hornung, *Japan's Potential Contributions in an East China Sea Contingency* (Santa Monica: Rand Corporation, 2020 pp. xv, 93.

[28] See Ministry of Foreign Affairs of Japan, *The Guidelines for Japan-U.S. Defense Cooperation,* as accessed July 19, 2018, at https://www.mofa.go.jp/region/n-america/us/security/guideline2.html.

[29] "Maps: Tracking Tension Between China and Taiwan: Show of Force near Taiwan and Japanese Islands," *New York Times,* August 7, 2022, as accessed August 15, 2022, at https://www.nytimes.com/interactive/2022/world/asia/taiwan-china-maps.html.

Ocean,[30] though closing the Miyako Strait could be reasonably construed by China to be an act of war by Japan.[31]

Of course, a Sino-US conflict over Taiwan, like any great power war (or any war more generally), would be inherently unpredictable. That extends to how Japan would react. Although it is the conclusion of this book that Japan would not hesitate to use for to defend its control of the Senkaku islands (and its other outlying islands), this book is not predicting that Japan would definitely refuse to militarily participate in the defense of Taiwan eventually, given the inherent unpredictability of war. What this book is rather arguing is that as of now there is very little evidence that Japan is planning or preparing to militarily participate in such a conflict. Although constitutional and legal restrictions on employing the SDF overseas to use force were somewhat relaxed (although they remain restrictive),[32] that does not translate into a will to use force overseas by political elites, much less by the public at large.[33] As Sheila Smith notes , "the political sensitivity over the use of force by the SDF—remains...None of the legal changes made recently have fundamentally altered Japan's desire to limit to use of military force to tasks that embrace its own security."[34] Furthermore, the more recent NSS and NDS of December

[30] Robert S. Ross, "Reluctant Retrenchment: America's Response to the Rise of China," *Naval War College* Review 76, no. 4 (Autumn 2023), as accessed March 11, 2025 at https://digital-commons.usnwc.edu/cgi/viewcontent.cgi?article=8382&context=nwc-review. Also see Robert S. Ross, "The Rise of China and American Security Policy," presentation for the Institute of International and Strategic Studies, Peking University, as accessed March 15, 2024, at http://www.iiss.pku.edu.cn/info/1005/4651.htm.

[31] As mentioned previously, Japan does not have the right under the Law of the Sea (including UNCLOS) to control or close the Miyako Strait, which at approximately 250 km in width, is an international waterway. To do so as a non-combatant could be legitimately construed as an act of war.

[32] Jeffrey W. Hornung and Mike M. Mochizuki, "Japan: Still an Exceptional U.S. Ally," *Washington Quarterly* 39, no. 1 (2016), pp. 95-116. Hornung and Mochizuki concluded that "Japan continues to impose strict restrictions on the use of force, power projection capabilities, and arms exports, and its national legislature remains highly intrusive in operational decisions.... While the SDF can do more overseas than it ever has previously, the security changes achieved by the Abe administration occurred in tandem with maintaining—and in some cases imposing new—restrictions on what the SDF can do" (pp. 109, 110).

[33] Paul Midford, "The Influence of Public Opinion on Foreign Policy in Asia: The Case of Japan," in Takashi Inoguchi, ed., *The SAGE Handbook of Asian Foreign Policy* (Thousand Oaks, California: Sage, 2019), pp. 381–404.

[34] Smith, *Japan Rearmed*, pp. 237–238.

2022 doubled down on territorial defense and did not even mention Japan exercising the right of collective self-defense.

Japan is shaping its forces for territorial defense, not for defense of Taiwan or participation in other overseas conflicts. Its authoritative defense documents from 2022 do not mandate or anticipate direct military participation in a Taiwan conflict, and there is no evidence that the LDP, the Kishida and Ishiba administrations have been attempting (or the previous Suga or Abe administrations had attempted) to build a political consensus in favor of the SDF defending Taiwan. Rather, with a very few isolated exceptions, their silence on this topic has been deafening.

One important unknown variable is whether during a conflict over Taiwan China would attack Japan, or US bases in Japan, or whether Beijing would conclude it would be advantageous not to attack either. Assuming that the US uses its bases in Japan for the defense of Taiwan, and that the SDF does guard US military assets, at least on land and in Japan's territorial waters and airspace, and perhaps beyond into the surrounding contiguous waters, there is a relatively high probability that China would launch attacks on US bases in Japan and perhaps even SDF assets, especially those guarding US forces or blocking Chinese access to the Miyako Strait. On the other hand, if China does not attack Japan during a Taiwan conflict, Japan would have a strong incentive not to become directly militarily involved. Instead, Tokyo, would have an incentive to "keep its powder dry" for the sake of defending its own territory.

Even if China does attack US bases in Japan or even SDF bases, Tokyo's response would likely be limited and measured. It can be expected that Japan would launch counterstrikes at the bases from which the attacks came, or at related military infrastructure to try to reestablish deterrence but would likely not go beyond that as the SDF would only have a limited number of Tomahawks at its disposal. Moreover, with China's advanced air defenses and dispersed base infrastructure, the impact of Japan's counterstrike options on China's military would be very limited in any case. As one senior Pentagon official remarked at a seminar on Asian security, China is "a Tomahawk sponge."[35]

Even against adversaries with less sophisticated air defenses, the effectiveness of Tomahawk cruise missiles has proven to be limited. During

---

[35] Harvard University, April 2023.

just the first day of strikes to suppress the ability of the Houthis to attack shipping in the Red Sea the US reportedly fired 80 Tomahawk missiles, yet even with follow-on strikes the results have been limited at best as Houthi attacks on shipping continued. Likewise, in 2017 the US fired 55 Tomahawk missiles at a single Syrian airbase.[36]

Given Japan's limited acquisition of 400 Tomahawks, and its lack for several years to come of other missiles that can effectively hit fixed targets on mainland China, it is likely that Japan would limit its use of Tomahawks to reestablishing deterrence and thereby preventing further attacks against itself, rather than using this capability to help defend Taiwan. Moreover, there is reason to doubt whether even the US would strike targets on the Chinese mainland. A Center for Strategic and International Studies (CSIS) table-top exercise found that in the event of a conflict over Taiwan even US decision makers were in some major scenarios reluctant to authorize strikes against military targets on the mainland or limited them to facilities (e.g. seaports and airbases) immediately involved in an invasion of Taiwan. Concern over provoking a nuclear weapons response from China was seen as a major reason, plus doubts about the effectiveness of such strikes and quantitative limits on the US supply of long-range precision munitions.[37] Compared to the US, Japan is likely to be more, not less, cautious in targeting the Chinese mainland with its limited Tomahawk arsenal.

[36] Mackenzie Eaglen, "Why Is the U.S. Navy Running Out of Tomahawk Cruise Missiles?" *The National Interest*, February 13, 2024 as accessed March 11, 2024 at https://www.aei.org/op-eds/why-is-the-u-s-navy-running-out-of-tomahawk-cruise-mis siles/. More generally see Marc Champion, "U.S. Preeminence Is Threatened by a Real 'Missile Gap'," *Japan Times*, January 5, 2024, as accessed February 29, 2024, at https://www.japantimes.co.jp/commentary/2024/01/05/world/us-missile-gap/. A related problem is whether US production capacity can rapidly supply Japan with 400 Tomahawks, given that the US is currently using these cruise missiles faster than it is replenishing its supply.

[37] Mark F. Cancian, Matthew Cancian and Eric Heginbotham, *The First Battle of the Next War: Wargaming a Chinese Invasion of Taiwan* (Washington, DC: Center for Strategic and International Studies, 2023), pp. 71–72, 150. P. 137. This wargame found that the US ran out of the LRASM anti-ship missiles within the first few days of the conflict. Meanwhile, the US has been firing Tomahawk missiles against relatively weak adversaries such as Syria and the Houthis in recent years faster than it has been procuring them, drawing down its stockpiles. See Eaglen, "Why Is the U.S. Navy Running Out of Tomahawk Cruise Missiles?".

146   P. MIDFORD

Even without Chinese strikes on US bases in Japan, Japan would support US military operations to defend Taiwan in several ways not involving combat. Although, as Hornung points out, permission for the US to use its bases in Japan to defend Taiwan would not be automatic, it would be extremely likely that Tokyo would allow Washington to use its bases in Japan for military operations in defense of Taiwan. It is also very likely that Japan would provide rear area logistical support for US forces. As a former Japanese official told the author, this would include defending US ships and planes in territorial waters and airspace. Japan might extend its defense into international waters beyond Japan's territorial waters, especially into contiguous waters around Japan's territorial waters, but whether protection would go much farther remains unclear, and likely would not include anywhere near all of Japan's EEZ. SDF defense of US military assets in international waters and airspace is second possible route for Japan becoming directly involved in a military conflict over Taiwan.

A third possible scenario for supporting US combat operations for defending Taiwan would be to allow the newly reorganized 12th US Marine Littoral Regiment based in Okinawa to temporarily deploy and to Yonaguni or perhaps Ishigaki, and use those islands to fire missiles at Chinese forces.[38] However, the MOD's statement to local residents about not deploying counterstrike missiles on Yonaguni makes that possible scenario look difficult (see Chapter 4), and US long-range missiles deployed to SDF bases on these islands would be vulnerable to Chinese counterstrikes and might put residential areas at risk. Given that Japan cancelled the Aegis Ashore missile defense system over concern that the rocket boosters from this system could fall on residential areas, it is clear that Japanese leaders and public will be very sensitive to agreeing to US deployments and actions that could lead to strikes on residential areas. Rather, for Japan, this US Marine Regiment appears purposed for helping the SDF defend the Senkakus and Sakishima islands.[39] A fourth

---

[38] Cooper and Sayers, "Japan's Shift to a War Footing; Giulio Pugliese, "In It Together Taiwan's and Japan's Security Are Linked," in Bonnie S. Glaser, ed., *Next-Generation Perspectives on Taiwan: Insights from the 2023 Taiwan-US Policy Program* (August 2023), p. 41, as accessed August 26, 2023 at https://www.gmfus.org/news/next-generation-per spectives-taiwan-insights-2023-taiwan-us-policy-program.

[39] Takashi Watanabe, "U.S. Marine Unit in Okinawa Gets New Littoral Combat Duties," *Asahi Shimbun*, October 18, 2023, as accessed at October 31, 2023 at

scenario for possible involvement would be the use of the SDF to evacuate Japanese and other civilians from Taiwan, and the possibility that SDF planes or ships could come under attack from Chinese forces.

Under any of these scenarios, a Japan that finds itself directly involved in a military conflict over Taiwan is unlikely to respond to such a conflict by committing the SDF on a large scale to defending Taiwan, and will likely prioritize defense of Japanese territory. The 2022 NDS and NSS politically (re)commit Japan to territorial defense, but these documents do not commit Japan to defending Taiwan. Of course, war is unpredictable, but based on the NSS and NDS, other pronouncements by Kishida and his cabinet, and more recent statements by the Ishiba cabinet, including the security commitments Japan has made to its public and internationally, Japan's current and envisaged capabilities over the coming decade, and the way the SDF will be shaped over that period, it is clear that Japan is not planning or preparing to participate in combat over Taiwan.

For example, as discussed in Chapter 4, Japan has been modernizing and expanding its electronic warfare capability. However, this is so far entirely focused on defensive measures (countering China's offensive electronic warfare capabilities) rather than offensive capabilities. Moreover, the centerpiece of Japan's electronic warfare modernization and expansion is the GSDF's truck-mounted NEWS system, a system that is not easily mobile beyond Japan's land mass. Moreover, the emphasis on territorial defense in the NSS and NDS means that major planning for direct combat involvement in a Taiwan or other regional contingency beyond Japan's borders is unlikely. The SDF's marching orders instead are to focus on territorial defense, especially in the Southwest. Building a defensive "wall" there is very different than defending Taiwan which is outside of that "wall."

In short, Japan's active involvement in defending Taiwan, even if it comes under attack from China, appears unlikely. Although there is

---

https://www.asahi.com/ajw/articles/15032051; "U.S. Marines set up littoral unit in Okinawa for islands defense," *Kyodo*, November 15, 2023, as accessed March 11, 2024 at https://english.kyodonews.net/news/2023/11/6ca78816e719-us-marines-sets-up-littoral-unit-in-okinawa-for-islands-defense.html; "GSDF, Marines Retake Island in Joint 'Iron Fist' Drill in Oita," *Asahi Shimbun*, February 23, 2023, as accessed December 14, 2023 at https://www.asahi.com/ajw/articles/14843309; "US Marines Set Up Littoral Unit in Okinawa for Islands Defense," *Mainichi*, November 15, 2023 as accessed December 14, 2023 at https://mainichi.jp/english/articles/20231115/p2g/00m/0na/033000c.

extremely widespread sympathy for Taiwan in Japan, that does not translate into a consensus for helping to defend that island. The evidence indicates that Japan is not planning to participate militarily in a Taiwan conflict, and clearly Japan is not preparing for such a scenario. War is inherently unpredictable, so Japan might get drawn into such a conflict anyway, but if so, that will happen unintentionally, with Japan not prepared militarily or politically for such a conflict. If Japan does become involved in combat with China, it will mostly be limited to trying to reestablish deterrence and to ensure Japan's continued control over the Senkakus and Sakishima islands.

DECLINING CONFIDENCE IN THE US DEFENSE COMMITMENT

The transformation of Japan's defense, including its emerging A2/AD strategy, reflects not only its own loss of uncontested air and naval superiority vis-a-vis China in the East China Sea that Japan had enjoyed until about 2010, but even growing pessimism about the US ability to maintain military superiority over China regionally. Former Prime Minister Abe's evaluation of the US policy of strategic ambiguity toward Taiwan reveals pessimism about US military capabilities, which also underpins Japan's A2/AD strategy toward defense of the Senkaku and Ryukyu Islands: "The policy of ambiguity worked extremely well as long as the U.S. was strong enough to maintain it and as long as China was far inferior to the U.S. in military power. But those days are over."[40]

Tokyo also appears to be increasingly concerned about US willingness to defend Japan. The open questioning of the Japan-US and other US alliances by candidate and then President Donald Trump has exacerbated Tokyo's fears of abandonment in case of a crisis. As Smith notes, "the political mood in the United States has unsettled the Japanese...As Japan faces increasing pressure on its defenses, the reliability of the United States seems less certain."[41] As Tobias Harris notes, "while unpredictability may be useful to keep adversaries off balance, it was a chilling prospect for an

---

[40] Abe, "U.S. 'Strategic Ambiguity' over Taiwan Must End."

[41] Smith, *Japan Rearmed*, p. 4. Regarding Trump's Negative Rhetoric about Japan and the Japan-US Alliance, see Tobias Harris, *Iconoclast: Shinzō Abe and the New Japan* (London: Hurst, 2020), pp. 271–272.

ally in need of help to deter China and North Korea."[42] It is also notable that Japanese security elites reacted to Trump administration calls to greatly increase the host-nation support Japan provides for the stationing of US troops in Japan by arguing that Japan should reject those demands and instead use the same funds to strengthen the SDF.[43] This reaction is an indicator that Tokyo may be coming to see additional investments in the SDF as a safer bet than additional investments in its alliance with the US.

As of this writing Japan is viewing the early second Trump administration with uncertainty and trepidation, concerned that Trump will use the image of an unpredictable madman to conceal an unwillingness to defend Japan.[44] Increased concern about US abandonment appears to be an additional factor encouraging Japan to double down on territorial defense, rather than more ambitiously expanding the country's defense horizons further afield.[45]

Summary

This book finds the ongoing Senkaku confrontation since 2012 that is characterized by frequent (nearly monthly) Chinese coast guard patrols into Senkaku waters has triggered major changes in Japanese defense policy, including the development of an A2/AD capability in the East China Sea. For the US, these major changes include the benefit of Japan potentially slamming shut the Miyako Strait as an access point to the Western Pacific for the Chinese military. The transformative impact of the ongoing Senkakus confrontation stems from the fact that it is the first direct physical threat to Japanese territorial integrity (i.e. territory

---

[42] Harris, *Iconoclast*, p. 272.

[43] Smith, *Japan Rearmed*, p. 233.

[44] "Abe moto shushō mo osoreta 'kurutte inai toranpu' dai 2-ji seiken no mondai wa barete iru koto," *Sankei Shimbun*, March 14, 2024, as accessed March 16, 2024 at https://www.sankei.com/article/20240314-QLAMNFW4PJNXTG6MZF D2YLR73I/?utm_source=substack&utm_medium=email; and Tobias Harris, "The Wages of Spring," *Observing Japan*, March 15, 2023.

[45] For an earlier argument that Japan is moving toward territorial defense, see Lionel P. Fatton, "A New Spear in Asia: Why Is Japan Moving Toward Autonomous Defense?" *International Relations of Asia Pacific* 19, no. 2 (2019), pp. 297–325.

150   P. MIDFORD

that it controls) since 1945. Consequently, since 2012, as Smith explains, "defense of the Senkakus became equated with the defense of Japan."[46]

The ongoing confrontation over the Senkakus has legitimated moves to loosen restrictions on the SDF, withdraw from extra-regional SDF contributions to global security, and the development of longer-range missiles that undermined Japan's hitherto policy of not acquiring long-range missiles that can attack targets in other countries. At the same time Japan's emerging A2/AD strategy faces several challenges, including the very slow pace of its roll out, the paucity of territory or flexibility in deploying mobile SSM missile launchers so they can survive potential Chinese strikes, insufficient of C4ISR, and the need to further develop electronic warfare assets.

Some observers have argued that Japan's three defense documents of 2022 and more muscular defense policies, such as a 60% increase in defense spending and acquiring counterstrike capabilities that supposedly "break taboos," reflect lessons it has drawn from the Russian invasion of Ukraine, lessons that also point to playing a military role beyond its territory as a "regional protector."[47] However, as this book as shown, the decisions ratified in the *Anpo San Bunsho*, such as the decision to acquire counterstrike capabilities, resulted from a decade of defense transformation stemming from the continual threat to Japan's control of the Senkakus, and from years of consensus building (which was also helped by Japan's emerging A2/AD umbrella over the Ryukyus that had already largely eroded the "taboo" on long-range missiles), consensus building most evident in LDP policy reports dating back to 2017 (see Chapter 5). Rather than learning the lesson that Japan needs to become a regional protector, the lesson that appears to have been drawn from the Ukraine war is the need to double-down on territorial defense, a trend that has been underway since 2012, when the new status quo of China continually challenging Japan's control of the Senkaku islands emerged. The three defense documents of 2022 represent a culmination of this trend.

---

[46] Smith, *Japan Rearmed*, p. 216.

[47] Yuki Tatsumi, "How Russia's Invasion of Ukraine Changed Japan's Approach to National Security," Stimson, February 16, 2023, as accessed February 29, 2024, at https://www.stimson.org/2023/how-russias-invasion-of-ukraine-changed-japans-approach-to-national-security/; Zack Cooper and Eric Sayers, "Japan's Shift to a War Footing," *War on the Rocks*, January 12, 2023, as accessed July 7, 2023, at https://warontherocks.com/2023/01/japans-shift-to-war-footing/.

To the extent that the Ukraine war has had an impact, it has been to make it easier for Japanese to imagine their own country being a victim of a similar invasion, rather than imagining Japan becoming the savior of another country that comes under attack.

If China thought that increasing pressure on Japan over the Senkakus islands would encourage Japanese concessions, such a strategy has clearly backfired. Japan's resolve to defend its control of the Senkaku islands has grown not shrunk. With the conflict over these islands driving a Sino-Japanese arms race and even a Cold War, the question becomes what steps can be taken to deescalate and manage this conflict, if not find a means for conflict resolution? Nonetheless, the focus of Japan's new emerging A2/AD strategy in the East China Sea is on defending Japanese territory, about which there is a wide consensus in Japan, not about helping to defend Taiwan or play a regional military role. Rather, the thrust of Japan's current strategy is to contribute to the defense of Taiwan and regional security in the Indo-Pacific region by ensuring Japan's ability to defend its own territory. According to the 2022 NDS, "if Japan possesses a defense capability to enable disrupting and defeating invasion, this capability, coupled with that of the United States, Japan's ally, will be able to deter not only invasion of Japan, but also deter unilateral changes to the status quo by force and such attempts in the Indo-Pacific region."[48] Or as General Banshō put it, "The greatest contribution Japan can make is to properly defend itself."[49] For Japan defense starts with the Senkaku islands.

---

[48] Cabinet Secretariat, Government of Japan, *National Defense Strategy* (*NDS*), December 16, 2022, p. 11, as accessed April 11, 2023, at https://www.mod.go.jp/j/policy/agenda/guideline/strategy/pdf/strategy_en.pdf.

[49] Moriyasu, "In Taiwan Crisis, Japan to Play Poland to Ukraine."

INDEX

A

A2/AD. *See* Anti-Access/Area Denial
abandonment, 7, 58, 119, 148, 149
Abe Shinzō, 41, 53, 134
   Abe administration, 12, 52, 53, 56,
     101–103, 144
   Abe faction, 123, 139
ADIZ. *See* Air Defense Identification
   Zone
Aegis, 91
   Aegis ashore, 96, 102, 108, 146
Afghanistan, 10
aircraft carrier, 75, 100
Air Defense Identification Zone
   (ADIZ), 51
airports, 117, 121
Air Self Defense Force (ASDF), 43,
   64–66, 68, 78, 79, 84, 88
Akita Prefecture, 103
Amami Oshima, 76, 78, 86, 91
ammunition depot, 67, 93–95, 121,
   129
Amnesty International, 96

amphibious
   amphibious assault, 46, 49, 54, 55,
     57, 62, 63, 76, 116
   amphibious landing, 55, 88
   Amphibious Rapid Deployment
     Brigade (ARDB, Suiriku kidō
     dan 水陸機動団), 62
Anpo San Bunsho (安保三文書), 108,
   122, 132, 133, 141, 150
Anti-Access/Area Denial (A2/AD, 接
   近阻止/領域拒否), 8, 74, 76
anti-Japanese protests, 40
Anti-Submarine Warfare (ASW), 50,
   86
ARDB. *See* Amphbious Rapid
   Deployment Brigade
Argentina, 81
Asahi Shimbun, 35, 47, 86, 92, 105,
   123–127
ASDF. *See* Air Self Defense Force
   9th Airwing, 64
   Southwestern Aircraft Control and
     Warning Wing, 65

© The Editor(s) (if applicable) and The Author(s), under exclusive
license to Springer Nature Switzerland AG 2024
P. Midford, *The Senkaku Islands Confrontation and the Transformation
of Japan's Defense*, Palgrave Studies in Maritime Politics and Security,
https://doi.org/10.1007/978-3-031-77727-1

154 INDEX

Southwestern Air Defense Force, 64
ASM-3A (anti-ship missile), 79, 85
Asō Tarō, 134
ASW. *See* Anti-Submarine Warfare
attitudinal defensive realism, 3, 12, 13, 130
Australia, 54

B

Balance of power theory, 5, 6, 9
Balance of threat theory, 9
Banshō Koichirō, 61, 138
base hardening, 121
Bashi Strait, 87
Basic Law on Oceans Policy, 36
Beijing, 32, 40, 48, 132, 136, 144
Biden, Joseph (Joe), 141
   Biden Administration, 105
Bōei Taiko. See National Defense Program Outline; National Defense Strategy (NDS) (Japan)
boots-on-the-ground deployments, 56

C

Camp Amami, 78
Camp Setouchi, 78
CCG. *See* China Coast Guard
Center for Strategic and International Studies (CSIS), 145
China Coast Guard (CCG), 41–43, 58
Chinese State Oceanic Agency, 43
Clinton, Hillary, 35
Cold War, 9–11, 46, 56, 82, 83, 86, 88, 89, 140, 151
collective self-defense, 2, 52, 115, 116, 132, 133, 136, 144
counterstrike, 2, 69, 93, 94, 96, 101–106, 108–111, 120, 122, 127–130, 132, 137, 139, 144, 146, 150

Covid pandemic, 43
cruise missiles, 100, 101, 104, 128, 144

D

deconfliction of fire, 66
defense autonomy, 108, 140, 141
Defense Buildup Program (DBP) (2022), 108
defense spending, 3, 53, 54, 108, 117, 118, 120–124, 139, 150
defensive defense doctrine (*senshu bōei* 専守防衛), 13, 100, 127
defensive realism, 8, 10
democracies, 126
Democratic Party of Japan (DPJ), 33–37, 39, 40, 46, 49, 50, 52, 53, 56, 86
demographic decline, 69
deterrence
   active deterrence, 83
   deterrence by denial, 85
   deterrent threats, 54
   nuclear deterrence, 119
Diet, 36, 103, 112, 134, 140, 141
   Lower House, 141
      Foreign Affairs Committee, 141
   Upper House, 103, 104
diplomacy, 17, 33, 35, 37, 54, 126
DPJ. *See* Democratic Party of Japan
drone. *See* Unmanned Aerial Vehicle (UAV)
Dynamic Defense, 50

E

E/A-18 Growler, 89
East China Sea, 2, 7, 24, 26, 29, 51, 65, 75, 86, 88, 91, 133, 134, 138, 142, 148, 149, 151
EEZ. *See* Exclusive Economic Zone

INDEX 155

Eisaku, Sato, 134
election, 103–105, 136
  election manifesto, 104
electromagnetic, 89
electronic intelligence (ELINT), 87
electronic support and measures
  (ESM), 87
electronic warfare, 86, 88–91, 147,
  150
  electronic attack, 88, 89
  jamming, 87, 88
ELINT. *See* electronic intelligence
Emery survey, 24
enemy bases, 3, 100–104, 109, 130
  enemy missile bases, 102, 104, 112,
  122
engagement, 125
entrapment, 7, 58, 106, 119
ESM. *See* electronic support and
  measures
evacuation, 97, 129
Exclusive Economic Zone (EEZ), 21,
  29, 36, 113, 146

F
F-15 (air superiority fighter), 49, 64
F-35, F-35B (air superiority fighter),
  100
Falkland Islands, 81
federated defense, 55
fire control, 66
  fire support doctrine, 66
Fish Hook Undersea Defense Line, 87
fishing, 21, 27, 31, 36, 38, 43, 49, 58
flag-state jurisdiction, 36
forward defense, 82, 83, 120
France, 54, 55
Fujian, 65, 68

G
gas (natural), 24, 26

Genron NPO, 47, 124, 127
Great East Japan Earthquake, 66
Gross Domestic Product (GDP), 3,
  53, 108, 117, 137
Ground Self Defense Force (GSDF),
  46, 49, 54, 57, 61–70, 76, 78,
  85–90, 92, 94, 96, 116, 117,
  128–130, 138, 147
  15th Brigade, 67
GSDF. *See* Ground Self Defense Force
  301st GSDF Electronic Warfare
  Company, 90

H
Hateruma Island, 121
hawks, 100, 102, 103
hegemony, 10, 119, 120
helicopter, 59, 87
  helicopter carrier, 100
Hokkaido, 56, 57, 88, 89
Hong Kong, 28–30
host-nation support, 149
Houthis, 145
Huangwei Island. *See* Kuba Island
Huangwei Yu. *See* Kuba Island
HVGP. *See* Hyper-Velocity Gliding
  Projectile
hydrophone, 87
Hyper-Velocity Gliding Projectile
  (HVGP), 74, 85, 103

I
in-air-refueling, 79, 100
India, 54
Indian Ocean, 143
intentions, 9, 14, 35, 38, 48, 51, 54,
  108, 132
  malevolent intentions, 132
interceptions, 68
international law, 4, 22, 104, 111,
  114

156 INDEX

inter-service rivalry, 66
Ishigaki Island, 32, 49, 59, 63,
    76–78, 94
    Ishigaki City, 69, 94
        Ishigaki City Assembly, 128
Ishihara Shintarō, 39
Izumo, 100. *See also* helicopter,
    Maritime Self Defense Force
    (MSDF)

J
J-16D, 89, 90. *See also* People's
    Liberation Air Force (PLAAF)
JADGE air defense radar, 43
Japan Coast Guard (JCG), 28, 30–32,
    36, 38, 43, 46, 52, 58–60, 65,
    66, 78, 112, 117
    Asazuki, 60
    JCG Senkaku Flotilla, 58
    Okinawa Division, 59
Japan Press Research Institute (JRI),
    123, 125
Japan-US Security Treaty, 24
    Japan-US 2+2 Meeting, 141
    Japan-US alliance, 55, 56, 106, 136
    Mutual Cooperation and Security
        Between Japan and the United
        States of America, 6
JCG. *See* Japan Coast Guard
Jiji, 104
Jinping, Xi, 54
jointness, 57, 65

K
Kan, Naoto, 33–35, 37, 38, 52
    Kan Administration, 33–35, 37, 52
Katsuren, 85
    Katsuren base, 86
Kingdom of Ryukyu, 22
Kishida, Fumio, 100, 111, 116, 118,
    135–137, 140, 147

Kishida administration, 108, 123,
    127, 128, 133, 136, 139, 144
Kishi, Nobuo, 134
Kita, Kojima (Bei Xiaodao), 29
Kitazawa, Toshimi, 36
Koizumi, Junichiro, 30, 35
Komeito, 101, 102, 105
Kōno, Tarō, 137
Kuba Island (久場島, China:
    Huangwei Yu, 黄尾屿/黄尾嶼;
    Taiwan: Huangwei, 黃尾嶼), 20
Kume Island, 77
Kyushu, 58, 62, 65, 76, 78, 81, 87,
    89, 121

L
Law on the Territorial Sea and
    Contiguous Zone (China), 28
LDP. *See* Liberal Democratic Party
Liberal Democratic Party (LDP), 28
    PARC Defense Subcommittee, 137
    Policy Affairs Research Council
        (PARC), 96, 137
    Security Affairs Research
        Committee, 100
Link-16 data system, 66
Low Intensity Maritime Conflict, 58

M
Maehara, Seiji, 32, 38
Mainichi Shimbun, 85, 103
maritime observation base, 69
Maritime Self Defense Force (MSDF),
    36, 50, 58, 59, 66, 67, 70, 88
    Izumo, 100
    MSDF Fleet Wing 5, 88
    White Beach MSDF Ocean
        Observation Station, 87
Matsu, 24
Meiji Restoration, 22
minelaying, 88

minesweeping, 88
Ministry of Defense (MOD), 85,
92–94, 101–103, 105, 118, 130,
139, 146
Minjinyu 5179, 31
Mischief Reef, 50
Miyako Island, 49, 76–78, 85, 87, 93,
94, 96, 129
Miyako Strait, 76, 77, 85, 86, 114,
133, 142, 144, 149
Miyazawa, Kiichi, 29
MOD. See Ministry of Defense
MOFA. See Ministry of Foreign
Affairs
Motegi, Toshimitsu, 141
MSDF. See Maritime Self Defense
Force

N
Nagasaki, 62
Naha, 43, 64, 65, 68, 77, 88, 129
Nakayama, Yasuhide, 141
Nancy Pelosi, 113, 142
National Defense Program Guidelines
(NDPG), 49, 50, 57, 58, 63, 76,
77, 80–82, 86, 96, 101, 102,
109, 115, 137
National Defense Strategy (NDS)
(Japan), 3, 108–110, 115, 116,
119, 136, 137, 139, 143, 147,
151
nationalism, 4, 44, 69
National Security Council (Japan), 2,
132
National Security Strategy (NSS)
(Japan), 3, 50, 108, 109
NATO. See North Atlantic Treaty
Organization
NDPG. See National Defense
Program Guidelines
NDS. See National Defense Strategy
(NDS) (Japan)

Network Electronic Warfare System
(NEWS), 89–91, 147
NEWS. See Network Electronic
Warfare System
Newsham, Grant, 8, 62–64, 75, 82
Nihon Keizai Shimbun, 34
Nihon Seinensha, 28–30
Nippon Television (NTV), 40, 53
Nixon, Richard, 134
Nixon-Sato communique, 134, 141
Noda Yoshihiko, 53
   Noda administration, 40, 61
North Atlantic Treaty Organization
(NATO), 86, 108, 117, 137
North Korea, 7–9, 12, 46, 47, 49, 77,
81, 91, 101, 103, 104, 119, 149
NSS. See National Security Strategy
NTV. See Nippon Television
nuclear umbrella, 120
nuclear weapons, 9, 125, 145

O
Obama, Barak, 54
Ocean Policy Research Institute
(OPRI) (Japan), 21, 25
offensive liberal, 12
offensive missiles. See counterstrike
offensive realism, 12
oil, 24, 26
Okinawa, 15, 22–26, 30, 55, 57,
62–64, 67–69, 74, 76–79, 81,
85–90, 92–97, 121, 128–130,
146, 147
   return of (to Japanese sovereignty),
23, 25, 26
Onodera Itsunori, 33, 101
Osprey, 63, 66
Osumi Landing Ship Tank (LST), 67

P
P-1 patrol aircraft, 70

158 INDEX

P-3C patrol aircraft, 70, 87, 88
passive pacifism, 56
Patriot missile defense, 92
 Patriot Pac III, 91, 93
Pentagon, 144
People's Liberation Air Force
 (PLAAF), 65
People's Republic of China, 23
Philippines, 50, 60
Poland, 116, 117, 138, 151
police, 30, 38, 116, 129
poll, 35, 38, 40, 46, 47, 52, 53, 104,
 122–127. *See also* public opinion
precision munitions, 145
preemption, 111
 preemptive strikes (先制攻撃), 111
proactive pacifism, 56
protestors, 29, 30, 129
public opinion, 4, 13, 37, 48, 53, 68,
 93, 104

Q
Qixiong, Zhan, 32
Quemoy, 3, 24

R
Rand Corporation, 57, 65, 66, 75,
 113, 142
rare earths, 33
recruitment, 70, 71, 91. *See also*
 Self-Defense Forces
Red Sea, 145
referendum, 69, 95, 128
remote island, 23, 49–52, 54, 55, 57,
 61, 62, 74, 76, 77, 80, 81, 85,
 86, 93, 94, 102, 103, 109, 112
Republic of China, 3, 23–26. *See also*
 Taiwan
Russia, 7, 9, 10, 13, 78, 124, 125,
 150

Ryukyu islands, 23, 24, 49, 65,
 74–76, 83, 84, 86, 87, 89–92,
 148
 Ryukyu chain, 74, 76

S
Sakishima islands, 2, 3, 11, 14, 18,
 49, 50, 55, 57, 61, 63–65, 67,
 69, 74, 76–79, 81, 82, 84, 88,
 92, 94, 95, 97, 108, 117, 119,
 121, 128, 129, 138, 146, 148
Sakura TV, 43
SAM. *See* Surface to Air Missile
San Francisco Peace Treaty, 23
Schelling, Thomas, 3
scrambles, 65, 68
SDF. *See* Self-Defense Force
seaports, 121, 145
security partnerships, 11, 12, 46, 54,
 55
security vacuum, 49, 50, 61
Self-Defense Force (SDF), 11, 13, 38,
 46, 50, 55–57, 60–63, 65–69,
 85, 95, 117, 121–126, 149, 150
Senkaku islands, 2–8, 13, 18, 20,
 22–25, 27, 31, 32, 35, 36,
 38–41, 43, 46–61, 64, 66, 68,
 69, 74, 76, 78, 85, 87, 103, 112,
 113, 116, 119, 127, 133, 142,
 143, 150, 151
Senkaku Paradox, 3, 58
Senkaku Pioneering Day (January
 14>[th]), 128
shelters, 97, 121, 129
shield-spear, 105
signals intelligence (SIGNET), 49, 78,
 87
SIGNET. *See* signals intelligence
Sinai Peninsula, 56
Sino-Centric system, 22
Sino-Japanese Treaty of Peace and
 Friendship, 27

SOSUS. *See* sound surveillance system
sound surveillance system (SOSUS),
    86
South China Sea, 8, 21, 50, 60, 61,
    74–76, 112, 120, 142
South Korea, 114, 115
South Sudan, 56
Southwestern Wall Strategy, 61
sovereignty, 5, 7, 8, 15, 21, 23–27,
    41, 43
Soviet Union, 57
Spratly islands, 8
SSM. *See* Surface to Ship Missile
stand-off, 62, 69, 77, 80, 81, 83, 84,
    90, 93, 94, 102–104, 106,
    108–110, 120
strategically offensive military power,
    12. *See also* tactically offensive
    military power
submarines, 16, 49, 50, 82, 86, 87,
    100
Suga Yoshihide, 15, 141
    Suga administration, 53
Surface to Air Missile (SAM), 76–79,
    82, 84, 90, 92–94, 129
Surface to Ship Missile (SSM), 76–78,
    82, 84–86, 90, 92, 94, 150
surveillance, 59, 60, 66, 75, 78, 86,
    87, 91
Syrian airbase, 145

T
T-12 SSM, 78, 79, 84, 85, 93, 129
T-3 Chu-SAM, 78
T-88 SSM, 77
taboos, 150
Tactically offensive military power, 12
Taipei, 6, 136, 138
Taiwan Strait, 15, 16, 113–115, 125,
    134, 135, 141
Taketomi Island, 121
Tamaki Denny, 67, 130

Tarama Island, 121
territorial defense, 3, 8, 10, 12–14,
    46, 56, 62, 74, 79, 83, 90, 94,
    95, 106, 108, 111, 112, 116,
    120, 121, 124, 126, 132, 133,
    137, 138, 140, 144, 147, 149,
    150
territorial integrity, 2, 7–9, 14, 43,
    100, 108, 112, 132, 149
threat envelope, 77, 81, 102
Three New Conditions for Use of
    Force, 109
three no's, 27
Tiaoyutai Islands. *See* Senkaku islands
Tokuchi, Hideshi, 91
Tomahawk (cruise missile), 105, 128,
    144, 145
    Tomahawk Land Attack Missiles
        (TLAMs), 110
    "Tomahawk sponge", 144
Treaty of Shimonoseki, 23
Trump, Donald J., 5, 119, 148, 149
    Trump administration, 5, 54, 119,
        134, 149
Tsushin, Kyodo, 35

U
UAV. *See* Unmanned Aerial Vehicle
UK. *See* United Kingdom
Ukraine, 9, 10, 96, 104, 116, 117,
    124, 125, 138, 150, 151
UNCLOS. *See* United Nations
    Convention on Law of the Sea
United Kingdom (UK), 9, 81
United Nations Convention on Law
    of the Sea (UNCLOS), 21, 29,
    41, 113, 133, 143
United Nations (UN), 24
    UN Peacekeeping, 11, 46, 56, 132
United States (US)
    US House Speaker, 113, 142
    US Marine Corp, 46, 49, 62, 64

160 INDEX

US Marine Littoral Regiment, 64, 146
US Navy, 16, 114
US State Department, 26
Unmanned Aerial Vehicle (UAV, drone), 59
Uotsuri Island, 20, 28

V
Vietnam, 60
Vietnam War, 10

W
Washington, 4, 6, 15, 58, 70, 116, 135, 145, 146
weapons of mass destruction (WMD), 12
Western Army, 61, 62, 116

Western Pacific, 75, 76, 142, 149
White Beach, 87
White House, 119, 141, 142
Wild Weasel, 89
World War II, 2, 7, 23, 62, 68, 97

X
Xiaoping, Deng, 27

Y
Yaeyama Islands, 74
Yomiuri Shimbun, 30, 33, 34, 46, 47, 53, 79, 104, 111, 122–124
Yonaguni Island, 76, 108

Z
Zemin, Jiang, 29

Printed in the United States
by Baker & Taylor Publisher Services